Route 66 Chronicles

Volume I

Shadows of the Past Over Route 66

Arizona ~ New Mexico

by
Gerald M. Knowles

edited by
Marilyn von Qualen

Title Page:

Winslow, Arizona 'Corner,' 1944

Author in a Winslow 'tuxedo'

Copyright

Publication date: February, 2002
ISBN 0-9717709-0-5
First Printing, February, 2002

Route 66 Chronicles, Volume I, Shadows over Route 66
Arizona~New Mexico / by Gerald M. Knowles p.cm.

ISBN 0-9717709-0-5
1. United States Highway 66—Nonfiction.

Printing:
Central Plains Book Manufacturing
Winfield, Kansas 67156
March, 2002

Dedication

The knowledge, experience and passion

that might be found herein is gratefully shared

with my children — Bob, Tim, Maureen, Gregory and Jerrell,

with my grandchildren — Christina, Christopher, Rachel and Kevin

and with all those travelers who find themselves enraptured by Route 66

Acknowledgements

Special appreciation is extended to the following individuals for their help in supplying information and identifying graphics used in this book:

> Janice Griffith, Director of the Old Trails Museum, Winslow, Arizona
>
> Garnet Franklin, the Navajo County Museum, Holbrook, Arizona.
>
> Laine Sutherland,Photo Archives Curator, Northern Arizona University
>
> Anne Mason Brothers, Archivist of the Ray Mason Photo Collection
>
> Janie Severson Cogdill
>
> Richard Mike, son of Navajo Code Talker, King Mike
>
> Joseph M. Meehan, Arizona Historical Society, Northern Division
>
> Doug Jackson, former Flagstaff City Councilman and local historian
>
> Joseph Sanchez, Curator, Museum of Raton, New Mexico

Deep gratitude is expressed to all my friends and the members of my family who have provided support and encouragement.

CONTENTS

Preface

It is a pleasure to share with you my memories of that famous, fabulous American highway, Route 66. Growing up near the Road in Arizona and New Mexico truly enriched my life, and if I can enhance, expand or deepen knowledge of it for the curious or the devotee, well, that only serves to authenticate the importance that the Mother Road holds for me.

The original motive for this work was the encouragement I received from my children to recount what it was like in the old days on Route 66. Once begun, over 7 years ago, the project took on its own momentum as I searched family archives, delved into history and explored the sites of the Route 66 region. So inspired, I spent much of my life fleshing out the mysteries hidden behind red mesas, the tales concealed within old buildings and etched upon canyon walls along the Little Colorado River. These tap roots, once discovered, sweetened the dregs at the bottom of my Route 66 reveries, and they offer a well-deserved salute to a long, winding landmark paramount in the lives of so many.

The bitter chill of January along the Little Colorado, the chocolate-colored rush of water near a toasty fire inspired my visions of mid-1800's fur trappers huddled in lean-tos, dining on bacon and biscuits. Memories of cooking on that river linger when I'm exposed to the ambiance of an eatery designed to recreate the Old West — as in the Museum Club in Flagstaff, where I sipped a pop while Uncle Ray and the folks swigged on bottles of beer. I remember my father telling me about the skull atop a rock pile that marked the most dangerous spot on Arizona Route 66 at Two Guns. I used to stroll along in Holbrook with my Mamasita within a stone's throw of two of the fiercest gun battle sites of the West — the bloodbath at the Bucket of Blood Saloon, and the Blevins' House gunfight, where one particularly violent episode of the Sheep-Cattle owners' feud took place. I explored The Cave of Death down in Diablo Canyon at Two Guns, a sad place considered to be haunted by ghosts of dead Apaches killed there by the Navajos.

In the 1940's, kids like me were mesmerized by the beguiling objects found at Rimmy Jim's in Two Guns and at the El Tovar at the Grand Canyon. Sugared oranges in miniature crates, colorful sweets in little glass cars fascinated us and were cherished treasures. The old trading posts, like the venerable Wolf's on the Little Colorado, tempted their enchanted 1800's travelers with champagne imported from Europe and other unimaginable wonders. Further down the river, Cameron's proudly offered Indian blankets, furs and silver – earthy mementos snapped up by 1900's tourists under the spell of the Southwest.

Many writers attempted to capture the quintessence of the West. Of an evening, I'd read Zane Grey's captivating stories, tales that breathed life into my Tucker Flat Gang haunts — the high desert mesas and Camp Geronimo Scout Camp along the Mogollon Rim. Grey infused excitement into our favorite stomping grounds, and we joyfully interpreted what Grey created so beautifully in his books.

Then, there were the purveyors of fine food, elegant ambiance and décor — the Harvey Houses along the Santa Fe Railroad. Even at an early age, the caverns of the Alvarado in Albuquerque and the halls of La Posada in Winslow were special to me. I was fortunate to see, even hear speak, luminaries of the old days who starred in movies that were made around Flagstaff and Sedona. Seeing Hopalong Cassidy at Foxborro Ranch south of Flagstaff left me speechless, and listening to Errol Flynn under near riot conditions on the stage of the old Orpheum Theater was an experience that I never, ever forgot.

Young as we were my friends and I closely followed the epic of World War II, beginning with the Nazi march into Czechoslovakia, the death of Roosevelt and the radio announcement of the first atomic bomb. I was in Albuquerque that day in July when the first bomb was set off near Socorro. My Uncle Bill Mason was a Seabee in the Pacific Theater, and I've always been drawn to the stories of the Navajo Code Talkers and their heroism during World War II.

For half a century, the Flagstaff Pow Wow thrilled me and thousands of others. The chants and the drumbeats of the Apache Crown Dancers and the Navajo Yeibichai dancers made our hearts be fast and filled the July 4th streets of Flagstaff to overflowing as giant thunderheads gathered over the San Francisco Peaks. I worked off and on for years at my father's soda fountain in Winslow, and consummated my Rite of Passage as a Winslow Bulldog on that famous 'corner in Winslow, Arizona.'

The allure of Route 66 is due in part to the inevitable infusion of detail and drama into the vast array of its diverse icons. The contents of this book provide juicy information about those icons and will deepen understanding for anyone seeking heretofore hidden dimensions of the Road. I identify accessible sources available for those willing to take the time and effort to probe them, and hope that this effort will educate and entertain both the casual reader and the researcher. May those near and far discover newfound joy ~ and 'get their kicks' ~ reading about that great old Route 66.

ONE
Lights and Shadows cross the Coconino Hell's Canyon

The historical backdrop for Route 66's passageway across north central Arizona is rife with spellbinding sagas of fascinating people and tumultuous events. Beneath the rough surface of lava, limestone and Painted Desert lie hidden tales of

Canyon Diablo

man and nature, tales that still cast shadows and spells across the haunts of the old Mother Road. (71).

The major geological formation encompassing the area is the Coconino Plateau, and cutting through its very heart lies Canyon Diablo — "The Canyon of the Devil." Diablo is, however, only one of the many geological marvels on this small patch of planet Earth. Consider for a moment the majesty of the Grand Canyon, of Monument Valley, Canyon de Chelly, the San Francisco Peaks and the Painted Desert — might one muse that Mother Nature created this astonishing gallery of sculpture by employing her awesome, elegant power in her very own experimental lab? (15)

Michael Curtiz, director of the classic film, CASA BLANCA, chose this region for the production of the

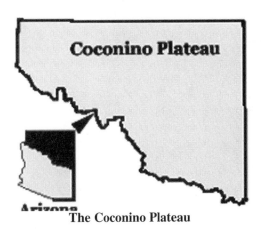

The Coconino Plateau

movie VIRGINIA CITY. It was the only area his location crew could find wherein distinct topographies depicting the four states of Nevada, Utah, Arizona and Colorado were within an hour's drive of each other. (91)

Beginning near Seligman and extending eastward, the Coconino Plateau terrain unfurls huge waves of ancient lava. As travelers move westward, the fifteen-million-year flows seen at Seligman give way to successive younger emissions. These lava emissions culminated in the creation of the San Francisco

Grand Falls of the Little Colorado

Peaks, which blew their titanic tops off two millions years ago. Lava spewing from those eruptions

Deep cracks in the Limestone

blocked the flow of the Little Colorado River, creating Grand Falls.

A thousand years ago Mother Nature retired her pyrotechnics career with a glorious finale —the eruption of Sunset Crater and the subsequent cloak-

Sunset Crater

ing of a vast region east of the Peaks with a mantle of fine, black cinders. Upon leaving these cinder hills, one enters beds of yellow-gray limestone deposited there eons ago by a vast Kaibab Sea, layers of which are clearly seen in the walls of Padre and Diablo Canyons. Percolation of rain and snowmelt over the millenniums eroded deep crevices into the limestone surface, and bones of unwary animals can sometimes be found in the cracks. Some fissures reveal underground steams that contain blind fish, suggesting the presence of deep subterranean caverns.

Just beyond Canyon Diablo, the Kaibab Limestone disappears under the red mudstone and sandstone of the Moencopi Formation. The Moencopi Formation, created during the Triassic Age by extensive fresh

Moencopi Cliffs

water flooding on top of the Kaibab deposits, was home to giant frogs, reptiles and salamanders who sloshed through the endless, shallow flood plain.

Ancient Messages

The Hopi Buttes

The unusual Moencopi formation, which appears as scattered islands just north and east of Canyon Diablo, changes into red cliffs at Winslow, and extends past Holbrook, Arizona almost to the New Mexico state line. A dark and very thin material called "desert varnish" coats these Moencopi Cliffs and allowed prehistoric peoples to etch messages upon them — messages which are still being deciphered.

Off in the distance, north of the red Moencopi Cliffs, beyond the Painted Desert and Little Colorado River Basin, one observes silhouettes of the Hopi Buttes which rose long ago like giant Kachina gods from the depths of ancient Lake Bitahochi. As one nears Winslow, the Chinle Formation can be seen from the highway, off in the distance to the north. At that point it dips down, covering the north side of the Little Colorado River Valley with its colorful pink,

prominently in the history of the region. Sometimes dry but more frequently wet, the river also percolates under ground.

Petrified Wood

In early days, Little Colorado River quicksand acted as a barrier to all travelers wishing to make their way across northern Arizona. A Norwegian missionary, Andrew Amundsen, commented that the river was the "same all the way, no plase fit for a human being to dwell upon—the most hostile desert lukking plase that I ever saw, Amen." The Mormon expedition called it, "a loathsome little stream, as disgusting a stream as there is on the continent." (84)

Painted Desert

purple, vermilion and white layers of Painted Desert. It is not unusual to find ancient horse and elephant bones in the Chinle Formation.

The formation at Winslow is protected from erosion by a layer of Shinarup aggregate, a cement and gravel-like hard rock thus named by Navajos due to the presence of specks of petrified wood in the formation — wood fabled to be chips off the lance of the Shinarup God. Just east of Winslow one crosses the Little Colorado River, a natural feature figuring

The Little Colorado Riover

Meteor Crater

Sunset Crossing, located a mile or so east of the present town of Winslow, was one of the few fordable spots across the quagmire of quicksand. One of the

Lake Bitahochi Sediments

Mormon settlements of the 1870's was located at the crossing. But, even before the Mormons, all of the trailblazers — from the Spanish Explorers to Army Pathfinders Whipple, Sitgreaves and Beale — crossed the Little Colorado at Sunset.

East of Holbrook, sediments of the timeless Bitahochi Lake can be seen at the Pinta Road exit.

This very old, Erie-sized lake, approximately 100 miles wide and 100 miles long, was fed by the ancestral Colorado River which at that time ran north to south in the approximate location of the present Little Colorado. Fish, clams, snails and beaver abounded in the lake, whose shores were lined with woods. Periodically, volcanic eruptions would issue forth from the lake, propelling sediment cones upward. Present-day Hopi Buttes, similar to the diamond-bearing molten lava conduits found in South Africa, evidence the many eruptions from the bottom of Bitahochi. Near the Arizona-New Mexico border, Triassic, Jurassic and Cretaceous formations blend vertically into the giant, multi-hued red cliffs that have so attracted filmmakers over the years.

Mother Nature added a final touch to the landscape by hurling a massive, 63,000-ton piece of the solar system into the Coconino Plateau. Originating somewhere between Mars and Jupiter 22,000 years ago, the huge meteor — 80 feet in diameter and approaching our planet at a speed of 133,000 miles per hour — slammed into the earth at a site south of Canyon Diablo. It blasted fragments of itself over a broad area, destroying all life within a 100-mile radius. It left a 600-foot deep, one mile in diameter crater that has been identified as the most distinctive impact of its kind on the planet. Anasazi ruins can be found inside the crater rim, along with the many names chiseled on it over time by those who lived there or who simply stopped by.

It wasn't until the discovery of meteors in 1886 that the origins of this meteor were confirmed. A Mr. Barringer, a mining engineer, searched for the main part of the meteor, thought to be hidden underground. However, only 10 % of it was found; 80% had either vaporized or splashed across the surrounding area.

Near the Meteor Crater landmark, off the Two Guns Exit, lies the longest subterranean cave in Arizona. Known as "The Cave of Death" it was the site of a gruesome encounter between the Navajo and Apache tribes.

Woolly Mammoths, Lost Peoples, and Mysterious Messages Left on Stone

The Lost Lance

There is some evidence to suggest that the first humans to enter the Coconino Plateau came from the San Luis Valley of Colorado. During what is known

Petroglyph

as the Paleo period of man in the Southwest, the woolly mammoth and giant bison roamed the region. A hunting and gathering period ultimately gave way, with fields of corn appearing amongst little stone villages. This abundant, pristine, peaceful scene would change with the onset of drought. (19)

These Anasazi (the Navajo word for "alien ancient ones,") would soon leave their open, exposed dwellings and begin climbing canyon walls, pots balanced on their heads. The increasing scarcity of corn brought about competition for food, and people moved to the relative security of cliffs and mesa tops, hoping to defend themselves from murder and cannibalism. Eventually, the "old ones" would disap-

Wapatki Ruins

pear altogether. Silence would engulf their stone apartments high in the cliffs, with only the moan of the wind through the piñons replacing tribal chants and the laughter of children.

Zane Grey, in his novel LOST PUEBLO, captures the mystery and allure of the search for the "ancient ones." Early pilgrims wending their way across Old 66 and its side roads looked carefully for things left behind by these mysterious people - their utensils, pottery, weapons, and, most interestingly, the messages they left on the Moencopi Cliffs and outcroppings. It is said that these petroglyphs and pictographs allow one to look "directly into the minds of those ancient ones."

What were they telling us? No one can really say. When were they communicating? There is a better answer to that question, because such "rock art" can in fact be dated. The cliffs are covered, or "patinated," with a coat of desert varnish — a thin layer of

Pictographs

brown, or bluish black, material. "Desert varnish" is the residue left by the bodies of dead bacteria — bacteria impregnated with iron and manganese salts leached from the rock itself over eons of time. A process of revarnishing, a study of the relative darkness of lines and carbon dating are used to determine age. Rock art style and symbols may then be related to a specific culture and period of time. (63)

Those who came after the Anazasi — the Conquistadors, missionaries, fur trappers, Mormons and sojourners passing along the cliffs on Old Route 66

Hopi Mesas, in Zuni villages, or on the cliffs at Acoma Pueblo — where legends and remnants of times past are alive today.

Glinting Heads, Weird Beasts and Shredded Rainbows

The Spanish Entrada

Coronado in search of the Seven Cities of Gold

also left their messages on the rocks.

What happened to these ancient ones is an enigma —a puzzle only somewhat allayed by the knowledge that their apparent descendants can be seen atop

One wonders what the prehistoric residents of the Canyon Diablo Region thought when, way off in the distance, what met their eyes was sunlight glinting off metal helmets! Most certainly, the sight of those

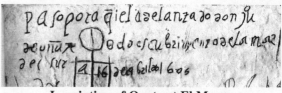

Inscription of Onate at El Morro

first Europeans straddling strange beasts, with rainbow colored flags flapping in the wind, had to generate both intense fascination and abject terror. The appearance of Spanish Explorer Coronado in the year 1540 marked the beginning of what was to become an incessant crisscrossing and eventual coveting of the native peoples' land — a coveting that persists as this book is written.

Hopi Mesa

The first of many frustrating attempts to cross Canyon Diablo was made by one of Coronado's officers, Capt. Don Garcia de Cardenas, who was searching for a large river described by the Hopis. His attempt to cross Canyon Diablo ended without much luck. Later, one Capt. Melgosa reached the edge of the Grand Canyon while exploring the Coconino Plateau areas. He traversed the Painted Desert, but, like Cardenas, was stymied at the edge of Canyon Diablo. (86)

There were legends of hidden treasures near Canyon Diablo, and there were hunts for the riches of the legends. Antonio Espejo was sent in 1582 for serious reconnoitering of the area, in search of precious metal. A group of Franciscan friars on their way up from Mexico were transporting a mule train packed with silver bars destined for Santa Fe. They traveled along the eastern edge of Padre Canyon, and when

"Taos Lightening" from Turly Mill

They Were Wild, Free and Resourceful

Those Mountain Men

TRACKING AT NIGHT IN THE RAIN

The entry of the Conquistadors and missionaries ended in Arizona, and Spain took over dominion of the region. However, during Spanish rule, pack trains of American explorers entered the Canyon Diablo area looking for gold and silver. They purposely left little trace that they had been there, because the land was still controlled by Spain.

However, when Europeans evidenced a penchant for beaver hats, companies and groups of fur trappers formed, spreading out across the American West. The Little Colorado at that time was lined with a heavy bosque of cottonwood and willow, and was resplendent with beaver. Taos was the disembarkation point for those trappers. They trekked into every nook and cranny of the Rockies, wandering over and into the Colorado and Little Colorado River Valleys.

Trapper Bill Williams ?

they reached the junction of Padre Canyon with Diablo they were attacked and almost overwhelmed by Indians. The legend is that they cached tons of silver bars in old ruins "near where Diablo enters the Little Colorado River." A cross embossed on a huge rock near the river records their passage that way in 1767. Although many treasure-hunting parties have scoured the area, only one silver bar has surfaced. (71).

Many Spanish inscriptions occur on rocks scattered throughout Arizona and New Mexico. The most striking examples may be seen south and east of Gallup, New Mexico, and at El Morro National Monument.

Prominent among Americans investigating the Canyon Diablo area were "Old Solitaire" Bill Williams, "Broken Hand" Fitzpatrick, Kit Carson, Antoine Leroux, Francois X. Aubrey and one who

Rendezvous

never left — Herman Wolf. The old fur trappers were the most free and independent souls ever to cross the Coconino Plateau. They were quite a sight in their beaded buckskin with wool or fur hats covering unruly manes of long hair, their feet wrapped in buffalo or horsehide. (42)

An extensive repertoire of survival tools was carried on their person — the famous "Green River Knife," a bullet mold, a pistol, a rifle, a powder horn and 25 pounds of powder. Occasionally they wore "buckskin armor," which was fashioned by letting wet buckskin dry and shrink into a nearly impenetrable body covering. Their traveling companion, the venerable pack mule, carried a hatchet, four traps, English wool

Bill Williams Mountain

blankets and eats. These men were cunning, strong and skilled in surviving the onslaughts of Mother Nature and unfriendly Native Americans. They did what they had to do to survive, and would sometimes

Wolf Trading Post

cut the throat of their mule to obtain life-giving moisture for their parched throats. It was said that Bill Williams could track animals, or men, at night in the rain. Many a fur trapper was the real hero of highly touted expeditions into the West.

Trappers often worked in small groups, and would "rendezvous" once a year at a designated spot where they staged medieval fair-like festivals. These magnificently barbaric, riotous celebrations would go on for weeks. The trappers traded their entire year's pelts for woolen blankets from England, powder from du Pont, lead from Missouri, rifles from Bolton

Inscription of 1820

Gun Works, gaudy colored shawls, bells and mirrors, and trinkets and beads from Italy for their Indian wives.

They bought coffees, sugar, tea and liquor ("white lightening") from Turley's Mill in Taos. This soiree of soirees was raw, crude and quite literally poisonous. The rendezvous was a place of buying, selling, haggling, cheating, gambling, fighting, drinking, palavering, racing, shooting and carousing. A whole year's work could be squandered in roaring debauches characterized by consumption of lethal whisky, reckless gambling, euchre, poker and occasional orgies of wild sexual abandonment. When they final-

Fur trapper fort on the Little Colorado River

ly sobered up, these fiercely independent souls feasted, raced some more and talked around campfires. Some such rendezvous were often held on the edge of Canyon Diablo.

Many trappers left either their name or mark on the Coconino Plateau. As one moves along the Little

Herman Wolf grave at Canyon Diablo

Colorado River, one can see small rock dwellings constructed by the trappers to ward off the weather and attacks by the Navajo and Apache. Some even inscribed their names on the rocks as a record of their passage. "Old Solitaire," Bill Williams had a town, a mountain, and a creek named for him. The Atlantic and Pacific Railroad perpetuated the tale that Old Bill was buried atop Bill Williams Mountain — a legend that persists to this day.

As late as the 1940's, the wilds of the Coconino Plateau continued to fashion the character of its residents. It was not uncommon in those days for groups of ten to twelve-year old youths to take off for days, exploring and camping by themselves along the rivers, creeks and canyons around Winslow. They possessed the same zeal as the old fur trappers in their desire for freedom, adventure, the testing of one's resourcefulness and a passion for what lies around the next bend. (see "Return to Tucker Spring," VOLUME. II, ROUTE 66 CHRONICLES)

In the 1840's, when hat fashion in Europe shifted from beaver to Japanese silk, the era of the fur trappers came to an end. Nevertheless, many of these men, who already knew the American West like the back of their hand, began to act as guides for the United States Army Survey Expeditions and the wagon trains trekking west. Some of them stayed and became traders to the Navajo, Apache and other tribes of the Coconino and Colorado Plateaus.

Such characters as Smith, Mitchell, Whitehead, Fitzpatrick, Gald Hall and Old Man Yellow Face Buck traveled together and went into other aspects of trading after the beaver trade stopped. Navajos well remember the mysterious appearances and disappearances of one Belaganna Sani (Old White Man) who was famous for his concoction of "fire water," consisting of one part pure alcohol and two parts water laced with tobacco juice and cayenne pepper. However, the old Little Colorado trapper who had a lasting impact on Canyon Diablo history was one Herman Wolf.

Charting Westward Passages to the Coast

The Great Pathfinders Through the West

Canyon Diablo played a formidable role in the pursuit of trails across northern Arizona. From earliest

The Beale Wagon Route

times, the Navajo used the east side of Diablo as a north-south route which passed by the present Two Guns site winding south through Chavez Pass and over the stark Mogollon Rim into central Arizona. After the United States acquisition of the region in 1846, the San Francisco Peaks, rising majestically on the horizon for a hundred miles in any direction, served as a guide to westward bound wagon train, but confronted travelers with Canyon Diablo. (see "Jewel of Old Route 66," VOLUME. II, ROUTE 66 CHRONICLES) Avoiding the probable impasse near Two Guns, they went downstream about two miles to find the ever-scarce water, hoping to locate a point where the canyon walls could be scaled on foot. There is a "barranca" crossing where many noted their passage through the Diablo on the faces of boulders, the earliest being 1830. Unfortunately, few knew that Canyon Diablo could actually be crossed upstream several miles south of Two Guns.

Leaders in Washington had visions of a railroad that would unite the nation from coast to coast. Jefferson Davis, then Secretary of the Interior, was prompted to authorize surveys for a transcontinental railroad route. A Lt. James Simpson carried out the first formal United States reconnoiter for an east-west route.

Accompanied by the old fur trapper, Francois X. Aubrey, he sought to lay out a wagon route from San Jose, California to Santa Fe.

Two events of special note occurred on that trip. The Indians traded fifteen-thousand dollars in gold nuggets for food, blankets and other commodities. The steep walls of Diablo blocked the traveling party at a point between the present Interstate 40 and the current Burlington Northern & Santa Fe Railroad bridge. The Indians told the party they would have to go further south to find a crossing. The Indians did not reveal the origin of their gold nuggets.

After the Aubrey-Simpson excursion, a whole succession of United States Army Topographical Engineers attempted to blaze trails suitable for a transcontinental railroad. In 1851 Capt. Lorenzo Sitgreaves, accompanied by yet another trapper, Antoine Leroux, came from Santa Fe to check the navigability of the Little Colorado River. The steep Canyon Diablo walls foiled yet another survey party, forcing them to go north to make their crossing. However, the pathfinder party's tribulations were not over. Later in the expedition Leroux was shot with an arrow, one person in the party was bitten by a rattlesnake, and, sadly, the weary travelers had to fend off starvation by eating one of their mules.

Next came the Lt. A.W. Whipple party in 1853, accompanied by a healthy Antoine Leroux and probably the most famous chronicler of the West, Heinrich Baldwin Mollhausen. The Whipple party

San Francisco Peaks

attempted to follow the 35th parallel as closely as possible. Yet allegiance to this route almost killed Whipple. The party came to Holbrook at the point where the Rio Puerco joins the Little Colorado (the original Holbrook settlement, named Horsehead Crossing), and went north of the Little Colorado to a fordable spot just east of present Winslow, Arizona, called Sunset Crossing (See "Mormons" below).

Whipple barely escaped with his life. One black night while trekking westward on the 35th Parallel,

Monument to Camel Dirver Hi Jolly

of the San Francisco Mountains and needed no temple made with hands within to worship our Creator." (84, pg.. 228)

In 1857, the famed ex-naval officer, Lieutenant Edward F. "Ned" Beale of the United States Topographical Engineers carried out one of the most famous and colorful expeditions across Arizona and New Mexico. His mission was to open a wagon route from Fort Defiance to California. Congress had granted Beale $30,000 for the procurement of camels, which animal Beale believed could handle the desert west better than horses. Alas, the first foray of the camel caravan was a miserable failure. The camels would not budge. No matter how much the American muleskinners yelled the camels ignored their English commands, looked at them with contempt and even spit at them. Beale was forced to import camel drivers from Greece and Arabia to handle the creatures. One such driver, christened "High Jolly," became a legend in Arizona history.

Whipple nearly walked off into the abyss that was Canyon Diablo. Whipple promptly gave the canyon its dark epithet — the Devil's Canyon, or "Diablo Canyon." Whipple's near tragedy had a strong influence on his later declaration that decent of the Canyon was impossible at the 35th Parallel. Whipple joined the ranks of the many that ended up going far to the north in search of an acceptable crossing.

After navigating the very shallow Canyon Diablo near present day Luepp, Whipple's party reached the foot of the San Francisco Peaks amid blowing snow on Christmas Eve. The setting sun gave the clouds of blustery white flakes a rather spiritual, rosy hue. The weary group toasted the day, themselves and the mountain with an eggnog drink concocted by one of the officers. In celebration, H.B. Mollhausen later reminisced, "We looked up at the sublime summits

During the sojourn of Beale's caravan across New Mexico and Arizona, many communities welcomed it with high excitement, perceiving it to be a circus. The flamboyant dress of Beale, the weird never-before-seen camels and the colorful drivers from Greece and Arabia were an absolute wonder to the folks in rural hamlets. The party arrived at Canyon Diablo on September 8, 1857. Beale, like his predecessors, found the Canyon "impassable" and went north to find an easier cross-over. Later, a second Beale party came eastward from Needles to Fort Defiance and used a rock dwelling on the west side of Canyon Diablo, opposite the present Two Guns, for operational headquarters. Camels proved to be much more durable than mules and horses. Contemptuous of the thirsty horses, they went days without water and easily consumed the desert fare, including prickly cactus. Some who wandered loose could be seen far off in the distance and were later

Wolf Trading Post on the Little Colorado River

discovered in the desert as piles of bleached bones. A monument to the camels' effectiveness and to the famous "High Jolly" has been erected in southern Arizona. The main streets of Arizona and New Mexico now bear signs reading "Beale's Road."

The Old Trails Highway, the first trans-Arizona auto route, was later superseded by Route 66. Both highways generally followed Beale's Road. In 1858, Lt. J.C. Ives traveled from Needles, California over the Beale Road to Fort Defiance and on to San Francisco. Like all his predecessors, Ives found the sheer walls of Canyon Diablo to be a huge impediment to progress. Further expeditions to plot a transcontinental route were halted by the outbreak of the Civil War.

Wine and Champaigne from Europe

post. Wolf was in business by 1868, and "Chi Hogan" was in such an extremely remote location that freight had to be hauled clear from Santa Fe and Albuquerque. That did not stop Wolf from bringing in champagne and wine from France to his oasis at the Little Colorado River in the Melgosa Desert. Such rich, unique goods were more than tempting to Apache raiding parties. Again and again, Wolf and his Mexican staff held off the marauders behind the thick stone walls of the Post.

The Apaches became frustrated and turned to more successful raids on the Navajo settlements north of the Little Colorado, across the Melgosa Desert. The last of those Apache raids prompted the most violent, macabre episode in the long-standing Navajo-Apache feud. The site of that holocaust, which became known as "Death Cave," is taboo today for both the Navajo and the Apache (see chapter four, "Cave of Death").

Wolf Trading Post

The Ageless Trading Post
The First Outpost of American Culture in the West

Trading posts came to the Canyon Diablo region on the coattails of the Navajos returning home after their release as captives in 1868 from Bosque Redondo at Fort Sumner. The Navajo Reservation had expanded to the banks of the Little Colorado River and the Colorado River. Herman Wolf, who had long before trapped beaver in the region, was the first to build a trading post in the area and did so at a point where the Navajo-Hopi trail crossed the Little Colorado River. The post was positioned where a strata of river bed stone allowed travelers to avoid the treacherous quicksand which often grasped wagon, horse and life itself from the weary parties.

The original name given Wolf's Post by the Navajos was "Chi Hogan," or "Beaver House," so named for the red beaver pelts that were hung out to dry. The Navajos later kept this name for Wolf's stone trading

If one happens of an evening to be at the Canyon Diablo ghost town, Herman Wolf's lonely gravestone may be seen, silhouetted by the setting sun against the Kaibab limestone ruins and the distant San Francisco Peaks. The Wolf Trading Post was passed down to other proprietors, including the Babbitt Brothers of Flagstaff. However, one Leander Smith,

Sunset at the Herman Wolf grave

an amateur archaeologist, placed a human skull in the Post's window, unaware of Navajo taboos about the dead. As a consequence few Navajos ever returned to the Post. The stone walls of the post still stand today, out on that lonely, nearly inaccessible site on the Little Colorado. Shell casings and broken champagne bottles were left behind, reminding the occasional wanderer of the violent confrontations that once occurred there.

Trading posts at other sites in the region — Black Falls, Cameron, Luepp, Sunrise, Canyon Diablo, Winslow and Two Guns — later succeeded Wolf's Trading Post. All would claim a niche in the notorious lore of the region. One interesting trading post and community was established near the Wolf Trading Post. A missionary named William R Johnston, associated with the YMCA, got off the train in 1896 in Flagstaff intending to bring Christianity to the Navajos. In the late 1900's, he focused on the Little Colorado area upstream from the old Wolf Post, a location known as Tolchalco, "Red Water Wash," by the Navajos. The Trading Post was intended as a campaign against other traders' high prices, their tolerance of gambling and their operations on Sunday. However, the scheme was not successful. Johnson's son, Phillip, was later to perform an even more significant role for the Navajo people with his recruitment of the famous Navajo Code Talkers. (4)

In 1905, a two-story dwelling was built at Tolchalco by a man named John Walker. Later on, the Babbitts owned the house, and Walker established a trading post at Old Luepp and Sunrise. At many sites across the Navajo Nation, trading posts still function as welcome oases amid the shifting sands, deep canyons and towering buttes of the Coconino Plateau. Some of the posts served both the Indians and the pilgrims of Old Route 66.

Enter Mormon Pioneers

Those First Real Towns

In the 1870's Brigham Young sent Jacob Hamblin to explore northern Arizona. Hamblin was to blaze a trail enabling the Mormon people to establish settlements along the Little Colorado River. In 1874, Mormon settlers traversed the Melgosa Desert looking for arable land, making their first crossing of the limestone gorge at Two Guns. Under the leadership of Bishop Lot Smith, settlements were established at sites named Ballinger, Sunset, Joseph City and Brigham City. All but one of these communities succumbed to the capricious Little Colorado. One settler remarked that the Little Colorado was "too thin to plow, too thick to drink." (30, pg. 5)

The Sunset Settlement

The settlers at the small hamlet of Sunset (east of Winslow, near the Homolovi State Monument) laid out a road southwest from Sunset some sixty miles to Mormon Lake, where they established a dairy and a sawmill. The road represented a direct line from the Little Colorado at Sunset. It bore south of Meteor Crater, crossed Canyon Diablo two miles above Two Guns and extended on to Mormon Lake and Mormon Mountain. One of the most interesting "trails" forged by the Mormon people was the famous "Honeymoon Trail" from Sunset to St. George, Utah. The trail crossed the Little Colorado at Grand Falls, a 180-foot high black lava obstruction to the Little Colorado River where the honey-

Early Mormon Home

mooners described the water is as "frothy cocoa." Remnants of an irrigation system and a small graveyard mark the location of Sunset. (30, pg. 6)

Joseph City, a small hamlet established on Old Route 66 by Mormon immigrants, has endured for over 130 years and remains the only surviving Mormon settlement. In 1996, excavation and restoration was launched at the site of Fort Brigham just east of Winslow on the west side of the Little Colorado

River. The author used to stay overnight at La Prad Ranch, the remaining vestige of Fort Brigham. He stayed with a member of the Tucker Flat Gang, Terry Newman, at that ranch when it was operated as the Newman Dairy. Zane Grey, in his famous novel

Fort Brigham Settlement

RIDERS OF THE PURPLE SAGE, used the Mormon society of the northern Arizona Strip (an area north of the Grand Canyon) as a setting for the book. The book was made into movies several times over. A TNT cable channel movie RIDERS OF THE PURPLE SAGE was aired in the 1990's. (45)

The Screaming Iron Buffalo and Its Depraved Offspring

The Railroad Bridge at Canyon Diablo

Throughout the 1870's, the steel rails of the transcontinental railroad crept slowly across New

Narrow Gauge Bridge at Canyon Diablo

Mexico and Arizona toward their rendezvous with the Pacific Ocean and a realization of national destiny. The construction of the Atlantic and Pacific Railroad continued through northern Arizona until its contractors reached the rim of Canyon Diablo at a point 2.5 miles north of the present site of Two Guns. Engineering complications in spanning the

canyon, along with financial problems, halted the advance of the Iron Buffalo for two whole years. Nevertheless, two years was all it took to ripen one of the most rotten towns the west had ever seen — the infamous Canyon Diablo.

The little settlement perched on the edge of the canyon was the typical railroad camp town. It's sole purpose, during its brief existence, was to clothe, equip, feed and entertain railroad workers. (4) This depraved offspring of the Iron Buffalo served its residents by roaring day and night clear through 1881 and 1882. Murder on the street was common, holdups happened almost hourly and newcomers got slugged over the head if there was any sign that they had valuables on their person. One chronicler of southwestern lore aptly summed up Canyon Diablo: "Tombstone, Virginia City and Abilene could not hold a candle to this end-of-the-rail depravity." (4, 84)

There were more people murdered in gun duels on the streets of Canyon Diablo than in Abilene and Tombstone put together. Things got so bad that Flagstaff businessmen requested that Army troops from Ft. Defiance come and establish martial law. But, before the Army from Fort Defiance could get there, the town died — almost overnight. The bridge was completed and the Iron Buffalo puffed and hissed onward toward California. Railroad officers proudly announced that "The Atlantic and Pacific Road is now completed to Canyon Diablo, 311 miles west of the Rio Grande River, where the dry chasm is being spanned by an iron viaduct 520 feet long and 254 feet high. The structure is designed to carry the heaviest consolidated engine, moving at a speed of fifty miles an hour." (81)

After the Canyon Diablo Bridge was completed, activity at the town turned to trade with the Navajo people. A gentleman named Algert from Pennsylvania opened a store in an abandoned rail car amid the railroad camp debris. Algert was later succeeded by Fred Voltz who ran a trading post at the site for many years. Voltz dabbled in precious stones, and also promoted tourism with excursions to snake dance ceremonies at the Hopi peoples' mesas.

Today, the only reminder of the grand days of yesteryear are cadaverous limestone walls and the endless howling of the wind. The single monument that marks old Canyon Diablo is a black granite gravestone, the last resting-place of Herman Wolf — who was the first to arrive and has never left! In his novel, THE UP TRAIL (1918), Zane Grey used the construction of the transcontinental railroad as his setting. Grey weaves plot, characters and incidents gleaned from a Flagstaff old timer, Lee Doyle, who had direct knowledge of the railroad's construction over Diablo. (45)

Held Up At Old Two Guns

Toured, Trapped and Fleeced, But Lucky to Escape Alive

Just off Interstate 40, 2.5 miles south and upstream from the railroad bridge at Canyon Diablo, there existed a notorious, rough-and-tumble settlement by the name of Two Guns. Two Guns was the site of some very significant and very violent events, including an Apache vs. Navajo confrontation in the 1800's, and a tragic, bizzare murder in the 1920's. It was the place near which Billy the Kid and the famous explorers Beale and Sitgreaves once camped. Beale in fact spent some time on the west rim at Two Guns during his second trip east from San Jose, California. Still another claim to fame for Two Guns, an historical distinction, is that it eventually became the very first tourist trap on Route 66.

This particular locale near Canyon Diablo was used by the Apaches and the Navajos to find water for their stock and as a place to hide from the United States Army and each other. Anderson Canyon, a small side canyon and tributary into Diablo, was the preferred site for the Navajo.

It's a toss-up as to whether Two Guns outdid Diablo in spawning episodes of violence, or vice versa. Passerby and residents alike insist that the never ending, howling winds are phantom voices of savagery that to this day inhabit Two Guns and Diablo. There is evidence, however, that Two Guns could claim prominence over Diablo. Certainly one of the most violent and macabre events in the history of northern Arizona occurred there in the 1870's. Forty-two Apaches were annihilated in a cave just below the old ruins of the village of Two Guns. (See chapter four, "Ghosts of the Cave of Death.")

The original entrance of this cave was high enough for horses to enter, the inside vast enough to hold forty-two Apaches and their horses. The cave is a

Approach to the Cave of Death

straight-line fissure, as opposed to being a water-created cavern. Spelunkers have explored the cave, probing as deep as 13 miles into its interior. Two theories suggest the origin of the cave. The first concept states that the massive impact of the Meteor Crater ruptured horizontal strata, creating cracks and fissures across the plateau. The second, and more plausible, explanation is that the cave was a consequence of intense volcanic upheavals combined with an enormous explosion of the San Francisco Peaks.

Various other aboveground cracks and fissures are evident near Two Guns. Deep, black arroyos crease the landscape, some extending from Two Guns clear down to the Little Colorado River. Some contain water from underground streams in which blind fish have been observed. These geological upheavals and the Apache massacre were only a prelude to the dark history of Two Guns.

Two Guns

Legend has it that Billy the Kid and his bunch, who were known to have stolen cattle near White Oaks, New Mexico, came to the region in the late 1870's

Aledged Habitat of Billy the Kid

hoping to sell stock to railroad contractors. Arriving near Two Guns, "The Bunch" took up temporary residence in a stone dwelling on the west side of the canyon. Their plan failed. Billy's bunch could not sell their stock to the construction crews since the crews were broke and had no idea when they would be paid. At the same time, the local stockmen had plenty of their own stock. That left the Navajos. Billy bargained desperately with them, succeeding only in swapping a few cows for a mere blanket or two. Eyewitnesses reported seeing the gang kill all the stock at Tucker Flat before heading back to New Mexico.

In hot pursuit behind the transcontinental road construction came entrepreneurs who established vari-

Billy the Kid

ous enterprises (or "tourist traps") at the Two Guns site. One of the most colorful concessionaires and

notorious tourist trappers, as well as the most likely progenitor of those latter-day billboard icons, was one Harry "Indian" Miller. Miller, who created most of the visible limestone dwellings at Two Guns (zoos and trading posts) who was rumored to have murdered one Mr. Cundiff, the first businessmen at Two Guns.

Adding to the somberness of the place, skulls were set on rock piles along Old Route 66 to warn the wary traveler. Notably, the highest rate of auto accident death on Route 66 was at the Two Guns crossing of Diablo. Old-timers and locals still believe that mysterious powers are at work near Two Guns, that there are forces hidden from the eye of the casual traveler whizzing by on Interstate 40.

The Diablo Theater of War
Combat Zones

For an extensive period during the 1800's, the Canyon Diablo region was a combat zone, a stage for numerous engagements between Apaches and Navajos and their confrontations with the U.S. Army. Both the Navajo and the Apache did most of their traveling south and north on the Navajo Trail. The

US Cavalry and Scout

Trail led along the eastern edge of Canyon Diablo from the Colorado River to the north, moving southward over the Mogollon Rim to the Verde Valley of central Arizona.

Canyon Diablo also served as a lookout, a refuge, and a base camp from which to launch attacks. Aside from the Apache massacre at Two Guns, most of the armed clashes occurred between the United States Army and warring tribal parties. As early as 1864, the Kit Carson Campaign against the Navajos was carried out successfully through the destruction of their crops and herds. The infamous "Long Walk" of the "defeated" Navajos to a concentration camp at Fort Sumner, New Mexico remains as one of the saddest and most brutal episodes of their long history, and is a black mark upon the record of America's treatment of the American Indians. The only benefit inherent in this tragedy was that the Navajo had at least escaped General Carelton's orders for Carson to wipe them out.

The United States Army fought with Apache marauders for two decades. In the year 1867, one such confrontation involved Company B and I of the 8th U.S. Cavalry, with Capt. J.M. Williams in command. Williams' troops chased an Apache raiding party over the Mogollon Rim and then north to Canyon Diablo, where a battle ensued. Thirty Apaches were slain.

Then, in September of 1869, an Army detachment from Fort Verde (near present day Camp Verde), intercepted a war party of Apaches packing loot taken from a raid on the Navajos. Moving along the edge of Canyon Diablo, the Apaches tried to avoid the Army by going west into the cinder hills and the San Francisco Mountains. Yet, thirty were intercepted and killed before they could reach the Diablo crossing.

In 1871, Companies A, D, and G, troops of the 3rd Cavalry under a Lt. Morton pursued a force of Apaches from the headwaters of the Verde River onto the Navajo trail, just below the headwaters of Canyon Diablo. The Apaches ran head on into the Army at a stagecoach crossing upstream from Two Guns. Fifty-six of the Apache band were killed, eight were wounded, and ten were captured.

Many other skirmishes between natives and interlopers have been recorded. In 1874, an Army scouting party found the remains of a destroyed immigrant wagon train near a Mogollon Rim military road. In July of 1882, the renegade Apache Natiotish was sighted southwest of Fort Apache with 75 to 100 warriors. Eight White Mountain Apache scouts were

sent out to arrest Natiotish but were instead immediately butchered by his group. Natiotish went on a rampage that rallied pursuit by combined U.S. Army forces drawn from Forts Whipple, Apache, Thomas and McDowell.

The cavalry made forced marches night and day to intercept Natiotish. The Apaches moved into the Tonto Basin, raiding those communities and wantonly killing stock and settlers. The marauders reached the Navajo Trail and, spying only one small group of soldiers, Natiotish decided to wipe out the troops by setting up an ambush at the upper fork of Clear Creek. At that point the trail drops 1000 feet into the canyon where it crosses Clear Creek, winding north through Chavez Pass.

The overwhelming numbers of the combined Army forces intercepted Natiotish, trapping his party against the steep canyon walls. Natiotish was killed, along with twenty-four of his warriors. This showdown was the last in that area between the Apaches and the U.S. Army. Much later, Mr. Albert Bailey, a Navajo from Kayenta, found a bit from a horse with a brass "US" embossed on it. Thwarted by the Army in the Mogollon Rim area, the Apaches shifted strategies and started focusing on Navajo sheep camps in the Melgosa Desert terrain, north of the Little Colorado River.

The Navajo people returned home after the Treaty of 1868 to the areas of the Melgosa Desert and the Little Colorado River. Their arrival was soon followed by intrusions into their land and theft of their sheep, horses and cattle. The Navajos began to resist. Seeking harmony with their neighbors and fearing a repeat of the "Long Walk," the Navajos would at first simply run off or rough up invading rustlers. These ploys came to naught, and the theft and vandalism continued.

In 1884 a cowpoke rustled some stock, and upon abandoning camp left behind arsenic in baking powder cans. Navajo women often foraged for camp remains, and this time, tragically, used the arsenic-laced baking powder to cook Navajo fry bread. An entire family of Navajos was poisoned to death. Enraged, the Navajos tried to ambush the arrogant cowboy but only succeeded in killing his partner. Ultimately, the cowboy escaped to Flagstaff, never to return to Navajo land.

The onset of the Spanish American War in 1898 prompted the formation of a local militia in Flagstaff. They were called "Flagstaff Blues" and served as regional law enforcers. On one occasion in 1889, the Navajos beat up a would-be-rustler, one

William Montgomery, who in turn filed an assault complaint in Flagstaff. Deputy Sheriffs Dan Hogan and Montgomery were sent out to serve warrants, picking up two more deputies from a cow camp on the way.

The "posse" proceeded to the rim of Elliot Canyon at the junction of Padre and Canyon Diablo. Locating the Navajo camp, the men walked into the canyon and surprised an old man tanning hides in a hogan (house). Navajos, hidden nearby, fired at the four men. Hogan was hit in the shoulder, Montgomery was killed, and one of the deputies was shot through the groin. In retaliation the men killed the harmless old man and hastily retreated. They wandered through the brush all night, finally arriving at the Canyon Diablo railroad station just in time to catch the dawn freight to Flagstaff. The episode caused intense alarm on the part of the Navajos and the Belaganniis (white men).

The Navajo, fearing that the Flagstaff Blues would hunt them down, sought refuge in Canyon Diablo. They traveled to Hogan Chee and asked old Herman Wolf what he thought would happen. Wolf told them that they should have no fear as justice was on their side. Three hundred Navajos gathered on the outskirts of Flagstaff, the residents totally unaware that their annihilation or survival hinged solely on a judge's decision.

The Navajos sent in a headman named B'ugoettin (Ba who' ah tin - No Teeth) and two others, all unarmed, to ascertain the verdict. B'ugoettin had ridden 100 miles from Black Mountain with a bullet wound in his chest to testify. The judge, who was impressed with the courage of B'ugoettin, ruled in favor of the Navajos, unwittingly saving Flagstaff from total death and destruction. Merriment prevailed when B'ugoettin and the band went back to Herman Wolf and related what had happened.

Bloodstains and Bitter Dregs

The Cattlemen and Sheepmen War — the Infamous Hashknife Outfit

The Canyon Diablo region had been used by the Navajos for eons as it offered excellent grazing land for both cattle and sheep. Following the railroad and the old Mormon Trail, various individuals brought steers into the area. A key event occurred when a Board of Directors member of the Atlantic and Pacific Railroad bought a million acres of the company's right of way — a vast track of land extending across the entire Coconino Plateau. The Aztec Cattle Company was formed and eventually operated by a bunch of Texas cowboys called the Hashknife Outfit, and every steer was branded with the Hashknife brand.

In the early 1860's, sheep were brought into the area along the Little Colorado and the rim of Canyon Diablo. In the late 1870's, the Daggs Brothers

Hashknife Brand

imported a huge herd of 10,000 sheep, and the chemistry for conflict was set up. Sheep and cattle didn't mix on the same grazing land, and neither did cowboys and sheepherders. The natural hostility between proponents of these two enterprises has been cited as the cause of an extremely bitter, legendary feud.

The famous Graham-Tewksberry conflict, with the sheep owners on one side and the cattlemen on the other, took place in Pleasant Valley, south of the Mogollon Rim near present day Payson, Arizona.

Cowboys on the range

This tense and lengthy feud was punctuated with numerous fights and murders, and there is evidence of involvement by what were at the time some of the most powerful forces in Arizona. Details of the feud are chronicled in Forest's account of the Pleasant Valley War. (33)

There is little doubt that the sudden presence in the 1880's of so many cowhands in the region gave rise

Sunset Pass

to rustling, robbery and gunfights. (see chapter five, "The Bucket of Blood Saloon") It did not take long for young cowboys to see train robbing as a means to quick fortune. Records detail the story of three men who robbed a two-family wagon party and got away with $1000 in gold coin. The gold has never been found. Stage robberies and train robberies became an almost recreational pastime for drifters and cowboys. Hundreds of thousands in cash, jewels and silver dollars are said to be stashed along Canyon Diablo.

The legend and lore of those times has been captured in many of Zane Grey's novels including SUNSET PASS, THE HASHKNIFE OUTFIT and others. The Tucker Flat Gang used an old Hashknife Outfit line cabin at Tucker Springs, west of Winslow, as their Mecca. It was a base camp for expeditions into the high desert of the Canyon Diablo region.

Diamonds and Iron

Caches of Precious Stones

Although myths about the Canyon Diablo region abound, there is actual evidence that precious stones and metals were hidden in the niches of its hills and canyons. Prospectors and gold seekers eagerly trailed into the area after the fur trappers left, but their successes, if any, are cloaked in secrecy and time. (87)

In 1886 two Hispanic sheepherders brought bits of a metallic substance they had found along Diablo to Fred Voltz of the Canyon Diablo Trading Post. The substance turned out to be meteoric iron spewed from the Meteor Crater impact. Voltz ended up shipping two railroad flatcars of these meteorites to California. Having sold the metal from outer space

for 75 cents a pound, he later was shocked to discover that the iron contained 2% platinum — which had been going for $36 per ounce! Meteoric iron later became popular when it was polished and set in rings and bracelets, selling for $25 per pound. Many members of the Tucker Flat Gang became the envy of other kids, boasting silver rings adorned with a meteorite or piece of petrified wood.

Diamonds were also found in meteors. Of course, any discovery of diamonds in those days was a closely guarded secret for fear of a "diamond rush." Still, prevailing rumors and yarns spun by the campfire attracted many in search of hidden diamond mines. These treasure hunters had no idea that they were actually walking over rough cut diamonds. The crystallized carbon bits were imbedded in a hard, stony slate-like material that had been "cooked" with great force and temperature by the impact of Meteor Crater and cast over the whole Diablo area. When broken open, pieces of this debris often revealed an industrial diamond.

One old prospector named Cannon was alleged to have gathered buckskin bags full of these diamonds over many years, stashing them in the caves of Canyon Diablo. Some surmised that the money he always seemed to have probably came from selling and shipping diamonds directly the out of the Canyon Diablo station. He was once seen with the diamonds in Winslow. Cannon's experience with diamonds proved to be fatal however, and one day he simply disappeared. His skeletal remains were later discovered in a gravel pit along the Little Colorado River, with two holes in his skull. No diamonds and no money were ever found. Yet, a story surfaced about a burly man who stumbled into a cattle line camp near Jack's Canyon with a buckskin pouch full of diamonds. Before the man died, he mumbled that he had found the Cannon diamond cache.

Voltz Trading Post at Canyon Diablo

The legendary tales of Diablo's riches did not end with the discovery of diamonds. In the 1890's, onyx was found in the canyon areas around Two Guns. Onyx was cherished at the time for use in creating jewelry, building facades and tabletops. Many prospectors made claims in the area, mining and hauling out the onyx with two-wheel horse carts. The onyx was then shipped by train from Canyon Diablo to Los Angeles and Chicago. Eventually, enough onyx was found in two Diablo offshoots, Grapevine and Deer Canyons, to meet the entire domestic need of the time.

Led by Precursors, the Mother Road Is Born

The California-Santa Fe Trail, blazed by early wagon trains and pathfinders, avoided Canyon Diablo and arced north across Arizona proceeding past Luepp on its way to Flagstaff. Mule trains, sometimes in a two-hitch series, rambled back and forth from the railhead to Flagstaff carrying freight and supplies. This means of transport to and from the railhead became tedious and expensive for the businessmen of Flagstaff. The problem compelled them to devise a shorter passage to Flagstaff, one routed to join the Winslow to Mormon Lake Road which crossed Canyon Diablo south of the Two Guns site. This was a lonely, winding road and a perfect setting for high-waymen and ambushes. In 1888, a horseback travel-er found a man hanging from the tongue of his wagon.

In 1907, just west of the upper Mormon crossing, a flat road was scraped out north to Two Guns where it wound down a long slope to the bottom of the canyon. An east side dugway was blasted up to the flat rim, but this road was impassable when flooded

Mormon Crossing at Diablo

water was deep in canyon, and travelers still used the old Mormon crossing. In 1914, a family named Oldfield appeared with their children and settled beside the new road. They built a rock house three miles south of Two Guns on the old road which became known as the Old Trails Highway, the pre-cursor to Route 66. At this site they conducted a small business from their home. Travelers, cowboys,

Navajos and sheepherders paraded through the Oldfield's front room, representing the first pilgrims on Route 66.

The arrival of automobiles and the railroad signaled the end of the idyllic western frontier. Tourism had begun in a big way. Fred Voltz at the Canyon Diablo Trading Post had experienced his first Hopi Snake Dance, and soon after began taking tourists to the Hopi mesas to see the dances. (see VOLUME. II,

Roadway Gouged into Diablo

ROUTE 66 CHRONICLES, "Uncle Ray.") He then established The Fields, a trading post halfway between Canyon Diablo and Orabi. In 1912 he sold the Canyon Diablo Trading Post to the Babbitt Brothers, leaving in 1922 to go to Route 66.

The 1920's clamor for highways initiated an intensive national highway building program. The National Old Trail Highway, proclaimed as "the golden road to the promised land," ultimately

Roadway westward out of Diablo

became the first Route 66, often referred to as "the Old Route 66." The first bridge was built at Two Guns to allow Old Route 66 to span the depths of Canyon Diablo. The new Route 66 was completed downstream in 1938, with a newer bridge transversing the Diablo. A plethora of rock dwellings, including three separate zoo complexes, are today a shrine to the fame of the Route 66 Two Guns site. Violence, mystery, enchantment, thrills and tourist trappings all melded into the many enterprises that came and went at the infamous Two Guns site.

The Crucible for Western Lore and Legend

Much of the allure of the southwest's segment of Route 66 is anchored in the fascinating western lore and natural beauty inherent in the area. Be it the pueblo architecture of a café, the curio shops and trading posts along the road or the rattlesnake eggs found in cans, the legends, the history and the loveliness of the environment thrilled thousands of travelers, imprinting forever upon their minds the many reflections of Route 66.

One cannot watch television anywhere in the world without eventually, in a movie or commercial, seeing Monument Valley appear on the screen. Although Bret Hart and other authors made the romance, adventure and lore of the American west famous long before the 1900's, it was Zane Grey who captured its magnificence, its seductiveness and splendor. Zane Grey's books, later made into movies, gave the American West a mystique and rendered it a preferred destination for world travelers.

No one contributed more to sketching the canyons and fleshing out the characters of the American West than did Zane Grey. Half of Grey's western books take place in Arizona. He aptly captured on paper its unspoiled natural beauty, unequaled anywhere in the world. Grey's characters and plots were based on real people and real adventures. In his novels, he consistently portrayed western frontier values such as the indomitable will to survive and succeed in the wilderness, a reverence for nature and the simplicity of moral codes and relationships. Grey imprinted the western character and the charm of the west in the psyches of both the local native and the international traveler. His books, subsequent movies and the fascination they generated launched a steady flow of international pilgrims to the western Meccas that continues to this day. (45)

The allure is launched

Grey is recognized for his unparalleled portrayal of the soul of the land. Arizona was the most representative of his settings and was the inspiration for innumerable plots. Arizona's endless, ever-changing vista of deserts, mountains, trees, roaring rivers, blue-white lakes and gentle meadow streams, its wind, sun, dust storms, rain, snow, withering heat and body-numbing cold all provided rich elements for plot and setting. Grey began his artistic command of western beauty, character and legend in Flagstaff, Arizona. Lee Doyle served for many years as a guide to those awesome spots, and was a source of lore for Grey's stories.

Grey's works were characterized by fictionalized romances based on actual historical events and authentic physical detail. He wrote about the canyons, the tribal lands, the deserts and the forests. Such titles as SUNSET PASS, THE HASHKNIFE OUTFIT, THE VANISHING AMERICAN, CALL OF THE CANYON, UNDER THE TONTO RIM, THE LOST PUEBLO, RAIDERS OF SPANISH PEAKS, THE RAINBOW TRAIL and ROPING LIONS IN THE GRAND CANYON were stories based upon actual, prominent Arizona sites.

In 1907, Grey came to Flagstaff and established headquarters at the Weatherford Hotel to do research on his book RIDERS OF THE PURPLE SAGE, a novel about the Mormon settlements north of the Grand Canyon in an area known as the Arizona Strip. In 1923, Grey introduced Arizona to the film industry with the production of THE CALL OF THE CANYON, filmed in Sedona and Oak Creek Canyon. Grey insisted in fact that all of the films of his books be done on location.

Grey wrote his novels from the depths of Oak Creek Canyon, from under the Mogollon Rim, overlooking Rainbow Bridge, among Anasazi ruins and amid the Navajo people in the most remote spot in the contiguous United States — Kayenta, Arizona. The Tucker Flat Gang were avid readers of Zane Grey. They brought Grey's imagination with them to Tucker Springs — and brought the ambience of Tucker Springs to Grey's landscape sketches of northern Arizona.

The RAINBOW TRAIL by Zane Grey

Zane Grey in Monument Valley

The Bridge at Canyon Diablo

TWO
Wilder than Dodge or Tombstone
The Screaming Iron Horse

Throughout the 1870's, the steel rails of the transcontinental railroad crept slowly across New Mexico and Arizona toward a rendezvous with the Pacific Ocean and toward their destiny — the railroad spanning of the nation. The Atlantic and Pacific railroad continued through northern Arizona, reaching the rim of Canyon Diablo at a point 2.5 miles north of the present Two Guns. Engineering complications at the canyon as well as financial problems halted the path of the Iron Horse for two whole years — but two years were more than enough to give birth to the wildest town the west had ever seen or ever will see — the infamous rail camp called Canyon Diablo.

Wagon Town

From 1880 to 1882, the town roared day and night. It supported resident construction crews and a bevy of ruthless characters, and acted as a railhead for Flagstaff, Prescott and other towns to the west and the south. Long freight trains of goods rumbled northward from the rail terminal, moving along the east rim of Diablo to the old crossing near the present day town of Luepp. At that point the trains turned west toward Flagstaff.

Freighters and stagecoaches made stops at Walnut Tanks and Turkey Tanks on the forty-mile haul into Flagstaff. There was a regularly scheduled stage from Flagstaff to Canyon Diablo, with other stagecoaches arriving daily with travelers. Various routes fanned out from Canyon Diablo in all directions. Busy freight wagons hauled clothing, equipment and food for construction crews and then headed westward, pulling trailers with merchandise delivered from the east by train.

The small community perchcd on the very edge of a canyon had become a bustling hub of activity, welcoming short passenger trains from Winslow as well as the long freights. Portable saloons, which had followed railroad construction camps from Kansas, Colorado and New Mexico, were unloaded and spotted on the main street to serve their new Canyon Diablo home.

Although its existence spanned but a brief blink of Western history, even towns like "Tombstone, Virginia City and Abilene could not hold a candle to this end-of-the-railroad depravity." Hourly holdups and murders were common occurrences. Newcomers were sought out and detected, and if there was even

a slight hunch that they possessed anything of worth, they were summarily slugged and relieved of their valuables. (84)

Hell Street

Canyon Diablo, the archetypal railroad construction shack town, consisted of two lines of buildings extending one mile eastward from the canyon rim. Situated on the north side of the tracks, its skyline was configured with a water tank, stock pens, a warehouse, and freight docks. Water was pumped up from the depths of the canyon. Even the hellish town setting used in the movie, HIGH PLAINS DRIFTER, painted red by Clint Eastwood, couldn't hold a candle to the likes of Canyon Diablo.

Its main drag was christened "Hell Street" in honor of it's fourteen saloons, ten gambling dens, four houses of ill-repute and two dance pavilions. These elegant shacks were made of green lumber covered by tin, tar or laced canvas, and many of them boasted eating counters. Scattered amongst these glowing tabernacles of pleasure were grocery and dry goods

stores. Though few of the establishments had signs, every one knew their names. There were saloons known as The Colorado and The Texas, and others with names such as Last Drink, Road to Ruin, Bughouse Joe's and Name Your Pizen. The main dance hall was the Cootchy–Klatch, whose green lumber slab boards reverberated all night long with the nostalgic strains of 1870's ballads. (71)

The favorite houses of prostitution were simply proclaimed Clabberfoot Annie's and B.S. Mary's, and on any given night residents might witness the hourglass figure of Clabberfoot or the six-foot raw-boned frame of B.S. Mary facing off from opposite sides of the street. The two madams would yell epithets at each until they ended up fighting in the dust and the dirt. Egged on by the profanities of men piling out of their saloon perches, Annie and Mary's screeching battles would fill the black night above the canyon, the frays reaching a climax when tufts of hair wafted into the chill air. Finally, bloody noses, black eyes and body bites would erode enthusiasm for vengeance, and the hostilities would come to an exhausting end. On one occasion, an angry Annie hit Mary in the buttocks with buckshot.

The Brief and Violent Tour of Town Marshals

A number of unorganized gangs and hard-luck drifters had come west to settle. They immediately noticed the strongboxes in stagecoaches, and they knew of the freight trains shipping gold and payrolls. These riches were seen as plums and easy pickings. Moving ever westward to avoid the law and civilized society, many of the bands included within the heart of their calloused crowd outright criminals and wanted killers. Pillage and plunder got so wild and out of control that E.E. Ayer, a Flagstaff lumber man, insisted on some kind of protection for his freight shipments. A freighter had been robbed and burned, causing some businessmen and sawmill people to request protection by U.S. Army military escorts out of Fort Defiance.

Failing in these efforts, victims decided to get organized and put money up for a Canyon Diablo Town Marshall. The ensuing rapid succession of marshals would have given the Earps second thoughts about accepting a position at Canyon Diablo. The first marshal's badge was pinned on his vest at three in the afternoon, and by eight that evening he was laid out for burial. The second marshal lasted only two weeks, while the third sneaked into a church with a sawed-off shotgun and shot several bystanders. His

More killings than Tombstone and Dodge

term was voided two weeks later when forty-five slugs hit him between the shoulders. The fourth Marshall, discovered to be making deals with the crooks themselves, lasted only six days, falling to the gunshot of an enraged victim's relative.

The fifth marshal's stint approached humoresque, near epic proportion. The sallow-cheeked, gaunt, consumptive ex-preacher marshal called "Bill Duckin" wore two guns slung on swivels and favored long, black coats. In one such coat the pockets had been taken out to allow instant access and firing of his pistols. One fateful Sunday, "Bill Duckin" forgot that the outfit he put on was his "Sunday" suit, which, to his great misfortune, had pockets instead of holes. The story told is that he was unceremoniously gunned down amid the screaming laughter of his assailants.

The sixth Marshall of Canyon Diablo, one Joe Fowler, managed to kill twenty men in the railroad town of Gallup—yet he lasted only ten days. After escaping perforation by lead, he managed to slip out of town alive, only to be hung later in Socorro.

The Heist of the Wells Fargo Stagecoach

Rogues, killers and thieves were not the only ones rampaging about at the Canyon's edge. Many a young cowboy in those days considered robbery a diverting pastime and a fast, sure way to amass a small fortune, and more than once held up stages coaches at Canyon Diablo in the hope of financing a rich retirement in Mexico.

Such was the case on the morning of May 10, 1881, when gathering thunderclouds sent an ominous message to passengers waiting to leave Canyon Diablo.

Wells Fargo Stage

They had disembarked from the comfortable coach in the A & P train where the tracks ended and were ready to board the red Wells Fargo Concord Stage bound for Flagstaff and Prescott. Earlier in the day, employees had stashed four mailbags in the boot at the back of the stage. The six-horse team finally pulled the Concord Stage out of the railroad station, heading in a southerly direction next to the rim of the canyon along a winding trail through the Kaibab limestone. (43)

The stage driver on that day was a man named John Hance, who would later win renown as a Grand Canyon guide and teller of tall tales. On this particular day he drove northward (near present-day Luepp), crossing a smooth, shallow part of the Canyon just before it joined the Little Colorado River. The trail then turned westward across the red sands of the Little Colorado River Valley, meandering through the black cinder hills and heading upward into the pinon trees and lush green forests covering the east flank of San Francisco Peaks.

As Hance eased the horses into a slow walk in the upward climb toward Flagstaff, five men appeared out of nowhere and surrounded the stage. They pointed their guns at Hance's head and demanded the loot. Hance told them that there was no loot. The bandits immediately selected two particular mailbags from the stage's boot and ordered Hance to pull out. Hance was puzzled as to why the bandits seized only two specific bags from the four in the coach. Even at that, he thought, the bags were only full of mail, and worthless.

When the stagecoach arrived in Flagstaff at five that afternoon, Hance informed the stationmaster and the marshal that some people would not be getting their mail that day. The stationmaster looked grim as the marshal informed Hance that the heisted mailbags had been disguised to hide a fortune in gold and silver. The bars of precious metal, he explained, had been packed into whiskey kegs and wrapped in paper. Wells Fargo was transferring money incognito from Albuquerque to San Francisco due to the increasing frequency of stage robberies. Finally, the officials concluded that the theft had to be an inside job, as only insiders would know which bags to take. A posse was formed and headed out in pursuit, but the robbers were long gone.

By a strange twist of fate, the Sixth U.S. Cavalry, Company D, was bivouacked south of the Mogollon Rim at Fort Apache. The commanding officer, Captain. E. C. Hentig, got word of the robbery and sent out Apache scouts to track the robbers. Hentig, Company D and the Apache scouts followed some lukewarm tracks to a spring on the San Francisco Peaks where they found five men about to mount their horses. Hance described one of the men as a red-bearded, burly sort. The sudden, deafening exchange of gunfire that ensued between the outlaws and the U.S. Cavalry resulted in five dead robbers.

As was the custom in those times, the dead men were swiftly dispatched into shallow graves near a spring, next to a cabin. Mysteriously, after a somewhat lengthy search, no loot was found anywhere. The bodies were later exhumed and identified by Hance. The robbery tale made for good storytelling, nourishment for the imagination on snowy winter nights in the small settlement of Flagstaff.

Prospectors were spurred into an endless, determined search for gold. One story is told about a strange father-son duo who were seen in caves near the spring, poring over a map by lantern-light. Confronted by a homesteader they claimed to be geologists, but following deeper probes they confessed they were hunting for the treasure buried by the stagecoach robbers. It was said that there was an inscription on the rocks near the spring, an inscription intended to identify the location of the buried loot.

Some claim to have seen a glowing, metallic image off in the distance near the spring site while sojourning on one of the myriad trails that traverse the area east of the Peaks. In 1913, one Short Jimmy McGuire appeared in a Flagstaff saloon, flashing $50 gold pieces and stating that he found the loot with a water witch. Rumor has it that Jimmy left Flagstaff one night, his coat bulging with gold coins, subsequently and ironically perishing of a heart attack from the exertion of carrying such immense weight in his pockets.

Many expeditions, both serious and frivolous, have probed the spring area for treasure. A gentleman named George McCormick, a Grand Canyon prospector, searched that area for many years. He was succeeded in his quest by his son, Melvin Mac McCormick. Melvin, along with a man named C.J. Hallidlay, looked repeatedly for the lost gold. The prevailing story suggests that C.J in fact found an inscription on a rock.

For nearly one-hundred twenty years the story has not changed — five dead outlaws leave no clues to $125 in buried loot — gold, silver bars and coins heisted from a Wells Fargo stagecoach buried near Canyon Diablo. Many interested parties and researchers question whether there was a holdup at all. No records have been identified in the Prescott newspaper, THE DAILY ARIZONA MINER, and cursory examinations of Wells Fargo archives reveal no proof of the Wells Fargo Concord Stagecoach robbery out of Canyon Diablo. (43)

A gentleman named Tony Richardson chronicled both the robbery incident and the quest for treasure in a pulp magazine. He claimed he was with Halliday when he found an inscription on a rock near the spring. Some researchers point to the fact that Richardson possessed a very active and productive imagination — one which resulted in three hundred novels and five thousand magazine articles during his writing career. (71)

Holdup of the Eastbound Santa Fe Express Number Seven

Arizona Territory tales romanticize the lives of cowhand buddies who, though not evil by nature nor innately criminal of mind, carried out single train robberies. Campfire glorification of these daring holdups captured the fancy of impressionable, adventurous young cowboys who saw in these bold ventures a chance to enter the ranks of the wealthy with what they viewed as a simple, low-risk train heist. (84)

One such unfortunate cowboy, named William Sparks, recounted one of the most intriguing train robbery stories ever to come out of Canyon Diablo lore. Although Sparks came to Arizona with the U.S. Calvary, he eventually ended up as a Hashknife Outfit buckaroo. According to Sparks, back then the cowpunchers hanging out at the Hashknife Ranch bunkhouse were not only broke, but also bored. They whittled away the hours dreaming about the good old hurly-burly days when they roamed the streets of Dodge, Abilene, Tombstone and Clifton. It seemed that life was passing them by.

With each faint ray that sank behind the peaks of Sunset Pass came the poignant realization that the glory days might be gone forever. Mere thoughts of the demise of those wonderful times brought on such a biting depression, such a profound sadness that the cowboys began to dream about anything, anything at all that would end the monotony of their existence. The romance of train robberies and the high esteem bestowed upon those who could pull them off did not escape the minds of Sparks and his Hashknifer pards. So it was that on March 21, 1889, four cowboys from that same Hashknife Outfit — John H, (Jack) Smythe, "Long" John Halford, Daniel M. Havrick and William D. Sparks — held up the eastbound SANTA FE FAST EXPRESS #7.

The four men met in high spirits at a predetermined site, the Chevron Hills Line Camp south of Winslow, but the blustery, stormy weather of the morning immediately eroded their enthusiasm. They gazed longingly over the Mogollon Rim, beyond which they knew lay the warmer desert of southern Arizona with its carpet of flowers and Palo Verde trees. Stronger gusts of wind coupled with stinging squalls of sleet and snow began chill their nerve even more. Sparks said later, "the winds screech, wail and cut like a knife," (75)

In spite of their discomfort, the recurring dream of leaving the cowboy life for untold ease and prosperi-

Lee's Ferry on the Colorado River

ty drove them northward, and they headed into the freezing wind and snow toward their inevitable destiny, the Canyon Diablo Station House.

Light streamed out a window, bestowing a golden hue upon a square patch of snow. As the train stopped at the station to get water, a fireman got off with a lantern and, blinded by the driving snow, almost walked off into the canyon. One of the gang shot at the fireman and the train staff threw up their hands in surrender. After subduing the crew, the four men blew open the express safe. They retrieved several packages of money, seven thousand dollars in watches and jewelry and a veritable fortune in jewels. A Wells Fargo agent reported that there had been $100,000 in currency, $40,000 in gold coin, $70,000 worth of diamonds and $2,500 in new silver dollars on the train.

The men headed to a point five miles south of the Station along the Canyon rim, and there lit a small fire to thaw their frozen bones. It was Sparks's birthday. They put the diamonds in a tobacco pouch, divided the riches equally into four piles and blindfolded Sparks. Sparks then randomly matched each pile with one of the men. Once each pile was identified with a man all the loot was buried either on the rim or down in the Canyon. They buried the rifles as well, wishing to maintain their cover as cowpunchers. It has been generally accepted that the site of the cache was very near the present site of Two Guns. Later, Smythe gradually lost the diamonds he had stashed in his tobacco pouch while absent-mindedly dumping his tobacco into cigarette papers.

The four men had first traveled south from Canyon Diablo in order to throw any pursuers off their trail.

They knew the trackers and a posse would pursue them posthaste, even in the bitter weather. They agreed to split up, and to meet in Wyoming. Two of the men took the road toward a place called Blackfalls, located on the Little Colorado River. The other two went north and then west to the Little Colorado River, where they let their horses drift with the current. Their slickers kept their cloths dry. All four crossed the Colorado River in the dead of night at Lee's Ferry, muffling their passage by covering their horses' hooves with cloth. They went up the Canyon walls in the dark, riding toward Wahweap Canyon (now the main bay and major access to Lake Powell).

They were certain that a posse had been dispatched to catch them, but they had no idea that the sheriff of Yavapai County (Diablo's locale at that time), would be Sheriff William O. (Bucky) O'Neill. O'Neill's Old West law enforcement acumen was acute. He was soon to gain fame as a Roosevelt Rough Rider, suffering a heroic death at the battle of San Juan Hill during the Spanish American War.

Sheriff William O. (Bucky) O'Neill.

Arriving at Wahweap near dusk, the group decided to stay with a Mormon colony encampment. Suspicious, the elders at the Mormon Camp challenged the four renegades and they narrowly escaped capture. In the meantime, Bucky O'Neill had reached another camp. The Mormons there warned him about the fugitives, hoping to get the reward that had been posted. Using this information, O'Neill cut off their escape and trapped them on a peninsula above the Colorado River. Desperate, Sparks raced down to the river on foot, wearing only one boot. This maneuver did not fool the trackers who followed his trail along the river. At length O'Neill surrounded the fugitives, handily catching all four of the men.

Captured and dejected, the four were escorted by deputies and express officers to the railhead at Milford, Utah. There they were put on a train to Salt Lake that continued on to Denver. At Raton Pass, the guards, exhausted from celebrating, fell into a deep sleep. Smythe was able to slip out of his shackles and escape. He stole a horse and headed east into Texas. He rode straight into a fierce blizzard, where he came upon a nearly frozen schoolteacher. His compassion in saving the schoolteacher proved to be his undoing as the act of kindness foiled his escape plans. Ironically, the Texas Ranger posse who had originally missed him in the blizzard stopped at the teacher's house and were told that he was there. Smythe was soon recaptured and joined his three compadres in the Prescott Jail.

The 25-year sentence in The Territorial Prison at Yuma that each man received was essentially a death sentence. Due to the inevitable onset of tuberculosis and the intense 120-degree heat at the Prison, the average life of a prisoner was only four years. One version of this tale claims that the young teacher, acknowledging that Smythe put both his freedom and his life on the line to save her, journeyed all the way to Phoenix on a mission of mercy.

There she allegedly pleaded for Smythe's pardon, which was granted by then Arizona Governor Hughes. There are those however that dispute the motive of compassion, contending that the teacher only wished to claim part of the reward. In the case of Sparks, an old friend of his from ranch days, a gentleman named Cutter, was now an Arizona Prison Commissioner. Hit hard at seeing Sparks languish within the walls of The Territorial Prison at Yuma, Cutter had him pardoned. There were no paroles in those days, and the only escape from disease and heat was a pardon from the Arizona Governor.

Pardoned Poet

Years later William Sparks wrote an account of his experiences, summing up much of his life through poetry. "The Last of the Pioneers — I am tired, and all day I've been dreaming; of a day and world that is gone; the world of the trail and the campfire that has passed to the West like the Dawn; and sinks in the wave throbbing ocean, along with the heroes that bore it along; and again we ride out westward till the dim purple mountain appears and the songs that were sung, and the laughter comes back as my memory clears, while my heart pulses through to the music that comes through the mist of the years." (75, pg. 175)

Commenting on his pardon Sparks wrote the following poem: "The Pardon — It is night and the gray walls seem fading. My cellmates have gone to their sleep. And the guards on the wall call their numbers as they tramp to and fro on their beat. For the prison has sunk to it slumbers and the mercy of night and of dreams now blots out the dull prison horror with all of its anguish and schemes, while I silently wait for my summons, that must come with the morning's first beams." (75, pg. 175)

The thieves had only $100 among them when captured. This fact has sustained the belief that the booty is still buried along rim of Canyon Diablo, or down in its gorge near Two Guns. Treasure hunting parties have generally explored the Canyon from Two Guns northward to the railroad bridge. Based on extensive exploration both in and along the edge of Canyon Diablo, the author has concluded that several lifetimes could be spent in examining and exploring every nook and cranny, every crack and cave of the sixty-five mile long Canyon — with little chance of discovering the robbers' cache.

Temporary Divine Providence

The Canyon Diablo area is resplendent with stories of robbery and mayhem. One tale tells of the outlaw who robbed a train construction crew's payroll. When the pursuing posse caught up with the bandit, they found he had lost the saddlebags. The fate of the robber was humorously described by his captors as a "suspended sentence," and he was summarily strung up with a rope around his neck. Just when a hand had been raised to slap the horse's behind, lightening hit the pine tree.

The vigilantes felt that the lightening was a sign of divine intervention. The traumatized thief was subsequently turned over to the law and incarcerated in the Territorial Prison at Yuma. Years latter a cowboy riding the range along the rim of Canyon Diablo sighted a piece of leather sticking out of a limestone outcropping. Pulling on the edge of the leather, out came a rotting saddlebag full of old money.

Winslow, Arizona circa 1890

Beyond the Bizarre

What would appear to be the most bizarre aftermath of any gunfight fatality in all of western history occurred at Canyon Diablo. On the moonlit eve of April 7, 1905, two cowboys, John Shaw and Bill Smythe, both dressed in business suits, entered the Wigwam Saloon in Winslow. It was after midnight on a Saturday. William Smythe was short, with dark hair and bronzed skin. Shaw was a six-footer capped with reddish hair and blessed with a broad, friendly grin, a grin that remained on his face even in death.

After the bartender poured their whiskey, the two cowboys suddenly stopped drinking and stared at the silver dollars on the side of the roulette wheel. Standing just in front of the wheel were two Hashknife cowpunchers named Frank Ketchum and Lucien Creswell. Smythe signaled Shaw with his eyes as they pulled their guns, and Shaw yelled, "Keep your hands in sight and nothing will happen." Stuffing the silver dollars into their pockets, they ran out the door of the Wigwam.

The two deputies on duty in Winslow, Deputy Pemberton and Deputy Giles, immediately checked Front Street, searched the alleys and buildings of downtown Winslow and then hastened to the train depot to warn the railroad ticket agent. Right near the tracks and the Santa Fe Division Headquarters, Pemberton saw silver shining on ground. The object turned out to be one of the stolen silver dollars. Six more were found another hundred feet down the track siding. It was decided that the fugitives had hopped a westbound freight and left the county. Pemberton notified Sheriff Henderson in Flagstaff and Sheriff C.I. "Chet" Houck in Holbrook.

At that time the only road west was used by horses and horse-drawn vehicles as it was far too rough for cars. The transcontinental railroad was the best and fastest means of transportation, so focus was on the trains. Sheriff Henderson searched the freight cars at Flagstaff, but realized the robbers could have gotten off before the Flagstaff depot and taken horses into the wilderness. They could also have jumped from the westbound freight and caught a train going east. In the meantime, Sheriff Houck had gone to Winslow, where just before dawn he telephoned Sheriff Henderson in Flagstaff. Having discovered no sign of the bandits in Winslow, Pemberton, or Houck, they decided to go to Flagstaff but found nothing there. In the late afternoon Houck and Pemberton caught an eastbound train back to Winslow. As they were approaching Canyon Diablo, Houck speculated that the two bandits might have gotten off somewhere in that area, stealing horses from a nearby ranch.

Their suspicions were heightened when the conductor declared that he had seen two men in the bushes several miles from Canyon Diablo. Houck and Pemberton left the train at a spot called Sunshine, four miles beyond Canyon Diablo. The two lawmen stopped the search at that point, giving in to the gnawing hunger in their stomachs. They headed west up the tracks to the Canyon Diablo Station to eat, entering a long, stone building, the Fred Voltz Trading Post. Voltz, who knew from a telegram about the fugitives, mentioned that he had seen a couple of bums hanging around the tiny rail town. Before Houck and Pemberton could exit the porch, E.F. Klee appeared in front of the trading post and declared that the two strangers were headed "thataway."

Houck and Deputy Pemberton jumped off the porch, crept toward the limestone corner of the warehouse and through the bluish haze of dusk barely made out two men headed in that direction. Houck and Pemberton abruptly came out from behind the corner and challenged the two men, announcing that they were officers of the law and demanding a search. The two bandits spun around and Shaw said, "No one searches us." Houck saw the tall one (Shaw) reach for a gun. Houck pulled out his own pistol, but

Passenger train over Canyon Diablo

Shaw beat him to the draw and fired, the slug going through Houck's shirt, creasing his stomach. At that instant Smythe drew on Houck. Pemberton quickly shot him in the shoulder, marring Smythe's aim and saving Houck's life. (82)

In less than no time, intense gunfight erupted, the two pairs facing off within several feet of each other. An amazing twenty shots were fired within the next few seconds — five slugs out of each man's gun. The firepower was so fierce that Houck's cloths were shredded with holes. Miraculously, neither the robbers nor the lawmen were killed in the heavy rain of bullets. Shaw, assuming that everyone was out of bullets but him, took dead aim at Houck, hoping to make a kill with his last bullet. He was unaware that Pemberton had a sixth bullet left in his chamber. Pemberton habitually kept a sixth bullet in the chamber with the hammer on, although most gunmen usu-

**Smith & Wesson .44 Caliber
April, 1876**

ally left that chamber empty for safety reasons. Pemberton fired his sixth cartridge, hitting Shaw in the side of the head and killing him instantly. (6)

Klee and Voltz later expressed amazement, saying that it sounded like all the bullets discharged simultaneously. Everyone found it incredible that the men, standing only 6 feet apart, had fired 21 shots and missed 18 times! Twenty-one bullets exploded in a split second! The only logical explanation that could be made for so many misses was that the gunmen fired too quickly, and that the powder flashes had blinded them in the dusky light. All combatants except Shaw later confessed that they were scared to death and literally shaking in their boots. Pemberton's sixth bullet saved Houck's life but ultimately lost him the Sheriff's job.

Because there were no embalmers at Diablo, Shaw was hastily put in a pine box, the lid nailed tightly and the coffin placed for eternity on the south side of the railroad tracks in Canyon Diablo's version of Boot Hill. Smythe, who had been wounded, was taken to the Winslow hospital.

Among the Hashknife cowboys present at Wigwam that fateful night were several that had little love for Sheriff Houck, whose brother was bitterly hated for hangings carried out on the range. Sam Case loathed Houck the most, claiming that the Houcks "liked rope and shots in the back." Lucien Creswell tried to dissuade Case from doing anything rash. Case finally stopped the threats and his bitter condemnation of Houck, blurting out that Shaw and Smythe had not had their drinks. "Them two boys paid for drinks and didn't down their whiskey. Was Shaw given a snort before they planted him?" Discussion went on into the night, and the bunch of cowboys were joined by many more including Hashknife wagon boss J.D. Rogers.

Finally, a long lonesome train whistle incited twenty-two intoxicated cowboys to jump on the on the next freight train to Canyon Diablo, one of the men shouting, "there is our iron hoss, let's go!" They went to the Voltz Trading Post, where Ketchum, Campbell, and Flake got shovels from Voltz. Voltz also supplied a Kodak camera to the unwieldy assemblage. They dug Shaw up out of the ground and stuck a shovel under the pine lid of his coffin.

Shaw's last drink

As the sun climbed over the Painted Desert the coffin lid was removed, revealing that Shaw, although somewhat disfigured by the bullet, still had a slight smile on his face.

The cowpunchers stood in silence looking at Shaw, musing about their own mortality. They began to cry, mumbling quietly that the dead man looked like any of the group and that he was in fact a pard brother. The general consensus was that he could have been any one of them, and that he certainly deserved a drink. Shaw's stiff body was immediately swung up out of the coffin. Campbell and Case poured liquor from a long neck brown bottle through Shaw's clenched teeth. Pictures were snapped and Case directed that they be presented to Houck, but Case took the roll back and later gave it to a Winslow attorney. The photographs were displayed in a Winslow tavern until 1940. Later accounts indicated that an editor of the local paper killed the story, believing it to be too farfetched.

One-hundred seventeen silver dollars were found on Shaw, and one-hundred fifty four on Smythe. Houck remarked about the familiarity of the men's names, speculating that the two were actually professionals using aliases. Smythe did concede that Shaw had been a crack shot. John Herrignton, the Flagstaff Coroner and Justice of the Peace, dutifully swore in

Shaw resting in peace

The chasm is finally breached

a jury several days later. The Jury's verdict was that Shaw died by gunshot wounds delivered by Sheriff Houck in the act of carrying out his official duties.

Smythe was sent to The Territorial Prison at Yuma for a fifteen-year sentence. Yet that same Smythe, whose real name was William Evans, had already been a prisoner at Yuma in 1897 and had been paroled in 1914. Pemberton, who later became a marshall, ended up killing Giles in a fight. Sheriff Houck lost his next election. Shaw still resides with a belt of whiskey in his mouth in his lonely, shallow grave at Canyon Diablo near the feet of Herman Wolf.

The boisterous, brutal nature of life at Canyon Diablo in the 1880's accelerated to such a degree that Flagstaff businesses asked the U.S. Army to establish marshal law in its streets. But before the Army from Ft. Defiance could get there, bridge construction was finally completed. The railroad moved onward toward California, construction crews, equipment and all. The wooden frame heavens of Hell Street were torn down or loaded on flat cars and disappeared into the West, bound for a new home.

The Finale

The depraved and barbarous town that Canyon Diablo had become died overnight. A terse announcement in the Railroad Gazette totally masked the demise of what might well have been the roughest little city in the West — "The Atlantic and Pacific Road is now completed to Canyon Diablo, 311 miles west of the Rio Grande River, where the dry chasm is being spanned by an iron viaduct 520 feet long and 254 feet high. The structure is designed to carry the heaviest consolidated engine moving at a speed of fifty miles an hour." (81)

A gentler and quieter Canyon Diablo arose amid the remnants of the original town. After the railroad was completed and the construction operation left town, a gentleman named Algert from Pennsylvania opened a store in an abandoned rail car and focused on trading with the Indians. Elaborate limestone dwellings were constructed, including a large trading post. In 1897 Algert sold the post to Fred Voltz.

Of an evening, off in the distance, one can see evening light fade over the tombstone of Herman Wolf — the only remaining recognizable grave in Boot Hill. Peering toward the distant silhouette of the San Francisco Peaks outlined against a rose hued sky, one can only muse about the dubious characters and violent confrontations that might still abide at

A heavy presence at old Canyon Diablo

that site. As dusk fades into darkness, the wails and whispers of the incessant wind seem alive and pleading. There is a heavy presence at old Canyon Diablo.

Mysteries yet to unfold

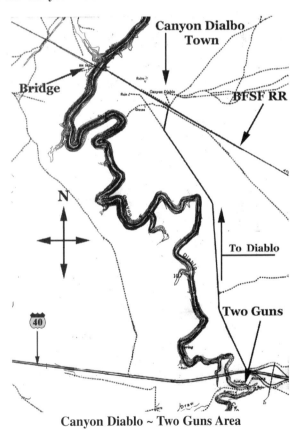

Canyon Diablo ~ Two Guns Area

Two Guns Zoo

THREE
The Dawning of the Mother Road Arizona
Murder at Two Guns

The centuries of travelers crisscrossing the Canyon Diablo region on foot, by horse, on wagons, inside stagecoaches and aboard trains made way for the ant-like line of autos that would later march in a steady flow on Route 66 to the edge of Canyon Diablo at Two Guns. It all began when Ed Randolph

First road across the Canyon

set up a business in a sector of Canyon Diablo, upstream from the present Two Guns site. Automobiles had begun crossing at Two Guns instead of using the Mormon Crossing two miles to the south. Flagstaff businessmen wished to shorten the lengthy route that followed the old Mormon Road to Mormon Lake before turning northward into Flagstaff. A crossing near Two Guns seemed the most feasible alternative to the southern crossing and road.

Consequently, in 1907 a flat road was engineered at a point west of Two Guns, pushing northward from there. At that locale it went down a long slope to the bottom of Canyon Diablo and up the east side through a dug-away which had been blasted up to the flat rim of the Diablo. Still, this crossing was not usable when flood waters in the Canyon were deep. The low-powered automobiles could not make it across the stream at the Canyon's bottom and up to its eastern rim. During these flood conditions travelers still used the old Mormon crossing.

First cement bridge at Canyon bottom

First Dwelling at Two Guns

The first ever "bridge" built over the canyon at Two Guns consisted of a cement structure across the steam bed which provided a solid base to prevent cars from sinking in the mud. As one roves over the Two Guns site, vestiges of those many early roads, the precursors of Route 66, can still be observed. Some trail up or down the bottom of the Canyon and others appear as cuts that have been carved up its sides, over the west and eastern rims.

Nothing could stop the westward rush of the horseless carriages. The concept of manifest destiny included a transcontinental automobile trail. In 1914 the Old Trails Highway was built and crossed at Two Guns. A family known as the Oldfields came with their children and settled beside the new road, building a square house three miles south of Two Guns on the Old Trails Highway. They conducted a small business from their living room, serving not only the dusty and weary bounding from their Model T's, but cowboys, Indians and sheepherders who showed up for repose and refreshment.

In 1922, four years before the debut of the Mother Road, Louise and Earl Cundiff arrived from Arkansas and paid $1,000 to get a claim at the Two Guns site. Cundiff, a veteran of World War I, claimed a 320-acre plot which defines the survey lines of the Two Guns site to this day. Cundiff built a large Kaibab limestone building as a living quarter on the west side of the canyon where the dirt road turned down into the Canyon crossing. He also put in a concrete dam which would serve as the solid base for automobiles to traverse the watery Canyon bottom. In 1925 the State of Arizona routed the highway directly past the front of Cundiff's store.

Later, a concrete bridge was built by the State of Arizona, the bridge providing the final link for the traverse of Old Route 66 across Canyon Diablo. Cundiff applied for and received a post office at Two Guns. He painted "Canyon Lodge" on his store near the bridge where he served as postmaster. This original Route 66, which had now been transformed into a transcontinental highway, brought many more tourists, thrusting Cundiff's tiny "Canyon Lodge" enterprise from obscurity and isolation into a booming business featuring gas and oil sales and a thriving cafe. (84)

Two Guns' legendary niche on Route 66 history really began in March of 1925 when Harry "Indian" Miller set foot there. Miller, who claimed to be a full blooded Apache — except for a smidgen of Mohawk — was well educated and a veteran of the Spanish American War in the Philippine theater. As time went on he proved to have a flair for gaudy publicity and fashioned a quintessential Route 66 tourist trap, maybe the first of its kind on the highway.

Cundiff store and Old Route 66 Bridge

It all began when he signed a ten-year site lease with Earl Cundiff, "Chief Crazy Thunder" as he called himself, and immediately began construction of an elaborate and extensive stone structure on the rim of Canyon Diablo. The structure was built facing the south. A zoo of wild animal cages and pens was constructed and Miller dubbed the operation, THE LION FARM. At the entrance to this first "zoo" he established a small store and living quarters. He also con-

The Kiva

structed a small restaurant and curio shop in additional buildings. Miller cleaned out the "Cave of Death," taking the bones to Winslow and selling some of the skulls as souvenirs. He built "ruins" inside the cave which he promoted as a tourist attraction.

Later, he hired Hopi workman from the Hopi Mesas to put up a pueblo type building above the cave entrance. This curio shop was appropriately christened HOPI HOUSE in honor of its builders and the architectural motifs. Tissue thin rolls of colored Hopi PIKI bread were sold in Hopi House in addition to jewelry, rugs and other articles. Fortunately for their mental health, few, if any, of the visitors to the subterranean hideout of the Apaches came close to imagining what really happened at that site. Miller began calling the stone building containing his zoo "Fort Two Guns," thus giving this ominous site on Diablo's edge its famous name. (9)

The violent encounter between the Navajo and Apache was embellished by Miller. He paved a path down to the cave's entrance and illuminated the cavern with electric lights by dropping them through cracks in the ceiling. Tourists were pulled off Route

Walkway to Death Cave

66 and drawn down into the depths, awed by thoughts of what they might see in the "Cave of Death." Apache skeletal remains were scattered both among fake ruins inside the cave and outside the cave. Travelers could buy soft drinks as they toured the phony setup.

Claims of ancient habitation eventually drew several archaeologist to the site who often completed their scrutiny of the Anazasi ruins with loud belly laughs. The tip-off to the fraud was the known fact that inhabited caves leave blackened walls from years of fire used for warmth and food preparation.

At one time Miller himself lived in the cave at Two Guns. The mysterious cave had not been carved by the action of underground water like Carlesbad Caverns. It is characterized by clean breaks and sharp edges with no rounded surfaces of stone com-

Fake ruins in Death Cave

mon to underground caverns formed by water. In the 1920's there was no evidence of any animal habitation, neither snakes nor bats.

From the very outset Cundiff and Miller fought over rights and boundaries. The bitter feud so poisoned their relationship that on March 3, 1926 Miller shot Cundiff to death and dragged his body out of his

Harry "Indian" Miller with a Gila Monster

house. Although Cundiff was unarmed, a jury acquitted Miller. "Killed by Indian Miller" was chiseled on the Cudiff's gravestone in the cemetery at Winslow. Infuriated by the damaging epithet, Miller in the dark hours of an autumn night came into the Winslow cemetery and painted out the reference to

him. He was jailed for grave defacing. In 1929 the interior of his big store burned. There are some reports from within the Navajo community at Luepp that Miller did not personally kill Cundiff, but hired a Navajo gentleman to do the job for two wagon loads of groceries. (59, 78)

Miller had acquired and housed every beast and bird native to Arizona in his zoo at Two Guns. Inevitably, either the curse of the Death Cave or the karma of Cundiff's murder caught up with him. First, he was nearly clawed to death by a mountain lion. Then he was attacked and nearly disemboweled by a lynx. Finally, he was bit by Gila monster whose poison fanged jaws, which characteristically lock on their pray, had to be pried off his arm. He suffered intense pain and a swollen arm as big as a basketball for six months. He spent months in the Winslow hospital. Next, his seventeen year old daughter died in an auto accident near Two Guns, punctuating the fact that Two Guns held the record for auto fatalities on Route 66. The reputation of Two Guns as a place of death resulted in the macabre practice of perching Apache skulls atop stone pyramids to warn drivers of the extreme danger of the Two Guns section of the Mother Road. Later, the skulls were replaced by small white crosses.

Business gradually lessened at Two Guns, finally dwindling to little or nothing. The final straw came when someone tore down Miller's signs. He closed the "Cave of Death" in 1930 and moved away to the New Mexico/Arizona Border. There he again put in a zoo and constructed yet another set of phony cliff dwellings which he dubbed the "Cave of the Seven Devils." Successors to Miller at the border site have

Old Trails Highway ~ Route 66's predecessor

come and gone over the years. Most likely, in any given year at that site, one will find a tourist trap not unlike old Indian Miller's. (71)

A signal maintainer for the Santa Fe Railroad named Hesch married Mrs. Cundiff, and they operated the trading post at Canyon Diablo until it burned in 1934. In 1938, a new bridge downstream from old one was constructed to coincide with the redesign of Route 66 at a parallel route several hundred yards north of Old Route 66. A "new" trading post building was constructed which Hesch moved to the high-

way side of the "new" Route 66. A restaurant and living quarters were erected and the zoo and lion farm were reestablished.

It was in that same year that a teacher at Canyon Diablo, Mrs. Ray Thomas, built a red sandstone house directly beneath the old Hopi House curio shop where she resided with her invalid husband for a number of years. The house was sold in 1950 to Gladwell Richardson, a chronicler of the history of the site and the author of numerous novels and articles about the surrounding region and northern Arizona. Richardson discontinued the zoo, and the building burned in 1963. At length the site and buildings were purchased by Benjamin F. Dreher under the tag of TWO GUNS, INC. Dreher offered to open the cave and haul sightseers through the "Death Cave" with a small train track but the project never got off the ground. In recent years a service station and KOA camp ground were established up on the hill on the southeast side of Canyon Diablo; however, at this writing there is no operating concession at Two Guns. U.S. Highway Interstate 40 provides an exit ramp to Two Guns, passing on over Canyon Diablo where the last Route 66 traversed the Canyon.

Many doors and windows

Windows into the past

ROUTE 66 MAGAZINE has copyrighted a Two Guns logo. For those who know the history of Two Guns and who used to repose at this Route 66 oasis of mystery and intrigue, wandering or even just passing near the old site never fails to fire the imagination and send chills down the spine.

The Navajo people have never been puzzled at Two Guns' bad luck and tragedies. The massacre of the Apaches in Death Cave, the wanton murder of Cundiff, the burning down of the big store, Miller's three time brush with death from wild animal attacks and the death of Miller's daughter as one of many of the fatal accidents near Two Guns all add up to their belief that the area is possessed by the **"Chindiis"** —the Navajo term for "ghosts of the dead." Navajos will immediately declare, "we don't go there, and you had better stay away."

More Two Guns at the Arizona border

Into the Cave of Death

FOUR
Ghosts of the Cave of the Death
Fated for Violence

The death chant became weaker and weaker throughout the night, changing with the hours into low moans and wailing. Finally, except for the lonely whispers of the incessant wind, dead silence fell over the canyon rim above the cave. The site, located halfway between Flagstaff and Winslow in a side canyon just below Two Guns, Arizona on Old Route 66, would forever hold a place in history as the host of one of the most violent, brutal confrontations that ever occurred between the Navajo and their cousins, the Apaches.

It was June of 1878. The Civil War had ended, and the Navajo People had returned home from their Long Walk and their internment at Bosque Redondo near Fort Sumner, New Mexico. A large number of the Navajo had settled north of the Little Colorado River in an area called the Melgosa Desert, now

known as the Painted Desert. Today, this area — part of the Navajo Nation — is referred to as either Red Lake or Tolano Lake.

This was a time in the Canyon Diablo region when the old fur trappers, who had once caught beaver up

Navajo People in captivity at Bosque Redondo

and down the Little Colorado, began to settle in as guides and traders. The evidence of trapper activity along the Little Colorado is manifested by the presence of their small stone structures, by the names carved upon the islands of Moencopi sandstone scattered about the Little Colorado River Basin. Herman

Wolf Trading Post

Apache warriors

Wolf, a fur trapper who remained in the region, built a trading post of red Moenkopi sandstone on a hill above the Little Colorado River. The post stood at a point where wagons could ford the river without being sucked into the depths of treacherous quicksand.

The Hopi and the Navajo had long used this crossing on the Navajo Trail. The ancient trail began in the north, near present day Kaibito, and extended southward past Blue Canyon, often referred to as Coal Canyon. It followed the east rim of Canyon Diablo

Mogollon Rim

into the pines and mountains at Chavez Pass, finally winding over the Mogollon Rim and down into the Verde Valley of central Arizona. In its solitary station at the river's crossing, Wolfe's Trading Post was both a symbol of security and a source of sustenance to the Navajos who had returned from the ordeal at

Bosque Redondo. The Navajos called Herman Wolf "Beaver" and the trading post "Beaver House" because of the beaver pelts that old Herman pinned up to dry around the post. (71)

Cousins, but Enemies

According to anthropologists, the Navajo and the Apache entered North America across the Bering Strait as Athapascan-speaking people. The two tribes eventually split up, migrating long ago to different parts of the Southwest. In spite of the fact that they were cousins with strong linguistic and cultural ties, over time they became bitter enemies.

Shell casing at Wolf Trading Post - 1800's

While the Navajo remained in northern Arizona and New Mexico, the Apaches went south and set up

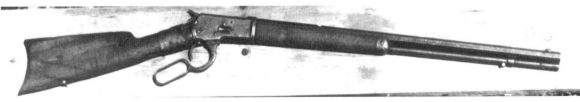

encampments just below the high pine country of the Mogollon Rim. They preferred the juniper tree-lined canyons and creeks of what are now Arizona and New Mexico.

The Mescalero and Chiricahua Apaches (the famed band of Geronimo) had strongholds in southern Arizona and New Mexico near Douglas, Arizona and Ruidoso, New Mexico. Apache Bands raided communities southward into Mexico and northward into Arizona and New Mexico, often attacking their cousins, the Navajos. One of the most potent weapons of all time has been christened "the Apache Helicopter." The Apaches were considered to be the most agile and fierce warriors of the old west and as such were not only revered, but also feared. Throughout the 1860's and 1870's, the Mescalero Apache raiding parties would attack sites throughout northern Arizona and New Mexico and then escape back to their lair over the Mogollon Rim between the Capitan and Sacramento Mountains of southern New Mexico.

B'ugoettin

Wolf's Trading Post was seen as but a ripe plum to the Apache raiders, and throughout the late 1870's they attacked it continuously. Nevertheless, the Apaches were never able to broach the defenses of Wolf and his Mexican workers. Wolf and his crew were able to hold out behind the post's thick Moencopi red sandstone walls, staving off any advance into the building with the heavy firepower of their Winchester repeating rifles. Early accounts of the trading post site describe the surrounding area as being covered by spent shell casings.

After a while, the frustrated Apaches gave up on their plunder of Wolf's Trading Post and directed their efforts to attacking Navajo communities that had settled in the Melgosa Desert, in an area next to Garces Mesa. The Apaches butchered anyone left in the Navajo sheep camps, stole what stock they could and would often take captives, particularly young girls, to enslave or torture. Many captives were horribly mutilated. (See notes below on torture)

Navajo leadership functioned at the local sheep camp level. The leaders were known as "Nataniis." There were three Navajo Nataniis who represented the communities in the Melgosa Desert and Garcia Mesa: B'ugoettin (Bah Gwo' Ah tin — "No Teeth"),

Nachise, "Crooked Jaw"

Natani, and Redshirt. B'ugoettin was the son of a Navajo Chief. Nachise, better known as "Crooked Jaw," a prominent Mescalero Apache and the son of the famed Apache chief, Cochise, led the raiding parties that ravaged the Navajo communities.

Retaliation

Apache attacks resulted in the torching of homes and possessions and the looting of the Navajo's sheep and horses. Captives, mainly women and children, were taken and tortured or brought back to New Mexico and forced into slavery. The pain and deep sorrow over their losses, particularly the rape and torture of their young daughters, helps to explain the Navajo's dogged determination to catch the Apache raiders and the rage they expressed on that grim night in 1878.

In the immediate aftermath of the Apache attacks, B'ugoettin and the other leaders would head toward the trails that led over the Mogollon Rim, hoping to intercept raiding parties at narrow passageways. The Apaches would disappear without a trace, leaving the ravished Navajo bewildered and bitterly disappointed. They began to believe the Apaches had such powerful medicine that they could vanish into thin air. Enraged at the torture and the theft of their stock

and crops, the Navajo never gave up in their quest for the retreating Apaches. Their persistence would one day pay off.

On a fateful day in June of 1878, B'ugoettin's sister and four children were captured in yet another Apache raid. When dawn broke on the hogans in the Melgosa, it revealed a scene of slain men, women and children. All members of the community were dead except for the captives. A band of twenty Apaches led by Nachise had attacked along the Little Colorado River, while a second group of twenty plundered hogans near Garces Mesa, taking no prisoners.

B'ugoettin, accompanied by the other leaders and a band of 25 warriors, followed the trail of the retreating Apaches into the cinder country just east of present day Flagstaff. At that point the tracks dispersed, disappearing across the finely grained black cinders. The Nataniis suspected that the Apaches were hiding in volcanic cracks in the earth, cracks common to the Sunset Crater region. On a hunch they sent out two scouts, Bahe and Begay, son of a chief, to search the area around Meteor Crater.

When the scouts drew near Canyon Diablo, they heard the faint sounds of voices and saw a slight curl of smoke rise out of the seemingly solid limestone. They crawled forward in the late afternoon sun,

Entry canyon to the Cave of Death

Original cave entrance

where they rested and dined on dry mutton and corn. For many years, the Navajo had used the shallower opening to the Canyon as a refuge and grazing area. Their discovery of the mysterious cave on that day in June 1878, was a complete surprise.

The cave is located within a small offshoot and side canyon of the main part of Canyon Diablo. The entrance to the cave is directly behind the present ruin of Two Guns, and had been concealed in 1878 by a solid stone natural bridge which had long since fallen in. The original entrance was a narrow tunnel-like passage leading under the bridge into the cave. The tunnel was wide enough and tall enough to lead a horse through and the stone walls of the cavern were higher than a man's head.

The cave was unknown to the Navajos in spite of their years of grazing and watering in the Canyon Diablo area. Later, exploration of the cave by spelunkers would reveal a crevice-like structure going back some 13 miles. The cave was created as a fissure in the earth, not as a cavern. Its origin is unknown, although it may have been caused by either the volcano activity of the San Francisco Peaks area to the west or by the violent impact of Meteor Crater. The cavern was large enough for 40 Apache warriors and their horses to enter and hide.

undetected within the tall grass and sage. They moved slowly toward the rim of Canyon Diablo to probe the origin of the sound and the smoke. Suddenly Bahe was startled by a rush of hot air coming from beneath his face, followed by the sound of loud voices from deep below him.

Recapturing his focus, his keen senses having been checked by these uncanny events, he looked down to see a crack in the limestone under his face. Begay slipped in beside Bahe, both warriors noting movement deep inside the abyss below the crack. From out of the crack in the ground they made out low voices conversing in Apache, the noise of horses and the odor of smoke and firelight flickering on the edges of the limestone crevice. The source of the mysterious smoke, light and sound was a ten-inch wide fissure which both men now straddled. Closer scrutiny revealed that they were on the top of a limestone ledge overhang above an opening in the Canyon wall. Carefully peering over the rim rocks, they saw Apaches entering and leaving the mouth of a large cave.

Sanctuary Uncovered

Bahe and Begay dashed to the Little Colorado River rendezvous and excitedly informed B'ugoettin, Redshirt and Natani that they had long last intercepted the Apaches. The three leaders put a war party in motion. The avenging band of Navajos moved eastward toward Canyon Diablo and the Navajo Trail,

Hole in Cave ceiling

Vengeance

The war party arrived at the Canyon's edge just as the glow of sunset marked the distant San Francisco Peaks. Approaching the site carefully, they saw the Apaches going in and out of the opening crevice under the natural stone bridge. The war party waited until the fullness of night shrouded the plateau and then made a plan to exact revenge. Chief B'ugoettin, grinning hugely at the thought of avenging the murder and torture of his sister and her four children as well as the destruction and death the Apaches had wrought on his community, said "We must kill them all."

Realizing that the Apaches were trapped and going nowhere, B'ugoettin and his men sent messengers back to the Little Colorado River for reinforcements and waited until predawn the next morning to make their move. They first blocked all routes of escape, and then shot the two Apaches standing guard at the cave entrance. The Navajo decided that the most vengeful strategy would be to burn and suffocate their enemies.

At the first light of dawn, when they could see to gather dry sage and driftwood from the bottom of Canyon Diablo, they gathered and stacked the grass and driftwood on the edge of the canyon just above the entrance to the cave. The mass of vegetation was set afire and pushed over the edge into the cave entrance, where the flames and the fumes would be sucked into the cave by a heavy prevailing draft. The desperate Apaches, realizing the horrible fate intended for them, made sorties into the passageway at the immediate entrance to the cave, resulting in immediate death by rifle shot for a number of them. Masses of fuel were ignited, feeding the smoke that was continuously sucked into the cave and could be seen to reappear out of several surface cracks.

Blood Money

The Apaches, peering up at the Navajos through one of the natural holes at the entry of the cave, pleaded for their lives and offered blood money, a customary trade of goods and valuables, in exchange for lives. The Navajos asked for "Crooked Jaw" and were told that he had left the day before for the southern encampment of their Apache band. The Navajos, while ridiculing the Apaches for begging for their lives, still hoped for and asked for the captive girls, not found earlier among the bodies, to be freed. Delays by the Apaches confirmed the Navajo's deepest fears — that the prisoners had been tortured and killed that first day for the amusement of their captors.

In a wild rage the Navajos poured a stream of bullets into the cave mouth, leaving even more bodies in the entryway. A second batch of grass and driftwood was therewith poured down into the cave entrance, feeding the flames and fanning them into a raging inferno. Soon more dense smoke plumed out of the cracks, darkening the starlit sky.

Desperate Maneuvers

It was then that events took an even more bizarre turn. The Apaches made a desperate attempt to save themselves. To block the scorching heat and suffocating fumes, they proceeded to kill and cut up their horses into large chunks which they stacked and stuffed, along with boulders, at the entryway. However, the heat and dense fumes had begun to take their toll. There was neither enough horseflesh nor strength among the remaining warriors to complete the blockage of the cave, and thus the Apache's last escape attempt failed.

In the middle of the night the fire was allowed to die down. The Navajos, looking through cracks, found that the Apaches had used what little water they had, as well as blood from the ponies, in an attempt to extinguish the fire at the cave mouth. With the onset of early morning, the gruesome cries of the Apaches became muffled. The cave floor was now strewn with bloody horse carcasses intermingled with the dead.

Dead Silence

The Navajo placed their ears on the limestone surface, sensing a finality in the death chants of the Apaches. Throughout the early morning, the solemn chants of the Apache raiders became fewer and weaker. It became difficult to distinguish the faint wail of the incessant Coconino Plateau wind from the dying chants of the doomed men. Finally, an ominous silence overwhelmed the bowels of the cavern. Death Cave or Cave of Death, as it was later to be called, had now become the final resting place of forty-two Apache ghosts. According to Navajo legend, these Chindiis still reside there.

Inside the Cave

It took until the following noon for the massive limestone to cool sufficiently for the Navajos to enter the cave, and the scene that awaited them was a terrible one. At the immediate entrance to the cave were the barbecued parts of butchered horses, the big haunches of quartered ponies piled about in the narrow entrance. The Apaches had not been strong enough to carry them beyond that point.

The Navajos used poles to punch holes through the boulders and horse carcasses so they could enter the second cavern, and again what awaited them was horrific. There were more quarters from slaughtered horses piled there, along with the bodies of Apaches who had been overcome and killed by the noxious fumes. The cavern displayed a macabre scene, with corpses splayed on stone ledges above the pony carcasses.

Some Apaches had bolted through a narrow passage into yet another cavern, but their panic had blocked the entrance. Five of them lay prone inside in grotesquely twisted positions, frozen in death while choking for a final breath of fresh air that never came.

The Navajos covered their noses and mouths with their bandannas, many retching at the stench of burned horse and human flesh. The bodies of the forty-two Apaches were stripped and loot from the raid was recovered for a return to the Melgosa and Garces Mesa communities. The Navajo party retreated very slowly and quietly, awed by the terrible destructiveness of their actions and fearing revenge of the dead. Still, the cruel torture and murder of their young girls had been avenged. The band of Navajos stopped at Wolf's Trading Post and recounted their grisly tale. They told old "Beaver" Wolfe that they now presumed the cave to be cursed by the tortured spirits of the dead Apaches. They vowed to never again go near that section of the canyon, and to warn others to stay away.

The Curse

The Apache raids on Navajo communities north of the Little Colorado River had come to an end with the killing of "Crooked Jaw's" raiders. The Navajo continue to avoid the Cave of Death area, and to this day advise others not to enter or go near it. In the early days of the old Mother Road, one would often see a fatal accident marked by skulls atop rock cairns, and many believed the skulls were those of the Apache warriors.

Years later, the Old Trails Highway was constructed and a bridge built across Diablo, launching a vast flow of automobiles near the cave entrance. The highest number of accidents later recorded occurred at this point on Old Route 66. A total of seventeen fatal accidents happened there, on one of the most dangerous curves on Route 66. In addition, as it has been noted, a long series of terrible events occurred at Two Guns — the burning of Harry Miller's store, the mauling of Miller by both a mountain lion and a lynx, and Miller's near brush with death from a Gila monster bite.

After Cundiff's successor Harry Miller acquired the property in the early 1920's, the bones of the Apaches began to disappear. There are several versions concerning the removal of Apache remains from the cave. One account claims that removal was ceremoniously completed by Apache medicine men. Yet another tale asserts that certain members of the Hopi Tribe removed bones, placing them inside fake stone walls built by "Indian" Harry Miller to depict Anasazi ruins. (Miller envisioned a Carlsbad Cavern-like enterprise. In the 1920's an elaborate tourist site with curio shops and zoos was constructed by Miller and became known as "Two Guns." Initial construction was begun to run a small rail tour into the cave. Archaeologists, drawn by stories of Anasazi ruins, left the cave laughing, cognizant of the fact that the Anasazi never built walls inside of caves because no fires could be maintained).

Deepest Cave

The Cave of Death is the longest known subterranean cave in Arizona. The cave was explored three to four miles back at an early date, but no chambers larger than the first two were discovered. Two Winslow men went in as far as 7.5 miles, reaching 9 miles on a second trip. There is an unverified story of spelunkers exploring back nearly 13 miles. Contacts were made with the U.S. Geological Survey in Flagstaff to confirm and obtain data regarding any explorations made of the cave. A letter was received saying that there were no records of such explorations. According to surveyors and hikers familiar with the Kaibab Limestone area, there are many deep and seemingly bottomless fissures that exist in the area. A recent rockslide occurred 500 feet from the Cave of Death entrance, blocking access beyond that point.

The origin of the cave remains a mystery, although two theories exist. The first is that the great meteor from Meteor Crater ruptured horizontal strata, creating cracks and fissures across the plateau. The second and more plausible concept is that the cave occurred as a result of the great upheavals caused by volcanic action and explosion of the San Francisco Peaks. There are many fissures evident throughout the area and northward towards Cameron. Deep, black colored layers and other great cracks reach clear down to the Little Colorado. Some of these fissures have water containing blind fish from underground streams.

There is no evidence of water erosion in the Cave of Death. The cave walls and ceiling are flat, with cleanly broken sharp edges. There is also no evidence of water running in the cave. The temperature remains a constant 50 degrees Fahrenheit throughout the year. Explorers have found it strange that no wildlife or insects inhabit the cave.

Lore about Two guns and the surrounding area mention the fact that diamonds, possibly from the Hopi Butte volcanic chimneys, were collected and stashed deep inside the cave. Yet another story suggests that the old prospector Cannon had cached bags of industrial diamonds in there. Such diamonds have been found in the stone debris resulting from the Meteor Crater explosion.

Many Navajo still avoid the cave site, believing that the Apache Chindi will forever reside in the cave. A descendent of B'ugoettin and delegate to the Navajo Nation Council wished to explore the cave, but found it blocked by a steel-bar gate placed there by the current property owners who feared liability that might result from an accident. In the late 1990's, it was maintained as an abandoned commercial area. An RV camp and gas station, the most recent development at the site, had been closed for several years.

The   limestone walls of Miller and Cundiff's multi-building complex on the edge of the canyon still stand, even though the last trading post building burned in the 1960's. To casual passerby on Interstate 40, the compound of limestone is a curious place and is often mistaken for Indian ruins. Few travelers in the days of Old Route 66 knew of the existence of the Cave of Death, and few travelers today are aware of what lies just over the canyon rim past the stone buildings.

Into the Bowels of the Cave

The author made arrangements with an old friend and realtor from Flagstaff to enter the cave and examine its depths firsthand. It was at this spot that a

group gathered one October morning in 1997. A mountain climber, a forensic archaeologist, a photog-

Phoney ruins

rapher and writer, the realtor and the author gathered their "spelunking" equipment and began to descend into Canyon Diablo. The group was fully equipped for a serious probe of the cave, carrying high-wattage lanterns and several thousand yards of twine to be unraveled as an escape contingency. And, of course, everyone in the group had cameras hanging from their necks and waists.

Overwhelming disappointment awaited the group's first entry into the original cave opening. A hundred feet inside they were met with a solid wall of rock and dirt. Spirits dimmed and solemn faces tried to hide the sudden disappointment. The cave doorway, which was the original opening used by the Apaches, had been closed off by a rockslide long ago. The group sat around the entrance looking at each other, trying not to feel discouraged and depressed. After thirty minutes went by, someone yelled from a limestone precipice in an adjacent canyon, "Here it is!"

The group crept up the ridge and tumbled down into a new canyon, immediately seeing the steel grated opening that indicated a newer entrance. In the narrow entryway sunrays poured through holes in the ceiling, providing a warm light which bounced off the cream and ocher-colored limestone. The author imagined the blazing barrels of Navajo rifles pointed downward over 100 years ago.

While some have doubted that forty Apaches and their horses would fit into such an area, once inside the cavern one could no longer question its capacity to accommodate both men and horses. The entry into the dark recesses of the cave revealed an almost rectangular solid that was fifteen to eighteen feet wide covered by a flat ceiling about eight to ten feet high. The large entryway went back about five hundred feet. At this point the cavern narrowed to such a degree that one would have to turn sideways and barely squeeze through in order to move further into the depths of the cave. The author attempted to navigate the narrow passage beyond the main room, but lacking both experience and the proper equipment, he abandoned any attempt to go further. The unpleasant thought of being accidentally trapped inside the dark recesses of the cave stopped him cold.

Having determined the cave's dimensions, the group turned to inspecting the fake Anasazi ruins that lined the second cavern. Contemporary knowledge of how the Anasazi actually lived made these walls seem ridiculous. Although past reports indicated no animal habitation evidence in the cave, there were a number of bats hanging from the ceiling.

At one point the author noticed a bright, sharp glint of light off in a deep side crevice. Thoughts of supposed diamond stashes crossed his mind. His lack of spelunking experience and dearth of equipment were apparent, however, and discretion overcame valor,

Tim Knowles near entrance

preventing him from crawling back into the area to discern the origin of the puzzling flash of light. Upon

Large room in Death Cave

examining photos taken in the cave, one shows a very tiny but extremely bright spot appearing off in the narrow recesses of one part of the cave.

Cave wall and floor

A large yellow bone was spotted on the back part of the second cavern floor, identified by the archaeologist as a horse bone. A number of pictures were taken, and various details of the second cavern were thoroughly examined.

The entire group moved back to the cave entrance area, leaving the author alone. Turning out his 100,000-watt torch, he experienced a peculiar sensation of being suspended in the center of something that was distinct and entirely separated from the outside world. He found himself engulfed in a totally dark, silent, and motionless void. There was

Horse bone on Cave floor

absolutely no sound. An overwhelmingly heavy, sinister and sad presence seemed to pervade every square inch of the area in which he stood.

The atmosphere in the cave quickly becomes so oppressive and suffocating that one becomes panicky and is frantic to turn the light back on. The author hurriedly left the cave entrance, shut the steel door and was soon bathed by the noon sun glowing off the Kaibab limestone cliffs — an especially welcome sight. Ham sandwiches on poppy seed rolls, coffee, orange juice and homemade chocolate cake revived the camaraderie of the group, the food and the sun concluding an extremely exciting, stimulating adventure.

Back in his office on the Navajo Nation, the author related his adventures at the Cave of Death. After all, he thought, one of the Navajo Nation Council dele-

End of an exciting day

gates from the area around the Melgosa Desert and Garces Mesa had tried to make arrangements to enter the cave, but had not known of the locked iron grate. Very possibly, fears of negative consequences after exposure to the Apache Chindi were only the result of superstition, and at any rate, they would not effect an Irishman. In the last analysis, the Navajo staff members were unresponsive, noncommittal and downright uninterested.

Two weeks after the trip to Two Guns, the author's car died 40 miles out of Kayenta. The car was towed into Kayenta where Navajo mechanics worked for two days, finding no apparent cause for engine failure. The car was towed 140 miles into Farmington. There, the Toyota garage found a cable to a vapor sensor wrapped around the exhaust pipe. There is still no explanation as to how the cable got that way.

Two Guns and the Cave of Death site are on private property and both are grated and locked at the time of this publication. A number of potential tenants and investors periodically explore the possibilities of developing Two Guns, a project that would include making the Cave of Death accessible once again to the interested explorer.

About Torture

A word about torture. As stated before, the Navajos and Apaches, although tied by culture and language, had become bitter enemies. Consequently captives, including children, were often tortured. While outrage and bitter vengeance to annihilate "savage Indians" has often been depicted in films (particularly in director John Ford's THE SEARCHERS) and explicitly expressed at times as national policy, torture had never been the exclusive prerogative of the Apache nor of Native Americans in general. History is replete with eras and episodes that evidence sophistication in torture by Europeans, Americans, South Americans and, for that matter, all human groups. The commonality in man that leads to torture of his fellow human beings does not lessen the horror of the practice. (25)

All tribes tortured in some form or another. Scalping was seen to exterminate the soul so it couldn't attack in the afterlife. Colonel Dodge, who lived, fought, befriended and often countered against injustice to Native Americans, maintained that "savage instincts and vindictive temper were often gratified by witnessing the agonies of the enemy undergoing torture." He maintained that this was not ceremonial or religious motivation.

Dodge went on to state that "Barbarism torments the body; civilization torments the soul. The savage remorselessly take your scalp, your civilized friend just as remorselessly swindles you out of your property. The progress of enlightenment of a people would seem to be measurable by their less or greater abhorrence with which torture may be inflicted. The actual cruelty is about the same in either case, but it is the case of the savage that comes up for judgment." Dodge also maintained that "Of all Indians, the Apaches have deservedly the credit of being the most ingeniously and relentlessly cruel and being the most capable in administering physical torture."

Dodge sites a case wherein a giant of a man from Mexico, the lone surviving defender of a large ranch, was captured by the Comanches and marched north to the Staked Plains. The raiding party stopped, and the captive was told to dig a ceremonial pit. He was then wrapped tightly and spirally by rope and planted upright like a post with dirt filled in up to his neck and tightly rammed down around him. Only his head was visible. He was then scalped, and his lips, eyelids, nose and ears cut off. The raiding party danced around mocking him, and later the tribe regarded this episode as an exquisite piece of pleasure. The man lived for at least eight days, revived at night by the cold of the high Plains, only to be driven mad next day by the hot sun beating on his scalped head and defenseless eyeballs, while a myriad of flies filled his wounds with maggots.

Navajo bear hunters ~ Chinle, Arizona Territory

Hashknife cowboys inside the Bucket of Blood Saloon

FIVE
The Bucket of Blood Saloon

The town of Holbrook came into existence as the result of a union of river and rail. Holbrook began simply and quietly, debuting at Horsehead Crossing one mile east of the present town of Holbrook. There, the westbound Rio Puerco River coming out of New Mexico joins the Little Colorado flowing northward from the high meadows of the White Mountains of Central Arizona. This particular spot was one of the few locations in the region where the hardness of the river bed could support horses and wagons, and as such it had been a crossing point for travelers since prehistoric times. In 1878, a Mr. Padilla came with his oxen to Horsehead Crossing and established a trading post and house. Padilla's arrival was closely followed by the ever expanding rails of the Atlantic and Pacific Railroad which had crossed New Mexico and arrived at Horsehead Crossing in 1881. In 1895, moving one mile west to its present location, the rail town became a county seat and was christened Holbrook in honor of the first engineer of the Atlantic and Pacific Railroad. The town's name, Holbrook, and the small cafe innocently titled "The Cottage" which perched just south of the railroad tracks masked a violent future which would compete with the more obvious reputation of its sister town, Tombstone.

By the mid 1880's, Holbrook had evolved into the "bibulous Babylon on the Little Colorado." (84, pg. 264) The town at that time contained two-hundred fifty people and had become a shipping center for cattle, wool, hides and merchandise for the U.S. Army. Its streets were packed with American Indians, cattlemen, and settlers. It had also attracted a full complement of social outcasts. Saloons lined both sides of the railroad tracks. Violence and law-lessness, whisky and misdealt cards spawned fre-quent gunfire. In its short life Holbrook had become one of the most lawless towns in the country. In one year twenty-six gunfighters were buried. Shooting brawls broke up dances and public hearings at least twice a week and it was not unusual for cowboys to gallop through town randomly firing their six-shoot-ers. (60)

The Invasion of Iron Horses, Steers and Texas Rowdies

Before Route 66 came along, Holbrook's story was all about cows, trains and their keepers. The U.S. government granted vast tracks of land for railroad construction. The railroad companies, lacking the capital to build a transcontinental railroad, financed their operations by selling right-of-way holdings to ranchers and settlers. In 1884 the Aztec Land & Cattle Company, the most expansive ranching enterprise ever formed in Arizona, was established near Holbrook. A gentleman named Ed Kinsley was a stockholder of the Atlantic and Pacific Railroad. He saw the lushness of the Little Colorado River Valley and secured 1.3 million dollars in capital for a cattle ranch. In 1885 the Atlantic and Pacific Railroad sold a million acres to Kinsley and the Board of the Aztec Land & Cattle Company for fifty cents an acre.

The Aztec's spread included two million acres of combined private and government land which was bordered on the south by the Mogollon Rim and extended westward from Holbrook all the way to Flagstaff. In no time a large herd of Texas cattle with a Hashknife Brand appeared on the huge ranch accompanied by some Texas cowboys — the Hashknife Outfit. The Aztec Land & Cattle Company at that moment was the largest ranch in the U.S. next to Texas' XIT ranch. The "Hashknife Outfit," the legendary and infamous name acquired by the ranch, ran as many as sixty thousand cows and two thousand horses on its land. The Aztec Land and Cattle Co. steers carried the Hash Knife brand which was likened to the knives used by camp cooks in those days. (84)

The Hashknife had enormous impact on the Holbrook area in the late 1800's. Its influence reverberated into the second millennium propelled by the force of the Hashknife cowboys, desperados running from the law. Along with the Hashknifers, the Aztec infused thousands of grass chomping longhorns onto the land which, in turn, attracted hordes of riffraff, hell hounds and cattle rustlers from out of Texas. Accordingly, after the spring and fall roundups, the streets of Holbrook were filled with money, six-shooters and rowdy cowboys. A 1936 federal report

described the town as a harbor for known killers and said that this rowdy bunch periodically rode through Holbrook with guns ablazing, screaming and yelling and shooting up all the dance halls. The author's close friend, whose grandfather lived in the region in those days, claimed that his grandfather and local citizens would hide behind the bars in saloons when the cowboys hit town. (6, 60)

Still, the superior numbers of the Hashknifers could not overcome the rustlers and small ranchers who hung around the outfit like wolves waiting to get their own stake. Such rustlers, although tracked and caught, were never convicted because of the prejudicial attitude that the community and its officials had toward the Hashknife Outfit. Also, the rustlers always seem to have buddies on the jury. Fourteen years went by without a rustling conviction. The community, who resented the immensity of the Aztec

Old Holbrook in 1880

Land and Cattle Company and always felt that it was grazing free on government property, was unwilling to punish its own citizens.

One of the Hashknife cowboys' range bosses, Burt Mossman, ended up firing half of the Hashknife crew and later became captain of the Arizona Rangers. Strangely enough and in spite of its vast land base and army of rowdy cowpunchers, the Hashknife Outfit was unable to profitably sustain the Aztec Land and Cattle Company and its brief life in northern Arizona sadly ended. The only remains of the Hashknife are the ruins of its cattle drive line cabins scattered over northern Arizona and an annual reenactment by modern day Hashknifers of a famous Pony Express Ride which starts in Holbrook, proceeds over the Mogollon Rim and winds its way into the Valley of the Sun, ending at Scottsdale.

The Bloody Anointment of Hell's Kitchen

A favorite haunt of Hashknife cowboys was the "Cottage Cafe" located on main street south of the railroad tracks. The Cottage lost both its name and its innocence on a cold, bleak day in November of 1881. Two Hashknifers named Crawford and Bell were playing monte with two Mexican gentlemen, Ramon Lopez and Rafael Chavez. According to an account reported in the ST. JOHN'S HERALD, a fist fight started, presumedly because of someone either

The Cottage ~ The Bucket of Blood

cheating or losing. Lopez struck Crawford over the head with pistol. Bell and Crawford were getting the worst of it when one of the more grotesque gun fights in Western lore transpired.

Crawford drew his six shooter first and shot Ramon Lopez dead. Gunfire raged and bullets whizzed all over the little cantina. Finally, Crawford also killed

Cowboy dinner

Rafael Chavez. Fearing prompt retribution from other Mexican cowboys, Crawford and Bell wanted to exit Holbrook right away. The bartender assisted by helping them to recoup their strength and by giving them horses to make their get-a-way. (68) It was said that the place where Lopez and Chavez fell had created such a large pool of blood that it looked like "a bucket of blood had spilled," (68) The grisly stain remained in the grains of the Cottage's wooden floor for a long, long time, and did in fact look like a spilled bucket of blood.

The same day as the Bucket of Blood incident occurred in Holbrook, a cattle roundup on the Little Colorado River range was completed. At a lake east of Holbrook, a herd was being held for transport to the stockyards. Suddenly, Bell and Crawford appeared on the horizon, loping slowly on horseback toward the roundup encampment. Crawford, who had a bandanna on his head, had obviously been seriously wounded and was weak from loss of blood. He yelled something at the mounted cowboys to the effect that the two had been "shot to pieces."

Crawford had been cut from his temple halfway around his scalp from the gun whipping and also had a bullet hole in his side. Bullet holes likewise had nearly shredded his shirt. A bullet also passed through his sleeve and grazed his side. He was so weak he had to be lowered from his horse. The cowhands put a flour plaster on his head to stop the bleeding. While ministering to Crawford his body revealed numerous scars of older wounds, raising the eyebrows of the cowboys about his past. It turned out later that Joe Crawford was identified as a cowhand from the Hashknife Outfit and George Bell was identified as a gambler. Potter, the captain of the roundup, took charge and asked what had happened, whereupon Bell related a detailed account of the fight. (68)

Bell told the group that a posse made up of the Mexican comrades of Lopez and Chavez was forming, and that he feared if the posse caught up with them they would be hanged. The outfit offered protection from the mob, but said that they must turn themselves over to the law. Bell agreed. Lunch was served from the back of the chuck wagon and Crawford got up and ate with the bunch. Tom South, another Hashknifer, galloped into the camp at midday to say that no inquest had been held because the Justice of Peace was out of town. However, he claimed that the deputy sheriff would come after them even without warrants. Several of the cowboys suggested getting out of the country. Crawford stated that he could ride, and that he and Bell should go pronto since no legal actions had been taken and they would not be fleeing arrest and prosecution. Roundup captain Potter agreed. Records indicate that Crawford and Bell were never prosecuted for the slaying of Ramon Lopez and Rafael Chavez.

Holbrook was without a church for its first thirty-one years, the only county seat in the United States with such a distinction. Judge Sidney Sapp decided to change all that. However, the cowboys voiced violent objections to a church and refused donations for its construction. Sitting atop the bar in the Bucket of Blood Saloon one of them proclaimed, "Who wants to bring women and children here, this is a man's country. Take your wife back to Oklahoma if you want her to go to church."(13) One of those historical ironies occurred when Holbrook got a church in 1913 and the Bucket of Blood closed that same year. It finally became a school.

The innocent looking Cottage Cafe perched across the tracks on Main Street Holbrook would forever be known as the ominous "Bucket of Blood Saloon." In its time the Bucket of Blood had been described as the most popular place in northeastern Arizona, and was the center of community decision-making. Yet many claimed, including the author's father, that as late as the 1930's the dark blood stain remained under the floor covering. In 1934 the author lived with his baby sitter, Irene Chavez, within a stone's throw of the infamous saloon.

Holbrook's The Darker and Bloodier Ground

No one in the 1890's doubted the deep impact that the Hashknife Outfit operations had on Holbrook. However, it was the famous cattlemen vs. sheepmen feud, (chronicled in Forrest's book, ARIZONA'S DARK AND BLOODY GROUND, 33) that set the stage for one of the most violent and controversial gunfights in the history of Holbrook and perhaps the entire West. Through it is not as well known as the gunfight at Tombstone's OK Corral, it may rival it in pathos and fury.

When word spread from cattle ranch to cattle ranch throughout the Pleasant Valley sector of central Arizona that sheep were coming into the Valley, a legendary era of violence was launched. Pleasant Valley, lush with grass and trees, was located in what was then a wilderness area under the Mogollon Rim, quite near the present day town of Payson. It is said that cattlemen, seeing the first herd of sheep coming from a distance into the valley, described them as "a great mass of maggots rolling down over the trail from the rim, (Mogollon) and swarming like a plague of locusts, devouring the grass, tearing it up by the roots and already (creating) a cloud of dust drifting up in the lazy morning air from the desert they left behind." (33, pg. 23)

This bitter disdain for sheep meant that true cattlemen rarely fraternized with sheep men. In those days, and in most cases, they faced each other only in violent confrontations. Cattlemen believed that sheep destroyed in short order what mother nature had taken eons to create. Sheep could ruin a cattle range in a matter of weeks by eating the grass down to the roots. Sheep also left a scent that precluded cattle from grazing on the same range for years afterwards. (40) There was no love lost between sheepmen and cattlemen for starters, even without the enhancement of historical personal feuds.

The famous "sheep-cattlemen's war" was not really a feud, but, according to one researcher (40), a long string of ruthless murders. The gunfights, ambushes and killing attributed to the Pleasant Valley War ended up with fifteen of the Graham cattlemen bunch and their supporters dead. The Tewksbury side counted three fatalities, those identified with the sheepmen. Lawmen of Apache and Yavapai county had consistently sided with the Tewksbury faction. The Tewksburys had always gotten off free with neither fine nor conviction. Credible evidence has been provided to suggest that all of the county sheriffs, most of the local media and the best legal minds of the Southwest joined with the power of the office of the Governor of Arizona (Governor Zulick) to protect the Tewksburys. Hanchett (40), provides evidence for a compelling theory that the murders of the Pleasant Valley Graham faction were part of a well designed conspiracy backed by moneyed interests from "The Valley of the Sun" (the Phoenix area and Salt River Valley). It has been ventured that settlers in Pleasant Valley were the object of a scheme entered into by land interests in collusion with politicians in high office to appropriate the lush land of the Valley for themselves. The important role of the supposed conspiracy had been played out in political decisions that ended up time after time exonerating the Tewksburys from any wrongdoing. The look-the-other-way attitude of officials permitted the ultimate destruction of the Grahams.

Numerous incidences have been documented to show that law enforcement only showed up in support of the Tewksbury side. The most serious charge and condemnation of those politicians was that lawmen were actually given the freedom to kill with impunity and annihilate the Grahams under the guise of their resisting arrest. Accusation has been leveled at J.D. Houck, Sheriff of Apache County, who appeared to pardon anyone on the Tewksbury side who happened to get imprisoned. The Tewksbury's hired hands, who received only $30 dollars a month, had retained "the best lawyers money could buy." This unexplainable element of the dynamic, combined with the shadowy presence of outside influences at the top of the state power structure, created a cloud of confusion about the Pleasant Valley War that has lasted over a hundred years. Bitter feelings and controversy rage on to this day.

The Blevins House Fire Storm

In northern Arizona in the late 1800's, the bitter Tewksbury-Graham feud flared up into a firestorm of brutality. The Sheriff of Apache County, Commodore Perry Owens, had become a source of great amusement to the citizenry of Holbrook because of his outlandish Buffalo Bill like costume and swashbuckling ways. Long-haired and handsome faced, pistol butt thrust forward on his fringed buckskin jacket, Perry was quite the dandy. Owens became the principal character in a famed Holbrook "shoot-out" and remains to this day a central icon in wild west legend.

Owens was from eastern Tennessee and grew up with an abusive father. He started out as a cowboy and ran through a number of pursuits including bronco buster and buffalo hunter. He ended up horse thieving in Texas with Andrew Arnold Blevins, although the friendship of the two fell out over women. Owens later showed up at White Oak, New Mexico and later surfaced in Arizona working for cattle ranchers. An 1885 robbery had left the Apache county citizens discontented with county officials and they began looking for a for new sheriff.

Consequently, Owens ran and was elected sheriff of Apache County in 1886. U.S. Army Colonel Grierson, stationed on the Navajo Reservation, asked

Commodare Perry Owens

Owens to catch Andy Cooper, who had stolen a horse from the reservation. Earlier, Grierson had refused to help Owens capture three Navajos accused of killing three posse members, whereupon Owens had threatened to bring a large posse onto the Reservation. Grierson retaliated by moving the accused killers to New Mexico and branded Owens as "a desperate, determined and ignorant man." (89)

During the period when Owens was forging a reputation in Holbrook, the Blevins family had moved to to

Arizona from Texas. Owens' arrival in Holbrook coincided with that of the Blevins. Andrew Blevins had changed his name to Andy Cooper. The Cooper-Blevins gang emerged as a faction of the Graham bunch and settled to the north in Holbrook. The original bitterness between Owens and Blevins (now Cooper) endures, magnified within the intense backdrop of the intrigue and butchery of the Graham-Tewksbury feud. So it is that this conflict set the stage for one of the bloodiest shoot-outs in the history of Arizona.

Andy Cooper had ridden north from Pleasant Valley to visit the Blevins house in Holbrook, boasting in saloons about killing two men in Pleasant Valley. (Cooper, in fact, had in fact led a band to the Tewksbury cabin and killed John Tewksbury and William Jacobs). On September 4, 1887 Owens appeared on the porch at the Blevins house to serve a warrant for the arrest of Cooper for horse stealing. He confronted Cooper, who, standing behind the partly opened front door, refused to surrender. Cooper then began to open the door with his pistol pointed outward. Owens immediately opened up with his Winchester, shooting through the thick wooden door, piercing Cooper's midsection and mortally wounding him. Cooper's brother, John Blevins, opened the door and fired wildly at Owens, hitting his horse. Owens spun around and fired from the hip, hitting John in the shoulder.

Next, a relative of the Blevins', one Mose Roberts, leaped out a side window just as Owens moved out into the street. Owens' Winchester cranked again and fired once more, killing Roberts. It was at this point that Sam Houston Blevins, a teenager of only fourteen, grabbed Cooper's pistol from his mother and ran out the front door to join the fight. But before he could aim and fire, Owens cranked yet another shell in the Winchester chamber and fired it, hitting young Sam Blevins in the chest and killing him instantly. Owens then calmly mounted his horse and left town. The inquest held later exonerates Owens of any wrong doing, citing the homicides as the result of Owens' carrying out of his duties and Cooper's resisting arrest. (89).

The Desperado Poet

Owens continued as the Apache County Sheriff, his stint punctuated by a humorous and colorful interface with Red McNeil, dubbed the "robber poet." McNeil had robbed the Schuster Trading Post in Holbrook and wrote a poem daring Owens to catch him. McNeil's poem reads, "I am king of the outlaws; I am perfection at robbing a store; I have a

stake left me by Wells Fargo; and before long, I will have more; Commodore Owens says he would like to kill me; to me that sounds like chaff; 'Tis strange he would thus try to kill me; The red headed son-of-a-gun; He handles the six shooter mighty neat; and kills jack-rabbit with every pop; but should he and I happen to meet; there will be a regular Arkansas hop." (88, pg. 194)

Another story involving Owens and McNeil recounts the time when Owens, in hot pursuit of McNeil, came upon a group of cowboys at a line camp. Owens spent the night and shared a bedroll with one of the bunch. Owens opened his eyes in the morning to the rising sun only to find the bunch gone and a note from McNeil pinned on his saddle blanket which read, "Pardon me, sheriff; I'm in a hurry; you'll never catch me; but don't you worry," (88, pg. 194) Owens had slept with McNeil.

Sheriff John Francis relates another tale about McNeil that occurred at a standoff at Clear Creek, south of Winslow. The posse in pursuit of McNeil was unable to cross a canyon gorge that was a thousand feet deep. They stood by helplessly, enduring the laughter and hand-waving of McNeil. Faithful to his code of poetic charm, McNeil left a note that read, "Although my name is badly smudged toward

Owens grave in Flagstaff, Arizon

these men I hold no grudge; and hope some day, a free man to stand; and grasp my combatants by the hand." (88, pg. 198)

In 1888 John Blevins, the lone survivor of the Blevins shoot-out, was sentenced to five years in prison but was subsequently pardoned. Owens ran for sheriff again but, probably due to the controversy over the death of the Blevins and his burlesque escapades chasing McNeil, he fell into local disfavor and lost the bid for reelection to his old deputy. In 1902 Owens ran a combination saloon and mercantile store in Seligman. Like so many men of the old West, Commodore Perry Owens died with his boots on in 1919, succumbing to Bright's disease and paralysis of the brain. He now resides at Block A, Tract J, Lot 13, Space 2 in the Flagstaff Citizens Cemetery.

C.P. Owens has been celebrated by most as legendary hero, while others have considered him the hired assassin of those county and state officials who wanted to get rid of the Graham faction. Many believed that he had no cause to gun down the Blevins boys and Roberts without giving them a chance, but none have doubted the courage of C.P. Owens that violent day on the streets of old Holbrook. (89)

Holbrook lays claim as the wildest town in Arizona, indeed, as the wildest town across the entire West. There is evidence that Holbrook far exceeded Tombstone in violence and lawlessness. The brutal tales about Holbrook do not end with that of the Bucket of Blood Saloon nor with Sheriff Owens' gunfight. One story relates how a druggist turned lawman named Frank Watron leveled a shotgun at a cowboy demanding that he give up his gun. When the cowboy flatly said "No," Watron hired him as a

est improved methods of scientific strangulation will be employed and everything possible will be done to made the surroundings cheerful and the execution a success." (84)

Another tale recounts how two law enforcers named Tex and Jenkins entered a saloon to quiet a gang of rustlers lost in gaudy merriment. Jenkins, a candidate for sheriff, saw big trouble brewing and demanded the firearms of the men. They were handed over to Tex, who put blanks in the guns. After the party had left Holbrook, the cowboys found out about the blanks. Furious over the episode with Jenkins and Tex, the cowboys shot up Chinese Louie's Washhouse and Restaurant with real bullets. Afterward, the cowboys set out to ambush Tex and Jenkins, wanting solely to chase the cowboys, grandstand with a few shots and then return to town. But, they fell into a trap set by the cowboys who had strung the trail with ropes geared to dismount the lawmen. The trap worked, and the cowboys tied up Tex and Jenkins and dangled their bodies in cold water. The whole town of Holbrook found out about the humiliation of the lawmen, and the daily street laughter in Holbrook nixed any chance for Jenkin's election as sheriff. (8)

Bucket of Blood ~ circa 1997

deputy rather than face his six guns in the future. That same Sheriff, Frank Watron, was reprimanded in 1899 by then U.S. President McKinley for issuing an ornate invitation to a hanging. The invitation read, "George Smiley, Murderer. His soul will be swung into eternity on Dec. 8, 1899 at 2pm sharp. The lat-

One bizarre episode was told over and over again. It was heard as late as 1934 by the author's father from many a customer sitting at the soda fountain in the Guttery Drug Store on Old Route 66. In those days, most victims killed in gun fights were dragged off to

the cemetery forthwith. Such was not the case with James Henry Walker, an Eastern-born cowpuncher known as the "Cimarron Kid."

The story goes that Walker had gone into the Bucket of Blood to fill a skein with liquor. An altercation with the bartender ensued, and the Cimarron Kid shot the bartender in the shoulder. With deadly speed, the bartender produced a gun and shot Walker in the forehead. The funeral cortège, containing Walker in a pine coffin, turned into a caravan convoyed by cowboys. A bottle of booze had been given to the wagon driver named Jersey. Jersey waved the bottle over his head screaming "Hurrah for Cimarron!" The yelling shied the team of mustangs and they bolted, throwing Jersey off the wagon. The dazed Jersey asked where his team of horses had gone. The cowboys said that Cimarron "had came to life and drove off with them." Jersey almost believed them until he spied the boys chasing the wagon which had been behind him. The popping guns caused the horses to cross a culvert and the wagon careened wildly. The coffin fell out and so did Cimarron, whose body went rolling through the prairie. Cimarron was finally retrieved and stuffed back into the rebuilt coffin, Jersey asking if he'd killed him dead this time. (90)

SIX
Requiem for a Belle

(A creative non-fiction tale that carefully follows the true events surrounding the tragic death of Norma Dean Shiply based on reports and eye witness accounts).

The City Cafe was quiet. Gone were the pungent smells of cooking charcoal fillets, the laughter of the crowd. The bright purple neon glow from the clock over the bar appeared pale and faded, it's slow tick keeping time with the dull thud of Shipley's heart.

World stage queen

The streets of Winslow were streaming with the runoff from late September monsoons; desert sand mixed with mud and water slithered silently through the night. Persistent drips of water fell from the sign in front of the restaurant onto the steps below.

The gnawing fear in Shipley's stomach began to eat away at his customary air of command. He became silent for several minutes, fixing his gaze out the window at the downtown lights reflecting off wet pavement. What is it? he wondered. And suddenly, he knew. The rendezvous at the restaurant was not going to happen. Leorena's arrival with the troupe

Winslow in 1920

coming in from the Petrified Forest was long over-due. "Vance, let's head out on 66," Shipley said to his friend and confidant. "We've been chewing the fat now for over three hours. That bunch should have been here long ago." Shipley's voice shrilled slightly revealing his anxiety, and he blushed.

The tall, gray-haired major and World War I French Medal of Honor awardee stood as a bastion of respect and strength in Winslow, his recent appointment as Chief Dispatcher at the Santa Fe Railroad further enhancing his prominence in the community.

Petrified Forest ~ 1927

All of Arizona knew of his deep love for his daughter Leorena, the belle of American Theater. The thought of any harm coming to her was unbearable.

"The gang does seem a little late," Shipley said, feigning composure. He tipped his hat to the waitress at the cash register and put his wallet away. "You know Leorena. As frantic as her theater travel gets, she always swings back this way, kidnaps May and charges out to her favorite Petrified Forest retreat. I guess she yearns for the taste of that red Moenkopi dust in her mouth. Anyhow, she can't get too far off

Painted Desert Inn

the beaten track with your brother and her mother to keep her in tow," Shipley said, his voice trailing off as he went out the door into the damp chill and rain. He hoped the weather would soon clear. Gully washers on the high desert plateau came suddenly and often disappeared just as quickly, leaving behind a bright starry sky. This evening however the downpour seemed unremitting. It added to the disquiet of the night.

Violinist in kindergarten

"Ah, take it easy, Shipley," Vance said, raising his voice above the patter of rain. He sensed an unusual panic in Shipley, who seldom lost his equanimity. "You know that Leorena's going to keep every one going until the cows come home, making sure, as always, that she sucks out every drop of excitement. And Tug is a good driver. But, if it makes you feel better, let's go anyway."

The Model T Ford passed the city limits of Winslow going eastward and the lights of the town became pinpoints in the rear view mirror. "The Harvey Indian Detours are doing a booming business," Shipley said. His voice was calm but expressionless. His whole being was concentrated on penetrating the gushing downpour, the black abyss of soaked highway in front of him. He hoped to catch the slightest appearance of lights in the distance, wanting to quell the fear seeping into his heart.

Roadsters of the 1920's

"Yep," replied Vance. His tone of voice revealed no apparent concern about their situation or the weather, but it sounded hollow and remote. The rain was hitting the windshield so hard that the wipers offered no clear vision of the road. The back wheels of the car swerved slightly as traction lost ground to the meandering rivulets crossing the highway. "You know, Shipley, the hoy poloy love it around here. The Hopis, the Canyon, the Petrified Forest and Painted Desert — why, we got more here than everything east of the Mississippi."

Vance felt it necessary to summon up a diversionary conversation to offset the sense of foreboding pervading the night. "Winslow's getting there. City Cafe is the finest eatery between Chicago and Los Angeles." After all, Vance thought, Winslow had become a resort destination of sorts, and Shipley's leadership was no small part of that achievement.

Shipley fell silent. The flashing reflections of small pools of water on the dark, wet highway were becoming hypnotic, the monotony granting Shipley a brief escape from an intensifying crescendo of dread. Scenes from the past flashed rapidly across his mind like the flickering images of a silent movie.

Belle of the stage

There was the move out from Iowa, with Leorena and her sisters M'Dell and Constance giggling and peeking out the window of the roadster. There was the time when his partner, Tom Pollock, perched on the brass-adorned engine cab of the Apache Line Shipley managed for him at McNary. Shipley's fantasy went deeper. "Leorena!" Shouts and sounds of clapping roared up from the inner recesses of his mind. He saw himself attending Leorena's violin solo at the Washington School Kindergarten recital. His senses were auto-piloting the roadster as his mind wandered through the past.

"Splendid and born to the part," the school paper had said about Leorena's leading role performance in the 1915 senior play, THE RUNAWAYS. By then, everyone had accepted the fact that Leorena was an extraordinary person. From the shadows of the old Rialto Theater came the sweet strains of "Claire de Lune" resonating from Leorena's clarinet. Shipley's mind caved totally into his compelling visions of days gone by.

Cottonwood Wash

Out past the edge of the headlight reflection he could almost see Leorena, easily imagine her ravishing the audience as she stood on stage in her lavender chiffon gown. He'd had it tailored for her at the House of Piermont in France. Thousands of pearl and lavender beads shimmered in Shipley's mind, just as they had shimmered long ago with each of Leorena's subtle movements across the stage.

A wrenching thud interrupted Shipley's reverie. The Ford twisted to the left through a hidden pool and a wave of water rolled over the windshield. The dashboard lights cast macabre shadows over the features of the two men now glancing at each other, glances seeking some sense of meaning and reassurance about the threatening, almost sinister onslaught of the night. The rasping ebb and flow of the torrential rain and the impenetrable void masking the high desert only magnified the eerie reality of the moment.

Last November, Shipley had gone along on the Petrified Forest trek, and he remembered how May had spent all day pumping Leorena for details of her theatrical escapades. He had marveled at the time how neither fame nor fortune had eroded the tight bond between May and Leorena.

Those long years away from Winslow, beginning as an amateur at the University of Arizona school of acting and stretching across time to her present acclaim as an international belle of the theater and the pending Hollywood contracts only intensified Leorena's passion for her roots. Shipley had been amazed at the art with which she romanticized the small railroad town nestled in the Little Colorado River Valley, at her ceaseless insistence that some unknown set of powerful forces converged at that particular spot on the planet. Even though he had fashioned her name, Leorena, by combining his own first name with that of a dear friend, he had accepted her choice of the stage name Norma Deane as charming and fitting. The name captured the essence of his daughter's sweet soul and delicate beauty.

The Ford slowed to a crawl as hailstones the size of mothballs began to pelt the car, covering the road in a blanket of two-inch slush. Shipley's mind lapsed back into the comfort of his trance as he attempted to restructure the events of Leorena's day. He mused that the troupe probably arrived at the Petrified Forest just after lunch. At that point they would have barely made out the San Francisco Peaks on the western horizon toward Flagstaff. A few innocent clouds would have been forming over the Peaks, mushrooming slightly upward. The Petrified Forest ranged over a large area and a tour of the National Park would have taken them several hours, including their short walks through the ancient fossilized logs.

Shipley was a realist and knew that he could not divert fate. He thought to himself, why hadn't the group seen the mushroom clouds over the San Francisco Peaks? Predictably, the clouds would have risen that morning at sixty thousand feet, within easy sight, eventually turning into a black, dense mass signaling an oncoming monsoon. Surely they would have heard rolls of thunder reverberating through the roadster windows.

Still, Shipley knew the exact conversation that had probably taken place between May and Leorena in response to the gathering storm. May would be pleading to get home, and Leorena would insist on dinner and drinks at the Painted Desert Inn. He could visualize the passionate, childlike persona of his daughter dashing here and there, mawkishly posing, feigning theatrical utterances and bouncing off the sixty-million year old logs.

Leorena's rich laughter and her elegant stage voice seemed to echo through the darkness. Finally, Shipley braved re-entry into the inauspicious stormy night, breaking the silence and his repose. "The routine never changes. It's chilidogs and chocolate shakes at Guttery's Drug in Holbrook. Della and I never could put enough nutmeg in her shakes. I know she posed for a photo on top of that big log she calls 'Rainbow.' She loves that part of the Park.

"May your star never dim"

Last year she and May played hide and seek in that ancient dead forest," Shipley said, looking at Vance with shining eyes and a slight smile.

"Yep," replied Vance. Vance's voice was low, revealing his resignation to the heavy mood wrought by the vile weather and the possible peril of the missing troupe.

"She said to May that life was short, that life was like a cactus wren flying from a storm into a warm cabin and then back out again to the lonely blackness. 'When it's your time,' she told May, 'you got to go on to another place, another stage, another production.'

Shipley's eyes were watery now, and Vance had no response. "The critics all the way from San Francisco to Salt Lake, even up in Calgary, say her performances are 'fresh, thrilling, vibrant, and touching.' She met Victor Jory and fell in love with him when they played starring roles in the romantic comedy, NANCY ANN," Shipley muttered, more to himself than to Vance.

"Watch it, Ship!" Vance yelled as the car fan-tailed through another deep pool on the road. Headlights gleamed dimly in the distance as the wave of water drained off the windshield. Shipley's gut began to relax a little.

Shipley rolled down the window to flag the oncoming car, praying strong that there would soon be a joyful reunion with Leorena and the troupe coming in from Holbrook.

"Didn't see anyone," the driver yelled, backing away from his open window to avoid the blowing rain.

Old wooden bridge

"Thanks anyway," Shipley said, his heart sinking. He crawled back into the car and avoided looking at Vance. He let the clutch out and slowly, without speaking, moved down the highway. Starting a conversation in a normal tone would sound shallow and stupid. He drove on lost in thought, his body filled with a tension he thought he had abandoned on the battlefields of France.

"Hey Ship," Vance said, finally breaking the silence. The sudden appearance of a car, of other human beings on Old Route 66 shattered the glum outlook he wanted to blame on a mysterious September mood of Mother Nature. "The rain might be hard, but if they take it slow they'll be okay."

Shipley turned to Vance and flashed a rare look of appreciation that revealed his vulnerability, his profound concern for his daughter's well being. Shipley could still remember the text of the telegram he had sent Leorena when she received outstanding acclaim for her performance of BAD MAN at the Speckles Theater in San Diego. "We are mighty proud of you. May your star never dim. Cling to your success by being a good girl." Shipley thought her achievements had only just begun and that soon he would see her on the silver screen.

His sharp, pragmatic mind could not sustain the illusion; the memories vaporized into the vastness of dark and damp. Tense and shivering, he succumbed to the terrible possibilities of the moment.

Rump, rump, rump. "That's the bridge over Cottonwood Wash," Shipley said. "We're now out almost six miles. It sure is slow going in this rain." Five miles north up Cottonwood Wash, runoff from the high desert gullies had gathered into a six-foot wall of water that was now rolling rapidly down the dry wash bed. A curtain of night hid the impending flash flood from the unsuspecting travelers.

"I see something, Ship," Vance said, wiping the fog off the windshield. Vance put his face up to the windshield. "Yes, there is something," Vance repeated a few seconds later.

Dim but perceptible points of light began to grow larger in the distance. "It has to be another car," Shipley muttered triumphantly to himself. He knew that the presence of another car meant that the road was okay ahead. Any company at all was more than welcome that night on the lonely stretch of Route 66 along the Moenkopi Cliffs, on that foreboding road spreading to the north from Winslow to Holbrook.

The Major recognized Leorena's car before she recognized her father's head sticking out the driver's side in the drenching rain. The relief was so great, especially on Shipley's part that they stood in front of the headlights in the soaking rain laughing, hugging and joking for ten minutes or more.

"Let's get back to Winslow," said Shipley. "Vance and I will lead the way. Tug, you take over and drive, just in case." The two cars continued slowly on toward Winslow, crossing Manila Wash. Rump, rump, rump. The wheels reverberated over the beams covering the bridge. Everyone relaxed and talked about getting a hot bowl of chili at the White Café, open all night. "We're lucky, Major. This rain can cause flash floods, but it looks like we're going to be okay."

The darkness and the driving rain would have obscured car headlights, spotlights, any lights pointed northward up Cottonwood Wash toward the Cliffs. There was no chance of seeing the roaring six-foot wall of water. Shipley and Vance had missed it by a minute.

Shipley, gazing through the back window, saw the headlights of the troupe's car fifty feet behind go straight up in the air. "Oh my God," he screamed., "Leorena!"

May said later (83) that Leorena's mood had turned merry after the reassuring encounter with Shipley and Vance. She was chattering excitedly, saying, "You got to come to the Apache in Phoenix in October folks and," May said her voice was cut short by a deafening "whop!" May described the car as jolting like a tilt-a-whirl, rising upward in front and turning to the right. The windows had cracked and splintered inward and gray, gritty water filled up the interior almost instantly.

May gasped in the suffocating silt, thrashing with her hands, trying to grasp anything within reach. She felt the top of the left side window frame and held on with a vise grip, hoping to pull herself toward the surface. Everything was slippery, impossible, sucking down at her body. The frantic grabbing and clutching for a solid handle, anything to lift her body upward and out of the mire seemed, for the first few seconds, to be a fruitless, hopeless effort. Terror and surrender to the inevitable rapidly replaced her expectations of escape.

Della was under May's body, struggling with a super human effort for release. She began to feel faint and resigned herself to a hopeless position. Tug later related to Shipley that he had reached up and could feel space, air and drops of rain. He pushed himself against the seat, lifting his body toward the driver side window. Tug said that he sensed Leorena's movement upward. He felt that she must have been pinned under him, and he prayed she could follow him out. But the bad luck of that night continued as the car began to slide even deeper into the turbulence. As they later surmised, there was a moving current of thick quicksand under the layer of water.

After screaming his daughter's name, Shipley immediately realized what had happened. He'd seen flash floods before and understood their savage swiftness and malevolent power. He hurriedly turned around and sped back to the edge of Cottonwood Wash. Shipley and Vance saw that the wooden bridge was gone, that Leorena's roadster was lying on its right side with only the left front corner breaking the surface of the muddy, surging waters.

A hand was reaching out the driver's window. Vance grabbed it and pulled his brother Tug from the car as it slipped and plunged further down into the gorge. Tug sat on the bank while Shipley and Vance jumped over to the back window. Shipley groped around in the water and felt an arm. It was May's arm, and he held it tight. The car shifted, sinking deeper and deeper as though a giant force was sucking it into a bottomless quagmire. Vance braced himself against

the bank, grabbed Shipley and jerked hard. Shipley fell backward, heaving May up and out of the window, pulling her to the shore with Vance's help.

"Della and Leorena!" yelled Shipley. Neither man knew where to start looking. Shipley lowered himself down into the back window. Holding Vance's hand, he searched and felt a leg. It was immobile. He grabbed the ankle with both hands. Vance, near exhaustion, pulled and yanked until a leg emerged from the back window. Both men grabbed the leg, retrieving a soaked, unconscious Della from the doomed vehicle. Tug was crying by then and yelling, "Get Leorena, get Leorena!"

Leorena had been knocked unconscious when her head banged against the dash board. Had she been conscious, Leorena would have been vaguely aware that attempts were being made to rescue everyone, and she must have felt, with her unshakable self confidence, that she would escape this nightmare either by her own power or that of her father. She would have begun thrashing upward, reaching her hands out, expecting to grab onto something, anything that would bring her back to her beloved world. Leorena's passionate heart and her love for life would never have permitted surrender.

As Shipley and Vance turned back to the car to go after Leorena, it slipped and disappeared under the water. Holding Vance's hand, Shipley jumped in and promptly sank up to his neck. His feet could not touch any part of the car and he became frantic. Tug had recovered somewhat and, grabbing Vance's other hand he jumped in. Both Shipley and Tug were neck deep in the water, kicking in all directions, but they could make no contact with any part of the vehicle. Five, ten, fifteen minutes went by and finally the men, overcome with fatigue and shock, decided that the two rescued women would have to be taken to Winslow at once if they were to survive. The agonizing reality of the moment suddenly hit Shipley. His chest became numb, his eyes drooped and a gush of tears ran down his cheeks.

Shipley's mind could not block the haunting vision of what his daughter's last moments would have been like. Leorena must have known that the car was sinking and would have felt the thick, cold sand suck at her body. She would have certainly hoped that someone was above her, that she could make a final push upward to make contact. The spirited twenty-nine year old was after all in her prime, with an energy that had faced and overcome all previous challenges. Defeat was not in her repertory.

Months after the tragedy, in long hours of discourse, Shipley and his friends reached the consensus that Leorena, regaining consciousness, must have braced herself against the right front door and pushed with all her might, holding on to life, feeling her body move toward the surface and safety. Halfway up she must have jolted to a stop. The fashionable elastic band around her waist, they discovered later, had caught on the gearshift and trapped her in a watery tomb.

Arriving in Winslow twenty minutes later, the men rushed Della to the hospital. They put out a call at the Police Station and at Santa Fe Headquarters for male volunteers. Men streamed out to Cottonwood Wash in their cars. Officials at the scene sent runners to probe downstream toward the Little Colorado River with the idea that the raging waters had perhaps washed Leorena there. Finally, rescuers placed a rope around a man's ankles and lowered him down into the surging stream. In time, he found the car and confirmed that Leorena was still inside. He could not remove the body.

A hundred men went to the edge of Cottonwood Wash and worked in shifts around the clock. The rescuers made many attempts to pull the vehicle out of the fifteen-foot quicksand but they were unsuccessful. They finally lowered steel plates, building a cofferdam to allow access to the sunken roadster. At long last, 72 hours later, the body of Leorena was taken from the car and wrapped in a blanket. Grown men wept in frustration. The roadster sank down into a quicksand grave, never to be seen again.

Hundreds of Winslowites lined the bank of Cottonwood Wash that tragic night. It was a somber, cold, wet procession of heartbroken spectators who greeted the dead theater princess on the 11th of September, 1926. Arizona's Mother Nature had taken many lives throughout history in blizzards, canyons, sweltering sun and floods, but the death of Leorena was especially difficult to accept and left a lasting scar on Winslow's collective psyche.

Leorena's funeral took place on the very stage where she had debuted as a kindergarten violin soloist. The Washington School Auditorium was filled with thousands of the lush American Beauty roses that the actress had so dearly loved. They arrived by railroad boxcars on the Santa Fe. The place was utterly silent. (90)

The businesses and the school had closed, and Leorena's casket was born by pupils she had joyfully instructed during her brief teaching career. Other students sang hymns, hoping to soothe the grieving hearts of townspeople who came to bid tribute to Leorena, to say goodbye to the local princess who never allowed her fame to dampen her love of Winslow. "A great soul of light was gathered into the Soul of the Supreme Light, shining on forever," read the last paragraph of the obituary. That balmy, clear September afternoon, Leorena Shipley, "Norma Deane," was laid down in Winslow Desert View Cemetery, where her body rests today.

Gowns, gloves, hats and other memorabilia belonging to the actress were sadly gathered up by the grief-stricken Shipley and a heavyhearted Della and buried in a storage trunk for forty-four years. A second tragedy struck Shipley in 1941 when Leorena's sister, Constance, was felled by an unexpected heart attack. Leorena's other sister, M'Dell, lived on to become a successful businesswoman in Phoenix until her passing in 1970. (38)

The trunks containing the memorabilia of Norma Deane's career were finally opened after all that time, the precious items preserved intact. L.D. Welsh, M'Dell's son and the only grandson of Major

Shipley, donated Leorena's remaining legacy to the Old Trails Museum in downtown Winslow. The famous lavender gown sewn in France, brought from Europe especially for Leorena, is now displayed in a glass case at the Museum.

Years later, a cement bridge was constructed over Cottonwood Wash. On the now abandoned segment of Old Route 66 east of Winslow, remnants of the old bridge remain. The stillness of the place is broken occasionally by the shrill chatter of wrens and the sound of trucks buzzing on Interstate 40 to the south. The site is heavy with an air of mystery, but blessed with a sense of respect. It's a peaceful place where the spirits of Old Route 66 seem to be frozen in time. The dry, sandy riverbed stretches northward among the Moenkopi sandstone cliffs that stand as a fitting and eternal monument to the forces of Mother Nature's waters.

Shipley often came out to this spot to relive his memories of Leorena and to seek some solace for his aching heart. One evening near sunset, at the point where the old bridge was located, he noticed that the banks were covered with the most beautiful lavender wild larkspur. His heart began to burn like the rosy orange sun fading off over the San Francisco Peaks. It was time to let go and say good-bye. He made his peace with the lonely place and headed back to Winslow.

SEVEN
Forces that Sculpted Monument Valley

A sculptor once explained his art as a process in which everything is carefully removed, thus leaving the artist's vision intact. Across eons of time, in a highly complex scenario, the art of nature orchestrated the miracle that is Monument Valley, one of those rare spots on the planet where natural forces have forged an awesome garden of massive buttes, spires, arches and mesas. (22)

Since the first human walked into the Valley this question has been asked: "Where did these layers upon layers of gorgeous red, brown and orange rock come from?" The Valley continues to fascinate visitors who come to the northeastern corner of Arizona to see for themselves this epitome of the American West, this glorious setting for commercials and western movies. (56)

Materials making up the Monument Valley seen today are not newly arrived pieces of a mystical planetary process. These substances are very old.

Long ago, Monument Valley was once a basin. The beautiful deposits of sandstone, rock and shale were

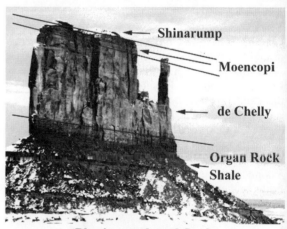

Shinarump
Moencopi
de Chelly
Organ Rock
Shale

Blowing sands and floods

placed there in ancient geological time, buried for a millennium before being exhumed from inside the earth and fashioned into magnificent monoliths.

If a slide show were to be made of ancient times, when the thickest layer comprising the cliffs of the Valley was being formed, it would show the shores of a onetime sea stopping just short of the Valley's western edge. To the north, in an area centered around Pagosa Springs and Ouray, Colorado, one would see the Uncompahge Range — the ancestral

Buttes ~ The Mitten

Rocky Mountains — and the geological time clock would read between 225 and 270 million years ago. (5)

The earth would be concluding the third level of five growing stages — the Permian Period of the Paleozoic Era — a time when vast seas inundated most of the American West. The Ancestral Rockies, on high ground above the sea, would be slowly ground down by the constant forces of wind and water. Granite material, exposed to the air, would be oxidized into various hues of red. Huge streams would carry the red sand grains to the sea, and from higher ground, the grains would be swept into lowlands along the sea's eastern and northeastern shores.

Incessant, seemingly never-ending winds would create enormous layers of sand as deep as a thousand feet thick.

This giant layer of sand was destined to become the sheer cliffs that characterize the monoliths of the Valley. The sand would be compressed into stone by

Dinosaur track

the weight of deep layers of material that would cover it during the fourth and fifth stages of the earth's development. The sandstone would be called the De Chelly (de shay') Sandstone, named after the famous Canyon De Chelly National Monument some seventy miles southeast of the Valley. A primitive four-footed amphibian creature several inches in

Spires ~ The Totem Pole

IBM desk atop Totem Pole

Today, such deposits make up the yellow, gray, purple and red layers of the Painted Desert of Arizona. Huge trees, floating on top of massive streams, were caught in the bends of rivers and sank to the floors of streams, buried in silt for incubation as the famous Petrified Wood.

The wearing down of a second Rocky Mountain Range created brown silt that was deposited in tidal flats on the edge of the ancient sea, settling to the bottom as very fine mud. Currents and movement over the sediments created wave patterns frozen in place by more sediment, fossilized for storage through the ages. This shallow layer of shale can be seen at the tops of the buttes as thin strata capping the De Chelly cliffs. The appearance of this Triassic mudstone was identified with a settlement of Hopi peoples at Moenkopi, seventy miles north of Flagstaff, Arizona — hence the Moenkopi formation. The Moenkopi formation spreads over a vast area of north central Arizona and is the predominate environment in Winslow, Arizona.

The least apparent but most important formation in Monument Valley provided durable, hardened capstone for all the monoliths, enabling and protecting the sublayers from the ravages of time, water and wind erosion. The top layer of the monoliths, part of

length would be seen moving through the sand. Sporadic patches of ferns and cone-bearing plants would be present, as well as some flying insects. (24)

Reddish-orange materials that form a base, or platform, for the huge monuments arrived at an earlier time and are actually mud hardened into shale by the same massive weights pressing down over the centuries. This reddish orange shale, called Organ Rock Shale, was created millions of years earlier by the same erosion process as that of De Chelly, except that the material was of a much finer grain and was deposited in shallow waters as mud. These broad bases appear as stepped pyramids forming a platform upon which the shear pillars could be displayed. Both of the Mittens depict the Organ Rock Shale and De Chelly in their classic positions.

Monument Valley would never have existed without the next layers of material. These two layers were deposited during the beginning of the fourth period of the planet's aging — the Triassic Period of the Mesozoic Era. The Triassic Period was characterized by vast floods of fresh water which carried and deposited silt all over the western United States.

Arches

the early Triassic flows of water, provides the most interesting story of all the deposits, even though little can be seen of it atop the monuments.

The topmost capstones of Monument Valley were deposits of gravel caught in the ancient bends of giant rivers. Settling to the bottom of the river, deep layers of the fine gravel were deposited. These sediments attracted fluids that seeped downward to form caches of uranium later compressed into concrete-like layers of rock. They were extremely hard and

"The land of time enough and room enough --"

resistant to the perpetual wind, water and temperature changes, and they protected the softer Moenkopi, De Chelly and Organ deposits.

Embedded in this gravel were bits of petrified wood which both the Navajo people and the Piute tribe of southern Utah and northern Arizona believed were weapons of the Great Wolf God, Shinarav. Given the name Shinarump Conglomerate, this layer of material made Monument Valley possible. Near Holbrook and Winslow, Arizona, the remnants of the Shinarump can be seen gleaming like a multi-colored marble-like blanket covering the Moenkopi hills.

If the Monument Valley configuration was buried deep in the earth under two eras and nine periods of geologic deposits of material, how was it uncovered? Unseen forces deep in the earth, always on the move, began to slowly push upward, creating a huge dome some forty miles by sixty miles. While the more vast Colorado Plateau had been pushed up by profoundly dynamic forces, this minor bulge, called the Monument Valley Uplift, surfaced like a giant nail through a layer of paint about 25 million years ago — just yesterday in geological time. The dry climate caused the huge bulge to crack, creating large fissures in all directions. Volcanoes emerged in areas surrounding the Uplift, releasing the molten rock underneath. Soon worn away by wind and water, the newly deposited material on top of Monument Valley was exposed, revealing the five layers that now compose the monoliths.

Nature then completed the sculpting process, removing substances around the buttes and spires protected by Shinarav, the Wolf God. Were these natural or spiritual forces? Monument Valley is old enough, and vast enough, to encompass all mysteries and theories. (48)

Merrick and Mitchell Buttes

EIGHT
The Lost Silver Mine

If the world's script writers could design the ideal setting for mystery and intrigue, they could not do any better than Monument Valley. One of the most fascinating of its strange and legendary stories, one told over and over around western campfires, concerns an event that happened in the latter half of the 1800's. That was the time Kit Carson captured the Navajo people hiding out in Canyon De Chelly. He took them into captivity and marched them in the famous Long Walk to Bosque Redondo at Fort Sumner.

Two of Carson's men, Merrick and Mitchell, were mesmerized by the gleaming silver bracelets and jewelry worn by the fleeing Navajos. They assumed that the silver came from the northwest Navajo land. From their patrols of the area, the two soldiers knew that no silver was being brought into the region, and they hadn't seen enough of the ore to account for the large amount used in the bracelets, necklaces and the thick bow guards strapped to the Navajo men's wrists.

Merrick and Mitchell became obsessed with a vision of silver bars that surely would be found to the northwest of Canyon De Chelly. When the Long

Walk of the Navajo people was completed, the two mustered out of the U.S. Army and headed north to pursue their destiny.

The former soldiers disguised themselves as trappers and entered Monument Valley. Throughout the spires and buttes they set their line of traps, but spent most of their energy looking for tell-tale signs of silver ore.

Canyons west of Monument Valley

Hidden from the prospectors was a band of Navajos led by Hoskinnini, a Navajo natani who had successfully escaped the clutches of Kit Carson. Hoskinnini approached and told Mitchell and Merrick to get out of the Valley and never come back, but lust for treasure and wealth had sunk deep into the souls of the two men. They were driven, and willing to place their lives on the line to find the huge cache of silver they believed must be somewhere in the Valley.

Hoskinnini

As the legend is told, Merrick and Mitchell did find the old silver mine and it was richer than they had imagined. They were gripped by both fear and joy. Hiding ore samples in their saddle bags, they took off for the nearest town, Cortez, Colorado. Their familiar, spellbinding tale was told over and over in the small hamlets of the west and spilled out once again at the bar of a small saloon on Main Street. The accounts of seemingly unlimited richness were drowned out by ooo's and aahs as ore samples were dumped on the poker table. Of course the location of the silver mine was to be kept a close secret.

Mitchell and Merrick faced one small obstacle in securing their riches. It would take a sizable sum to set up mining operations to extract the silver, and they had no money. They spent months trekking in and out of the tiny towns of southwestern Colorado, hoping to make a deal. The mining town of Dolores, the lumber town of Mancos and the coal mining town over the mountain in Durango were visited

more than once. But it was in Cortez, where the treasure find was first announced, that a backer made a commitment to finance the mining operation. Other investors followed, but there was one hitch — the two had to go back to the mine and return with a second set of samples to verify the mine's existence.

The lives of Mitchell and Merrick were pulled by the excitement of becoming millionaires on the one hand and of meeting their deaths on the other. They had told no one that Hoskinnini and his band had given them a second warning, insisting that the prospectors never return to the Valley.

The two were deeply concerned about Hoskinnini's warning and mused about the danger of going back. Their bravado and saloon bragging had given them special status and they felt pressured to prove themselves in the eyes of the men in southwestern Colorado. After all, they had the financial support to run the mining operation. They took the risk and reentered Monument Valley.

The entry and extraction of new ore samples from the mine seemed so easy that Merrick and Mitchell were lulled into a false sense of security. Their joy in finding fortune led them to question their early concerns about the Navajo band. Hoskinnini had probably moved out of the area, they thought.

Unfortunately, like many who came to the West, Merrick and Mitchell totally underestimated the ability of native peoples to know exactly what was happening on their lands. Navajo scouts had seen the two prospectors enter the mine. Hoskinnini told his warriors that adequate and fair warning had been given and, like many white men (hostein belaganiis), that these two ex-soldiers failed to heed the word of a tribal chief. They, not the Navajos, had sealed their own destiny.

The story goes that Mitchell and Merrick had built a campfire and were cooking bacon and beans. Firelight was reflected off the large butte under which they were camping. Anticipating the good life they danced like grotesque giants with glee and laughter, their bodies silhouetted on the wall of the butte's De Chelly sandstone. Hoskinnini and his warriors lurked in the darkness outside the circle of campfire light. Their sudden plunge into the camp changed the laughter of the two men into low screams of surprise and fear as recognition of their doom overwhelmed them.

Merrick took a bullet and fell face downward with a thump into the sand of the Valley floor, kicking up a fine cloud of red dust in the firelight. Merrick Butte

Dredging for gold on the San Juan River

marks the site of his death, and his grave probably matches those of pharaohs for the magnificence of his memorial.

Mitchell lurched outside the circle of light. He felt searing pain from a bullet in his side but managed to escape to a nearby butte, hiding in a small crevice created by a slab of De Chelly which had slid down the cliff. Mitchell had all night to ponder on his poor judgment and the fate he would face in the morning. Hoskinnini waited until daylight, and when Mitchell ran out of ammunition the Navajo warriors finished him off. Mitchell Butte, a gigantic tombstone, is named for this ill-fated prospector.

The ironic fate of the two prospectors soon reached the ears of anxious investors awaiting their return in Cortez. A posse was formed and twenty or so men left Cortez, heading due west through McElmo Canyon and on across the flat country through Bluff, Utah and down into Monument Valley. The Navajo band took them to the gravesite of Merrick. The investors moved the red rocks covering the body but

found no silver. Then they were taken to Mitchell's burial site and found a sample of the rich ore in his grave.

The Navajos fabricated a story of a renegade band of Piutes who had killed the prospectors, covering their own actions to keep the military out off their land. They said that Mitchell and Merrick had come to Hoskinnini for food and water and later camped under Merrick Butte. At sunrise, having mounted their horses, the two prospectors had been challenged by a band of Piutes who accused them of taking tribal water. One warrior asked for tobacco and when Merrick reached for it, the warrior grabbed his gun and shot him. Mitchell escaped to the rocks under another butte, was wounded and eventually died of thirst, starvation and his wounds.

The posse knew the real story, but did not want a confrontation, so they reburied the bodies under the buttes that bear their names. The Navajos kept the secret, and the posse finally left the area in 1881, abandoning their search for the silver mines.

Reinactment of the signing of the Treaty of 1868

The legendary tale of Mitchell and Merrick was told in saloons all over the West and even on the east coast. Many white men ventured into the Valley in search of the silver mine. The Navajo nataniis

(Chiefs) met and decided to cover the mine with sand and rock, and so the location of the silver lode passed into eternity with the last Navajo "natani."

Legends never die — nor do the dreams of the adventurous. There are more tales about riches deposited near Monument Valley. For example, a

gentlemen named Height circulated a rumor that gold could be found in the silts of the San Juan River. Enterprising gold seekers went so far as to pull up a dredge to a point some 50 miles above Kayenta. For many years the dredge could be seen sticking out of the mud. It has now disappeared under the dark sand , and with it, the great hopes of striking it rich on the San Juan River.

Movie making in Monument Valley

NINE
Ford Brings Monument Valley to the World

The striking image of the Mittens of Monument Valley surely represents the world's image of the American West. If it weren't for an impassioned lover of the Valley and a slight twist of fate, this beautiful natural wonder might have remained hidden. (58)

Harry Goulding, his wife "Mike" and the Navajo people living in Monument Valley were struggling to survive the Depression. One evening over radio KTAR in Phoenix, Harry and Mike heard an announcement that United Artists were looking for a site to film a western movie.

The Gouldings packed up bedrolls, coffee pot and grub and motored on Old Route 66 to Hollywood. Harry had with him a large portfolio of pictures that friends had taken over the years. Harry was told that it was silly to think he could get into United Artist

Studios unless he knew someone real well. Harry said that he was going to get in to talk to someone or go to jail.

When told by the receptionist at United Artist Studios that he couldn't see anyone, Harry went out

Gouldings Trading Post

to the car, brought in his bedroll and grub sack and tossed them on the floor. The receptionist warned Harry that an important executive was coming down to throw him out. Behind him an agitated man, fuming expletives, came busting through the door. As

Harry turned slowly around, the man asked him what he had there. Harry produced two bundles of pictures from under his arm. As he turned around a magnificent scene of the Mittens caught the attention of the man, who turned out to be the location manager for the movie, STAGECOACH.

Having spread Harry's pictures over three rooms on the second floor of United Artists, the production manager spent an hour quietly studying each scene. He asked Harry if someone else could look at the pictures, and he and Harry were soon joined by director, John Ford and producer Walter Wagner. The group talked into the wee hours of the morning about the sites, the terrain and whether or not those were real "Indians" on horseback. One day later, John Ford and the location manager flew out to Monument Valley to see for themselves.

Harry was dumfounded when John Ford asked him if he could handle the logistics supporting the filming of STAGECOACH in Monument Valley. The filming was to begin in three days with an entourage of one hundred people. Harry mentioned that he was short on funds and Ford had a check issued. Harry later pulled out the check to cash it at a gas station and ended up getting credit. The check was for five thousand dollars.

Plane near Monument Valley

"Three days? A hundred people?" Harry said. "Gosh, them old rocks have been out there an awful long time, and the Indians ain't going to move. Wouldn't a few more days be about as well?" (58, pg. 149) Three days later Harry was in the office of an frustrated James Babbitt in Flagstaff who was trying to fill an order to pack eleven trucks bound for Monument Valley hauling John Ford, John Wayne, a movie company and eight carpenters.

Ford told Harry that they would shoot the next day and would need "theatrical clouds." When Harry found out that meant "fluffy" he said it would be no problem to contact medicine man Hosteen Tso, who would work with smoke signals to assure the clouds would be there. The first scene of the famous Academy Award winning STAGECOACH was done on schedule the next day with beautiful white clouds in

Stuck in the sand

the background. The celluloid saga of the west and the upgrading of westerns from "B" rating to classics were now in place.

The relationship between Navajo medicine man Hosteen Tso, "Fatso," as John Ford affectionately came to call him, is legendary. During the first week of shooting John Ford requested blowing clouds to follow the fast moving stagecoach and showed no particular surprise when the company was presented with a large cluster of fast moving clouds moving northeast at the next day's shooting. About four o'clock after each day's work, Harry and Tso would go up to the upstairs room above Goulding's Trading Post to talk to Ford.

Babbitt Brothers Trading Company

On another occasion Ford mentioned that they needed a sandstorm to give variety to the stagecoaches' journey. Harry interrupted the troupe's lunch break the next day by announcing that a sandstorm was coming. He announced that the troupe would miss it unless they got out to the proposed site on the ridge to film it before it passed. After two runs in the violent sandstorm, people couldn't see their hands in front of them and filming was ended for the day. Several days later, Hosteen Tso, using chants and

HosteenTso

rattles, turned a sandstorm from a path that would have destroyed the large circus-like tents used by United Artists for storage and the company cafeteria.

Snow in Monument Valley in October

It was clear at this point that while Ford had great affection and respect for Tso and defended him vigorously if anyone questioned his power, many mem-

Gouldings upstairs

bers of the company questioned the weather making. They felt that it just couldn't be. On what was to be the last day of the filming, Harry approached John

Ford and asked him if he and Tso could come up to talk with him. Ford thought for a moment and told Harry that the only thing lacking in their shots was a snow scene in Monument Valley. He smiled at Harry, knowing it was early October, the wrong time of year. Snow usually came to Monument Valley in

Cowtown movie set

early December. John Ford went to his second floor room in Goulding's Trading Post and slept with the blinds pulled, his usual custom.

That morning, John Ford looked eastward to the magnificence of Monument Valley blanketed in snow. "My goodness, Harry, I owe you an apology! I thought you were just kidding me about that old medicine man!" United stayed another day to shoot

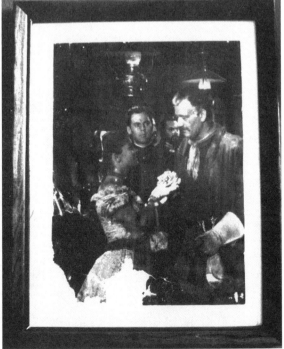

SHE WORE A YELLOW RIBBON ~ RKO

Twentieth Century Fox

the snow scene. Although Hosteen Tso received the same fifteen dollars a day pay like everyone else, John Ford give him a big wad of bills when he shook hands to say good-bye at the end of the filming of STAGECOACH.

Wayne and location manager

John Ford came back to Monument Valley to make many more films. In the early days, Harry wondered why the film troupe did so well way out in nowhere away from the comforts and excitement of Hollywood. He found out that Ford carefully

Film Crew for HARVEY GIRLS

screened and selected his film crew for their interest in and love of the scenery and people of the northern sector of the Navajo Nation.

The filming of each picture was accompanied by a host of movie tents and Navajo camp fires. Feasts and festivals were frequent, and Navajo actors and extras participated time and again over the years and became close friends of Ford, his crews and the actors. The economic impact of movie making in the area was enormous. Navajos survived one very long and bitter winter only because the pay they received from a Ford movie filled their hogans with food and necessities. One August, with another severe winter forecast by medicine men, Harry contacted John Ford who felt that maybe it was time to make another movie in Monument Valley.

The author's cousin, Jack Bean, co-engineered the layout of the movie village that supported the filming of MY DARLING CLEMENTINE, made in 1948. Jack Bean related how his troupe got stuck in the sand and spent the night several miles south of Monument Valley wondering if they would ever see "civilization" again.

COMANCHEROS

John WAYNE

Jimmy AUSTIN

Michael Curtiz, Director

20th Century Fox

Ford came to the Valley in 1956 to make the film SEARCHERS. Led by Lee and Frank Bradley, John Ford was made an honorary member of the Navajo Tribe. Accompanied by John Wayne and Ward Bond, Ford sat on a deerskin for the inducting ceremony of the Navajo medicine men. Wayne, Bond and Ford feasted on three barbecued steers and mutton stew with their long time Navajo friends.

In 1971 John Ford returned to Monument Valley to make a documentary, DIRECTED BY JOHN FORD. A large feast was held down below Gouldings. It would be John Ford's last trip to the Valley. As Seth Bigman tells it: "The last time Mr. Ford came back out here, we had our big feast down here at Jake Charlie Holiday's, my father-in-law's place, just below Goulding's. John Ford and John Wayne came out, and also another character, he always played comedy, I forget his name. The three of them came out, and this is where they had their feast. Then we heard Mr. Ford was passed away. Before that my father-in-law passed way, but they had a happy meeting. They fed a lot of people and they gave a lot of money away. Everybody went home happy." (58, Pg. 163)

Mrs. Lillian Smith, whose brothers played key roles in making local arrangements for Ford, attended a memorial at Ford's birthplace in Maine. The impact of Ford's movies on Native Americans is controver-sial and has gendered much discussion. While the movie, SEARCHERS, depicts rage and revenge against inhuman "savages," CHEYENNE AUTUMN attempts to make amends by showing the arbitrary and negative impact of the U.S. Government's treatment of Native Americans. However, it was no secret that John Ford had deep love and respect for the Navajo people and their country. (21, 85)

Wagons never ending ~ circa 1960

TEN
Sacred Ceremonials

It was summertime in Arizona. The smooth, rich voice of Howard Pyle resonated through the atmosphere, wending its way into a tiny radio in a small flat in east London. "And now, friends, we see the awesome, mysterious Crown Dancers from the White Mountain Apache Nation. Moving to the drum beat of an ancient chant, four shadowy figures dressed in russet leather aprons with black hoods over their faces are coming out of the black of night into the campfire light here in Flagstaff, Arizona," (94)

Pyle, the future Governor of Arizona and a prominent radio announcer for NBC-KTAR in Phoenix, was beaming the first international radio cast of the famous Fourth of July Pow Wow from Flagstaff, Arizona. The fame and allure of Pow Wow had accelerated throughout the 1930's, and by 1938 thousands of tourists from all over the world were making their summer pilgrimage to the appealing lit-

The sheer magnitude with which the Pow Wow had grown over time awed even the local leaders who had initiated the formal celebration many years

Apache Mountain Spirit Dancers

before. By the late 1930's, as many as twenty-five tribal groups from all over the United States, Canada and Mexico had begun an annual trek to the cool pines at the foot of the San Francisco Peaks. In one of its July, 1938 editions, the front page of the COCONINO SUN proclaimed that 800 "Indians" had arrived and were camped out in City Park. It was noted that "Jim Mahoney, a 113 year-old Hualpai Indian, scout for the federal forces during the Apache uprisings, will be back," (94) Joining Mr. Mahoney, the Sun stated, would be Chief Watahomogie, leader of the Havasupais and Chief Chee Dodge, a distinguished leader of the Navajo Nation.

The Pow Wow celebration encompassed a frenzied three-day non-stop schedule of parades, rodeos, and evening ceremonies. Extensive campgrounds, covering most of the area on the west side of town below Observatory Hill (of Percival Lowell's Martian studies fame), were filled with campfires and tarp lean-to's. Smoke wafted across the hills and up into the pine tops, infusing the air with the scent of coffee and charcoal roasted lamb. The organesque beat of the merry-go-round carried softly through the woods from noon till midnight, when the drums and the singing began. The forty-nine songs of the Plains tribes and the chants of the Navajo reverberated with a calming effect into the night air.

During the day, streets and businesses were jammed with shoulder-to-shoulder parade watchers with the Reverend Shine Smith holding court in the middle of the street. Shine had spent decades as a missionary to the Navajo at Shonto and knew their language and culture like few others. All the celebratory events, including one of the southwest's largest carnivals,

took place amidst mobs of U.S. and foreign tourists in Flagstaff, a pretty, popular Arizona town nestled under the San Francisco Peaks.

The "Peaks" stand at the southernmost tip of the Rocky Mountains, and represent the highest point in Arizona and on Route 66. Throughout history, because of its location on a natural trail and an east-west route, Flagstaff had been a gathering spot. It's tall pines, lush forests and inviting springs were a camping choice for native tribes, the United States Army, early settlers and the railroaders.

The first Fourth of July celebration occurred in the 1870's when settlers, Army Engineers and local

Going to the Pow Wow ~ circa 1955

tribes came together to celebrate the hundred-year anniversary of United States independence from England. The occassion also acted as a way to return harmony between Flagstaff residents and the follow-

Navajo camp at Gallup Ceremonials ~ circa 1950

ers of B'ugoettin following the altercation that could have destroyed Flagstaff. The Pow Wow tradition

Parade ~ circa 1960

also had long been established through frequent rendezvous held by fur trappers and tribes on the eastern rim of Canyon Diablo. Hence the deep origins of the Fourth of July celebration, one which beckoned folks from near and far to enjoy each other and the festivities.

To many a Navajo family the Pow Wow and the pines of Flagstaff offered an oasis of repose from the summer heat of the Painted Desert and the red rock canyons of northern Arizona. Extended families and

Hopi Tribal Band

clans reunited each year in the foothills surrounding the town. Local businesses poured forth bolts of velvet and cotton cloth, saddles, Mexican saltillos, watermelons and soda pop in exchange for the cash that silversmiths and artisans had received for such things as turquoise squash blossom necklaces, sheepskins, moccasins, exquisite pottery and kachina dolls.

Various Pueblo tribes came into Flagstaff from outlying mesas scattered across Arizona and New

Mexico. Apaches of the Mescalero, White Mountain, San Carlos and Jicarilla bands left their creeks and valley haunts below the Mogollon Rim and brought traditional costumes, dances and ancient chants with them to the celebration. Navajo families in their canvas covered wagons moved in slowly, literally spending weeks in transit from their sheep camps spread across the vast Navajo Nation.

The Pow Wow Committee of Flagstaff, comprised of local officials and businessmen, were called upon to

Zuni Tribe ~ circa 1960

manage complex logistics resembling those of a large city. One of the dedicated members of the POW Wow Committee, a vigorous supporter of Indian culture, was a man named Jack Fuss. A local artist, Mr. Fuss was the force behind the Pow Wow throughout its most impressive years. Andy Wolf, whose booming voice could be heard out across the Flagstaff skyline, became known as the voice of the Night Ceremonies.

The daily parade through the streets of Flagstaff was a time of frenzied excitement to first time visitors and old timers alike, previewing as it did the varied and distinctive costumes, dances and chants for each of the participating tribes. That night, presentations flourished in an ecstatic crescendo of movement, color and sound around huge, glowing campfires. Soon, the crowd would hear the Navajo and Hopi tribal bands off in the distance, the bright sound of John Philip Sousa marches filling the summer air.

Impressive, colorful, full compliment bands from the Hopi and Navajo Nations suddenly emerged from around the block, marching in front of groups of people gathered in pickup beds or sitting on lawn chairs. In their radiant satin and velvet red shirts and kerchief head bands, the tribe member's instruments would blare out various John Phillip Sousa marches, some of which were based on the ancient chants of those Native musicians. By the end of the four-mile parade on east Route 66, the rigors of the "fast step," along with the hearty playing of instruments would find the bandsmen with sweat pouring off their faces.

Suddenly, the blaring of bands, the beating of drums and a steady background echo of parade watchers became but a backdrop for the thunderhead clouds that formed around noon. Appearing like magic in the clear, sunny sky, the thunderheads signaled with a loud clap the arrival of nature's air conditioner. This daily blessing by the gigantic rain clouds cooled the forest and settled the dusty streets and ceremonial grounds with sporadic, welcome showers.

The seemingly unending parade of vibrant, energetic dance groups presented distinct spectacles and new sensations to viewers who packed the sides of the street four and five bodies deep. Each group offered a totally unique portrayal of costume, dance and song rarely seen in the Southwest and totally unknown to European visitors.

Experienced parade watchers anxiously anticipated the appearance of elegant maidens from Acoma Pueblo who moved gracefully down the streets, effortlessly balancing huge pottery jars on their heads. Gliding across a paved surface was simple compared to climbing up and down the steep cliffs of Acoma with jars full of water.

Eerie-looking Navajo mud dancers in loincloths, wearing kerchief head bands and covered with dried, gray mud, moved as a pack, droning the ancient YE BE CHE chant to the Holy People. Their singing stilled the crowd's chatter, awakening in them perhaps some deep, primeval memories.

Zuni maidens hauling water ~ circa 1960

Excitement heightened at the distant sound of the powerful, super-energized Kiowa fancy dancers who would appear around the corner frantically spinning, bending, and twirling. Bells ringing, feather bustles swishing and eagle feathers bobbing atop their heads, their feet would hit the hot July pavement in perfect time with every beat of the drum. Behind the dancers was a line of gently swaying women, beauti-

Navajo fire dancers ~ circa 1950

ful in beaded buckskin, fanning themselves with eagle feathers in the hot morning sun. At the sound of clapping the entertainers would stop and perform a Kiowa war dance, echoing the spirit of one of America's fiercest warrior groups.

Intense stimulation from an unending variety of performers generated an almost unbearable ecstasy within the huge crowd of Pow Wow observers. All the performers were extraordinary, but the Hoop Dancers of Laguna Pueblo were unrivaled for the complexity of their routine. Anthony Purly and his children would move in and out of various intricate body contortions, emerging with grace and ease out of an impossible mesh of twenty or more hoops.

The Jemez Pueblo dancers, with deer horn crowns on their heads and juniper branches in their hands, wound their way down the street, zigzagging in perfect unison with knees bent and both feet bouncing off the hot pavement. People in the audience who knew the purpose of the dances, and even those who intuitively sensed a deeper meaning to the ceremony, connected the dance to the pleasurable onset of afternoon showers.

Chills ran down many a spine, and muffled cries could be heard when a certain drum beat and distinctive rhythmic chant — ta - tah', ta - tah', ta - tah', ta - tah' — seeped into background chatter and became louder and louder. What they heard was the familiar, awesome sound of the Apache Mountain Spirit Dancers (often erroneously termed Apache Devil

Dancers). Black hooded, bedecked with large white lattice-like crowns, dressed in ochre buckskin and

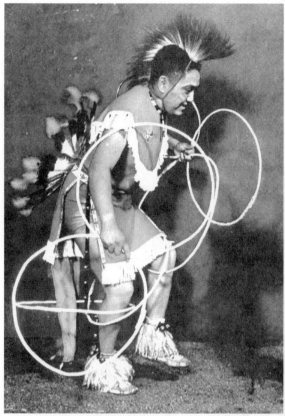

Anthony Purly, Laguna ~ circa 1955

curl-tipped moccasins, they moved down the street like a giant, slithering snake. Young people and panicky children streamed back, away from the front of the parade crowd.

The last dancer, his face covered with a white hood, swirled a stick in the in the air that sounded like a huge bumblebee, a stick designed to frighten away the evil spirits. Many years later the author discov-

Plains Indian dance ~ circa 1960r

Plains Indian fancy dancers

ered that the last dancer was the leader and chief medicine dancer — not a clown as so many people believed. It was this last dancer who would always "capture" someone from the crowd, usually a young person, and dance down the street with them.

The number of tribal groups represented in the parade was almost unbelievable. They came from New York, central Oklahoma, Florida and Mexico, each group unique in costume, colors, dance and song. In the 1960's, a new ceremonial dimension was added to the Pow Wow by Aztec dancers from Mexico. Their graceful hopping, bouncing and soaring gestures down the streets added a special charm to the parade.

The appearance of a horse drawn wagon signaled the parade's finale, and first time watchers were struck with momentary sadness at its waning. Happily, they came to realize that this initial wagon was only the first in a procession of over a hundred Navajo covered wagons, each filled with elders, mothers and children amid bales of hay and Indian trade blankets.

Ultimately, in the late forties, the use of iron-rimmed wooden spoke wheels gave way to automotive tires, and finally, in the sixties, only a handful of wagons

participated in the parade. Most Navajo families had abandoned the use of the wagon for the more mobile

Buffalo dancer ~ circa 1941

and much faster "chitty" (pickup).

Navajo wagons under July thunder clouds ~ circa 1960

When the last wagon disappeared down Aspen Avenue, the crowd scurried to grab a seat at the nearest soda fountain or restaurant. Bedlam prevailed in downtown Flagstaff until the crowd dissipated and trudged on toward City Park, where a whole new phase of the Pow Wow began. It was time to search for treasures offered by the various tribal vendors, time to munch on native delicacies such as fry bread, roasted lamb ribs, green chile posole and red chile "popovers." There was never enough time though to both "trade and dine," and many a tourist would agree prematurely to the price of a Navajo Squash Blossom necklace in order to find a seat at the start of the afternoon rodeo.

American Indians had become some of the world's best horsemen. The lengthy, frustrating attempt by the U.S. Army to subjugate the Apache attested to the Native Americans' superior horsemanship. Navajo dominance of the Four Corners area and New Mexico, reaching to the banks of the Rio Grande, affirms the power they wielded in the West. Fierce Kiowa and Comanche warriors ruled the plains east of the Rocky Mountains, and the Yaqui 10,000-man cavalry was one of the most feared forces in southern Arizona and Mexico.

Alas, the excellence of Native American horsemanship was concealed by prejudice and went unrecognized for many years. Due to lowered social position

their civil rights were trampled, and it was not until the 1950's that tribal groups were allowed to purchase liquor and vote like other American citizens.

Nonetheless, Native Americans distinguished themselves, fighting valiantly for their country during

Aztec from Mexico ~ circa 1960

both world wars. One noted, indeed critical, contribution was that of the Navajo Code Talkers working against Japan in the Pacific War Theater. A member of the Pima Nation was part of the group raising the United States flag on Mt. Surabachi, Iwo Jima.

Flagstaff police faced enormous challenges during Pow Wow, including gridlocked traffic, Native American fellows in town for a good time (downing pints of booze before it could be confiscated), and masses of tourists overwhelming the local services infrastructure. Many a tourist expressed disbelief at the $30 price of one watermelon, until they found out that it contained a fifth of whisky hidden in a hollowed out compartment.

Many Native Americans, both men and women, ended up incarcerated in a specially constructed "hoosegow" located on the Pow Wow grounds. The jail, which was intended to accommodate only a dozen or so individuals, was often stuffed with twice as many bodies. Many were not released until the Pow Wow was over, several days later.

The booming sounds of the rodeo announcer and the screams and applause of the crowd reverberated over the tree tops, filtering into the author's back yard on Aspen Avenue across from City Park playground. It was in this back yard, armed with potato salad, ham and soda pop that people-watching was honed to a fine art.

Rodeo festivities included a real old-time BBQ, consisting of beef wrapped in burlap that was then buried deep underground in a bed of coals where it was allowed to cook slowly for days. The tender juicy meat was served with a special BBQ sauce

Navajo rug sales

made by local Basque-Americans, and was complemented by potato salad, beans and home made bread.

Rodeos continued to be a prime sport for Native Americans, extending into the 1980's and 1990's when they became as popular as basketball and football. As the years passed by, various Native Americans attained exceptional skill and national reputations as cowboys. The Apaches were particularly known for their love of and the number of the horses they possessed.

Time out for lunch ~ circa 1950

Each small community on the Navajo Nation began constructing its own rodeo grounds. Navajo cowboys started to win big in rodeos across the nation. Stories about the feats of Native American horsemen were shared into the wee hours at campfires out among the pines and scrub oak. Some of the favorites were the myths and exploits of Kiowa horsemen, and each year the stories were a little more exaggerated. A case in point, and a favorite of the old timers, was the tale of a band Kiowa warriors who supposedly removed a kidney from the back of a live steer before it collapsed on the ground. The rodeos presented a somewhat relaxing respite from the feverish excitement that engulfed the small town of Flagstaff each Fourth of July from the 1930's into the 1970's.

One of the great pleasures of both tourist and native was a walk through the camp grounds spread all over Mars Hill, an amble through the cool Ponderosa Pine forest. The hundreds of camps of individual Native American families evidenced more about Native American people than all the parades and ceremonials combined.

The Pow Wow Committee, a group of volunteers crosscutting a broad spectrum of Flagstaff's community, worked year around to plan events and confirm the appearance of dance groups. In turn, Native Americans spent all year planning and looking foreword to the Fourth of July Pow Wow. Silver dollars and coins were stashed in old coffee cans. Sheep were sheared, wool was spun and woven into rugs and buckskins were tanned. Hammered silver and cut turquoise were fashioned into beautiful rings, bracelets and the famous Navajo Squash Blossom necklaces — the dream, and, once obtained, prized possession of every woman in Northern Arizona. The

The Jail

whole year was devoted — especially by the Navajo and the Hopi — to preparations for the trek to Flagstaff and the great craft market.

The tradition of gathering at mid-summer in Flagstaff was neither conceived nor motivated by commercial interests in Flagstaff. The Pow Wow had been instituted in the early 1800's to celebrate the mutual cooperation between the Native Americans and the old Fur Trappers who shared the bounty of the Little Colorado River. Back then, Rendezvous were held on the east side of Canyon Diablo where hides, jewelry and rugs were traded for hardware and food.

Although that first Pow Wow in Flagstaff was held in the late 1870's, the tradition of meeting, celebrating and trading at the foot of the San Francisco Peaks had been going on for a hundred years. It was the

Pow Wow Committee who formalized and presented the rich and exciting Native American cultures to the rest of the world.

Before the Bureau of Indian Affairs carted Navajo children off to their schools and dormitories, many of youngsters would spend the entire year at home in their family's sheep camp. To such children, going to the Pow Wow was like an American traveling to New York or Paris. Some Navajo families from way out on the Navajo Nation — at Kayenta, Chinle, or Kaibito — started their journey in horse drawn wagons as early as six weeks before the Fourth of July. The author's associate from Kayenta related how the 1950's July treks to Flagstaff always involved stuffing the whole family into the pickup cab and bed (along with the sheep and blankets), to head off for Flagstaff where the Pow Wow camp was set up.

Apache Mountain Spirit Dancers ~ circa 1960

"Rhet pop," was the standard response the author got from all the Navajo children moving back and forth from the City Park to downtown Flagstaff. The author ran a Koolade business in front of his house during the Pow Wow days. Strawberry Koolade — "rhet pop" — and lemonade, an option for the belaganiis (white people), were the only two choices. Occasionally, peanut butter cookies were also available.

The camping grounds were packed solid with individual compounds, each characterized and distinguished by the particular customs and culture of its Native American residents. Fires burnt day and night. The elderly would sit for hour upon hour playing some enigmatic card game. Others, wrapped in

Summer fun at Pow Wow camp

blankets, leaned and dozed against the pines, the flickering campfires casting mysterious shadows across their bronzed faces.

Large cuts of round steak "rations" hung like clothes put out to dry. Most families brought live sheep to slaughter and cook during the Pow Wow, while the Pow Wow Committee's rations came in the form of beef round steak, flour, lard and baking powder. The smell of roasted corn, blue corn cakes simmering in bacon grease and coffee steaming from spouts of blue enameled coffeepots mingled with the pungent whiff of sheep ribs broiling on the grill. The attack of the Pow Wow camp on the senses of "civilized" tourists was a hypnotic potion that lured them back every year. Some even came back to stay.

Along the road leading to City Park, in groups outside the bleacher area and throughout the pines, one could find Navajo Rugs, exquisite Hopi jewelry and traditional cowhide moccasins and beaded buckskins, as well as all sorts of other items sold by the Native American craftsman who made them.

The commingling of Native American, local and visitors' children created an unconscious sense of unity. A frequent sight would be two Navajo girls packed together in the Tilt-a-Whirl with a white boy and a Mexican boy, all four screaming and giggling at the top of their lungs. Their youth and shared experience often created a bond that superseded and extended beyond the brief time they spent together.

The carnival was anticipated all year long and must have seemed the ultimate thrill to the young Native Americans. Surely, to many a Navajo child, heaven was a carnival. The multi-colored point of lights way

off in the pitch darkness of a summer night were absolutely and forever burnt into the minds of enthralled Native American children.

The organ music of the merry-go-round, the barker's shrill call at the baseball throw, the chatter of Navajo children and the voice of the ceremonial announcer combined to overwhelm the senses of the celebrants. A deluge of professional artists, photographers and writers seemed to be everywhere, commingling with tourists, locals and Native Americans. Those sights and sounds were etched in the memories of all during the unforgettable days of summer on Old Route 66 in Flagstaff, Arizona.

The night ceremonials provided a varied and intense exposure to Native American cultures. The FEATHER DANCE of the Navajo never failed to awe the audience, and was the subject of conversation for days afterward. A feather placed upright in a wedding basket would rise and appear to move under its own power with the rhythm of the dance and the sway of

GallupCeremonial Parade ~ circa 1930

a Navajo maiden's long hair. To this day, the FEATHER DANCE remains a mystery, a secret closely kept.

The sudden appearance of the Apache Crown Dancers, coming from four directions out of the darkness into the light of the huge bonfires, added a surrealistic dimension to their already awesome countenance. The Deer Dancers of Jemez Pueblo, zigging and zagging in perfect rhythm and synchronization, suggested ancient tales about pueblo cultures, stories of unity and their long trust and dependence upon the deities for the rain and corn that resulted from their prayers and dances.

Navajo mud dancers chasing each other with juniper fire brands induced roaring laughter and screams from the huge crowds in the grandstand and out on the perimeter of the ceremonial grounds. Every presentation by a Native American group was wonderful, indescribable, each seeming to exceed the charm of the preceding exhibition. The grandstand audience was totally mesmerized during the four-hour ceremo-

Navajo "Natanni" ~ circa 1941

nial.

Melancholia hovered over Flagstaff when the final day of the celebration came. Carnival vendors began to disassemble the Tilt-a-Whirl. The Navajo wagons started to leave for their remote sheep camps scattered about the Navajo Nation. Sad farewells were shared, everyone aware that they would not meet again until next summer. The forest across from the Pow Wow grounds and the park on Aspen Avenue were silent once again. The drum beat and the laugh-

ter that had echoed from the recesses of the jack pine thickets ceased. A fresh morning alfalfa-like scent moved in to refresh the air, replacing the smell of hot coffee, fry bread and roasted lamb.

No one would have imagined that the Pow Wow of 1974 would be witness to the last dancer, the final bronco busting and the farewell spin of the Tilt-a-Whirl. Members of the American Indian Movement (AIM) assaulted and overwhelmed Andy Wolf in the announcer stand during the night ceremonials in July of 1974. The confrontation by AIM was in protest of what they deemed to be white control of and excessive local merchant profiteering from the efforts of Native American Pow Wow participants.

However, the reasons for not continuing the Pow Wow embody far more complex issues than the lone intercession by the American Indian Movement. The additional causes for its termination have never been explained or confirmed. A hundred-year tradition would cease with the last drumbeat on that cool summer night of 1974 in Flagstaff. Many individuals, including the author's father, were very upset about the death of the Pow Wow.

The GALLUP CEREMONIALS share the same deep-rooted traditions and international prominence of the Flagstaff Pow Wow. They follow a similar pattern with daily parades, rodeos and nighttime ceremonials. The Red Rock State Park setting east of Gallup boasts a high desert butte topography similar to that found on the Navajo Nation at Monument Valley and

Navajo women in Gallup Cerimonials ~ circa 1930

Fun on the Titlta-Whirl ~ 1942

Canyon de Chelly. The Gallup Ceremonials, seen as a critical element in the economy of Gallup, continue to this day and are held in mid-August. (3, 4)

One of the more interesting, paradoxical observances honoring Native Americans were the SMOKI PEOPLES CEREMONIALS held in Prescott, Arizona. The Smoki were local white people who, like the Mummers of Philadelphia, made their own costumes and executed their own dances in ritualistic performances. Many of their routines reflected the Hopi people's snake dances. Needless to say, with the emancipation of Native Americans following their brave efforts during World War II and their attainment of voting status, the Smoki People faded away, ironically in honor of their namesake.

The increasing adoption by non-Native Americans of the traditions and culture of Native peoples is felt to be intrusive and is of some concern to Native people. Few imitators or "Want-to-Be's" — as they are often refereed to by the Natives — realize that Native American culture is not superficially accessible, that it begins in the genes and the womb. The culture cannot be subsumed by someone outside the distinct biological, cultural and social context by which Native Americans attain their being and identity.

In fact, the kindness, generosity and open acceptance given by many Native Americans to outsiders is often mistaken for approval of the use, or abuse, of their culture. Indeed, the Hopi people have often expelled individuals who have attempted to assume leadership or priestly roles, persons who reveal with impunity their secrets to the rest of the world. There are many ways to honor, assist and support Native American peoples without intruding in their lives or attempting to adopt their ways.

Unfortunately, many an author writes of the essence of Native American life while contributing nothing to the welfare of those same individuals. Artists and photographers spend hour upon hour capturing the people and their land without so much as mentioning the name or place of their artistic subjects. It is a tragedy that for all the exploitation of the Navajo's culture, beautiful wool blankets and jewelry, their relative standard of living has not changed appreciably in comparison to that of the rest of the United States.

William Boyd ~ "Hopilong Cassidy" ~ circa 1935 at Foxboro

ELEVEN
Cinema Superstars on Route 66
Hollywood, Arizona?

Northern Arizona

In 1911, Cecil B. DeMille and Jesse Laskey decided that New York was not a good place to make movies. They packed up their personal effects and their motion picture company and headed west on the Santa Fe Super Chief toward Flagstaff, Arizona. Upon their arrival, they found to their delight a Currier and Ives hamlet nestled under the majestic San Francisco Peaks and thought it a great place to set up shop. Unfortunately, the unloaded equipment was stacked on the depot platform bricks for only a brief moment when an icy wind swept off the Peaks and passed through downtown Flagstaff, piercing their meager coats and freezing their ears. A miserable, depressing drizzle followed the frigid gusts, coating the two men and their company ensemble with a light layer of ice. Enough was enough. DeMille and Laskey boarded the next train for the West Coast, dooming Flagstaff's chance of ever becoming the movie capital of the world.

Thanks to novelist Zane Grey, Northern Arizona and New Mexico were to become hubs for Hollywood westerns, veritable Meccas for a world enthralled

Flagstaff Santa Fe Depot

with celluloid drama and idols of western lore. Grey used Flagstaff, Arizona as headquarters for the research and writing of many of his books. Movies subsequently filmed in Oak Creek Canyon — on the lofty red rocks north of Gallup and amidst the massive cliffs of Monument Valley — stimulated an incessant flow of cinematic pilgrims wanting to see where Errol Flynn or John Wayne had actually stood.

An old timer named Lee Doyle spent many years as a cowboy and guide in northern Arizona. He knew firsthand the picturesque, unusual sites of the area, was well versed in the lore and legend that distinguished these spots and was happy to share his

Cecil B. De Mille

knowledge with Grey. Grey used both lore and land to craft his compelling tales of character and scenery

Weatherford Hotel ~ Flagstaff

found in these hidden niches of Arizona and New Mexico.

Grey's novels, consisting of fictionalized romances based on actual events, rang with authenticity and detail based on the history and physical beauty of his settings. He wrote about the canyons, the tribal lands, the deserts and the forests of Arizona and New Mexico, his descriptions enthralling readers all over the world. Northern Arizona locations were the inspiration of a number of Grey's novels. Those locations can be enjoyed in the books SUNSET PASS (south of Winslow); THE HASHKNIFE OUTFIT (the expansive range from Holbrook to Flagstaff); THE VANISHING AMERICAN (the area around Kayenta); CALL OF THE CANYON (Oak Creek and Sedona); UNDER THE TONTO RIM (the area directly below the Mogollon Rim); LOST PUEBLO (Navajo National Monument); THE RAINBOW TRAIL (Rainbow Natural Bridge and Lake Powell) and ROPING LIONS IN THE GRAND CANYON.

Zane Grey in search of stories

In 1907 Grey made Flagstaff his research headquarters while writing RIDERS OF THE PURPLE SAGE, a story of Mormons living in a secluded area north of the Grand Canyon called the Arizona Strip. In 1918, three of Grey's books were made into movies. These early films were a beginning association between Grey's work and the motion picture business that eventually spanned five decades and produced one-hundred thirteen films. Plot, character, natural beauty and of course romance were transferred to this exciting visual medium. In fact, half of Grey's western books were situated in Arizona — a state that for Grey encompassed the most unspoiled natural splendor of any place in the world. Arizonans he had

Grey captures western beauty

lakes and gentle meadow streams beset by wind, sun, dust storms, rain, snow, withering heat and body-numbing cold.

Grey wrote in Flagstaff's daily paper, the COCONINO SUN, "An intense rivalry is already established between big motion picture producers to see who will get their first and utilize the scores of attractions, scenic and ethnological, this section has to offer. They realize it is a virgin field. They are coming here in a drove to capitalize on it." Grey became a major investor and owner of the Monte Vista Hotel, which, along with the Weatherford, was frequently used as a headquarters for stars and film production crews.

Literature and film helped make the West famous. Zane Grey's book, CALL OF THE CANYON, was written both in Oak Creek Canyon and on the top floor

Mathew's Lodge in Oak Creek Canyon

known became living characters in his novels. They were individuals portrayed as possessing the indomitable will to survive and succeed in the wilderness, living within plots that displayed a profound reverence for nature and absolute simplicity in moral codes and relationships. Grey's novels were a celebration of distinct American values and the overriding importance of the land.

Grey insisted that the integrity of his novels be preserved. He wanted his stories filmed on exact locations, with complete adherence to character, plot and story line. He was a major figure in creating a perception of the West, and often employed the Western formula plot: conflict, pathos and the ascendance of the hero or heroine. Within the simplicity of his stories, Grey's near mesmerizing description of natural scenes and beauty fired the imagination of a world audience who anxiously awaited movie premiers showcasing the actual sites depicted in the novels.

Most of Grey's early films were made in Arizona. In the end, two thirds of the films were based on books with Arizona settings, and thirty-two films were produced between 1918 and 1929. Grey saw Arizona as an unparalleled example of the soul of the land, and he portrayed it as an endless, ever-changing vista of deserts, mountains, trees, roaring rivers, blue-white

of the Weatherford Hotel in Flagstaff, in a room now known as the Zane Grey Room. Oak Creek and Sedona were the settings for the 1923 film, CALL OF THE CANYON, the exact title of Grey's book. It was the first film of many to be filmed in Oak Creek. Film exposed the world to the charm and beauty of Sedona and Oak Creek, establishing them not only as world wide resort destinations but also as centers of international new age spiritualism.

The author camped up in the West fork of Oak Creek in the early 1960's, in a place where walls rise to over 500 feet. Exploring a wide spot in the gorge, he detected the stone remnants of Grey's cabin and noted the high-pitched call of an eagle echoing off the canyon walls. Quite possibly, Grey's vision of the CALL OF THE CANYON was born upon hearing the wild, screaming serenades of soaring eagles.

Far above the clean, clear water running through the West Fork of Oak Creek Canyon, the canyon walls level out at the pine forest surrounding Flagstaff. Far

Movie set at Foxboro Ranch with Hopilong Cassidy and Gabby Hayes

below, one may find oneself at the bottom of a canyon no wider than 12-15 feet, with walls that rise over a thousand feet. Fresh trout are abundant, bear are common and the sweet smell of wild flowers fill the air. Oak Creek is an awesome environment. It's easy to understand why the place stimulated the

Movie set at Foxboro Ranch

muse of an author like Grey, why celebrities and movie stars returned to stay at a two-story log cabin called Matthews Lodge.

Actor Gabby Hayes at Foxboro ~ circa 1935

Twenty minutes into the 1940 movie LEAVE HER TO HEAVEN, the glorious red rocks of Oak Creek Canyon and Sedona were introduced to the world. Top stars of the time — Cornel Wilde and Gene Tierney — strolled within arm's length of the

Foxborro Ranch ~ circa 1997

Paramount Pictures

sandstone creekbed was filmed at Slide Rock, now known as Oak Creek State Park. Sunbathers and picnickers of today ride down the same strip of water.

Alan Ladd was often seen at the Cedar Motel located at the Sedona junction where the road turns south to Interstate Highway 17. In the mid-1930's, William Boyd, otherwise known as Hopalong Cassidy, posed for the author's father at a movie set near Foxboro Ranch. His perennial sidekick, Gabby Hayes, also posed for the camera that sunny summer day. Hayes made a long run of movies with Boyd and was present the day the author and his father visited the set.

author's family Buick. A romantic scene on horseback had just concluded, and the stars were walking back to the movie camp of small cabins and a warehouse-like sound stage.

Jimmy Stewart made BROKEN ARROW in lower Oak Creek, in a valley with a set designed to depict Cochise's Stronghold. A longtime friend of the author, one Kenneth Cogdill, hitchhiked from Flagstaff as a teenager to play a role as a U.S. Cavalry soldier but got to the cast screening session too late.

Locals watched as Richard Widmark, starring in LAST WAGON (1956), acted out a gun battle on a western town set located in an area of Sedona called Coffee Pot. The famous fight scene of two grappling men being swept down a narrow channel in a red

Jane Withers

The Foxboro site had been camp for boys before being purchased by a wealthy New York City enter-

Schnebly Hill Above Sedona ~ Oak Creek

tainment mogul named Fox, who spent the warm months there hosting summer stock theater.

Foxboro Ranch is located a few miles from Schnebly Hill, from the top of which one can see the entire panoramic view of lower Oak Creek and the Sedona Red Rocks. The most probable motive for using this site was that three distinct natural settings — the pine forest, the lodge and the red rocks — could be accessed. Most movies of that time were made in California at Lone Pine, on the western side of the Sierras.

The Monte Vista Hotel at the center of downtown Flagstaff hosted many a star over the years and now showcases rooms that they once occupied. One can stay at the Monte Vista in the "Bogart Room," the "Jane Russell Room," or the "John Wayne Room." In 1937, Leo Carillo and child actress Jane Withers, in town for the making of "Arizona Wildcat," stayed at the Monte Vista. One summer night in 1937 the cast joked, danced and sang "South of the Border down Mexico Way" in the center of Flagstaff on the steps of the Coconino County Courthouse.

The most classic western movie ever made in northern Arizona and New Mexico was VIRGINIA CITY. The filming of VIRGINIA CITY was accomplished in November of 1939, at a myriad of sites within a one hundred-mile radius of Flagstaff. The movie had all the necessary elements of the time — an authentic

western story, the cinema icons of the day and incredible scenery and direction by the man who crafted *Casa Blanca*.

Monte Vista Hotel ~ Flagstaff

The decision to film in the Flagstaff area was a close call. At a movie location meeting, a Mr. Barry, the site location official, was asked to identify a single area where four distinct state settings typifying Nevada, Kansas, Colorado and Arizona could be

164 MOVIE PEOPLE ARRIVE TODAY

Search For Bruce Crozier Continues In Rugged Country Near Promontory Butte

Big Program Of Work Starts At Fort Tuthill
At an estimated cost of $31,154, a program of improvements at Fort Alexander M. Tuthill, four and a half miles south of here...

The Coconino Sun Celebrates Its 57th Birthday With This Issue
Today is the 57th birthday of the Coconino Sun. The Sun has served Flagstaff and Coconino county for more than half a century, and proof that The Sun is...

Dolan Given Fine Complimentary Vote Saturday

Warner Bros. To Film Story Of "Virginia City" At Nearby Locations In Next Three Weeks

Headline of the Coconino Sun, Flagstaff ~ November 3, 1939

Statue of Humphrey Bogart

found. The scenes in the movie shifted to events in all four of those states. Barry sat in a depressed silence, totally stumped. Suddenly, he thought of Flagstaff, Arizona, a place he had visited twelve years earlier. Barry remembered the Flagstaff area as the only known place in the United States that afforded a wide variety of scenery, all within a radius of 50 miles.

He won the decision for Flagstaff over strong opposition from those who had their hearts set on another site. Other members of the group were still resisting the Flagstaff location when Barry brought Director Michael Curtiz to Schnebly Hill to see the "unparalleled beauty of Oak Creek Canyon from that spot,"

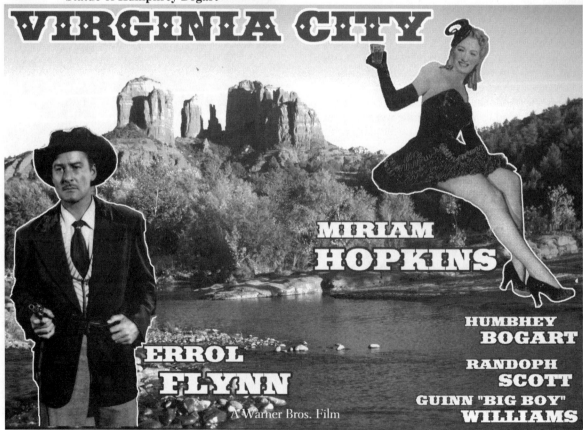

Warner Brothers Film, VIRGINIA CITY

November 19, 1939

Dear Mr. Marsh:

Sunday, a day of rest for most of the country, but not for the majority of us up here in Northern Arizona on location with Warner Bros.' "Virginia City" troupe. Location companies, you know, work Sundays and holidays. I'm more fortunate than Miriam Hopkins, Humphrey Bogart, Randolph Scott, Alan Hale, Frank McHugh, Big Boy Williams, Moroni Olsen, John Litel, Director Mike Curtiz and the rest of the troupe, for I got the day off. They didn't.

So, trite though it may sound, I really mean it when I say we're having an exciting time and we wish you could be here.

Best wishes.

Cordially,

Errol Flynn

Errol Flynn letter writen from Flagstaff on location for film, Virginia City

Barry recounted how he and Curtiz sat on a rock overlooking Oak Creek, both of them enjoying the view.

At that moment Curtiz was sold on the Flagstaff location. He could not believe such scenery existed in the United States. He even changed the film's script so more shots could be taken from the Schnebly Hill overlook. Thus, the famed scene with Errol Flynn and Marian Hopkins overlooking Lower Oak Creek and Sedona was captured for eternity. Curtiz also directed Flynn in Robin Hood, Charge of the Light Brigade and, later on, Dodge City.

On November 3, 1939, the Austrian-born Michael Curtiz, director of Casa Blanca — one of the top films ever produced — arrived in Flagstaff to film Virginia City. The movie starred Errol Flynn, Miriam Hopkins, Alan Hale, Randolph Scott, Guinn 'Big Boy' Williams, child actor Dickie Jones and the spectacular and daring stunt man, Yakima Canute. The cast, with few exceptions, was same as Dodge City, except that Miriam Hopkins played the heroine opposite Flynn instead of his perennial favorite, Olivia de Haviland. Haviland and Flynn, who made a number of films together and who were rumored to

have had more than a professional relationship, said "good-bye" both professionally and personally at the conclusion of the filming of Dodge City.

The Orpheum Theater ~ Flagstaff

The entire troupe and all the equipment — actors, multi-ton rigs and a four-score team of horses — traveled to Flagstaff in a special streamlined diesel train. The group set out to break the speed record set by "Death Valley Scotty" for the Santa Fe Railroad's Super Chief passage from California to Flagstaff.

Red Rock Crossing in Oak Creek Canyon

Intending to get from Burbank studios to Flagstaff in 12 hours, they came within minutes of breaking the record, only to be foiled by a hot box that delayed the train 50 minutes. The hot box incident happened on Scott and Flynn's car. Awakened by smoke, they had pulled the emergency cord. The Warner Brothers company of actors, cameramen and technicians, 164 in number, finally rolled into the little Flagstaff alpine station at 6:00 A.M. on November 3, 1939. Curtiz, a no nonsense taskmaster, immediately began rolling film.

The story tells of a group of southerners that sneaked out of Virginia City during the Civil War with a gold shipment bound for Richmond, Virginia in an attempt to stave off the ultimate defeat of the Confederacy. While all the characters are fictitious, the story of the gold shipment is true.

Errol Flynn plays a Union officer who escapes Libby Prison in Richmond and heads west to Virginia City to block the transfer of the gold. Scott, the Libby Prison Commandant, also travels to Virginia City to lead the group back to Richmond via a dangerous southern route. Miriam Hopkins, ostensibly a dance hall girl in Virginia City, is actually a southern agent

assisting in the gold transfer. Humphrey Bogart, who felt miscast and hated every moment of his roll, played Merrill, a Mexican bandito.

Dry bed of Little Colorado River

Dickie Jones, an eleven-year-old child actor, played the son of one of the southerners. As the wagon train full of gold rolls on, he makes a dash across the west-bound train for Richmond and becomes a key figure in the dynamic of the plot. Yakima Canute actually survives what appears to be an unbelievable

Cinder Hills east of Flagstaff ~ setting as Nevada

stunt. In fact, the crew included nine stunt people, including Opal Ernie and Ione Reid, two of the most daring stuntwomen of the time. Flynn's chums in

drivers, and stand-ins. And fifty-five miles away, up at Cameron, there is an overflow of twenty-five or thirty members of the company,"(Ref: Flynn)

Actors were quartered at the Weatherford as well as the Commercial and Monte Vista hotels. Bogart stayed at the Monte Vista in a room later named for his occupancy. Warner Brothers had taken all available reservations in Flagstaff, including most motels,

Black Cat Cafe

many films, Alan Hale, Sr. and Guinn "Big Boy" Williams, round out the cast and narrative with their usual comic relief.

The film's production was headquartered in Flagstaff. As Flynn recounts in a letter written in Flagstaff during the filming, "To house the invasion from Hollywood, three hotels and five auto camps are filled with actors, actresses, cameramen, stunt men and women, cowboys, grips, electricians, property men, wardrobe experts, makeup artists, truck

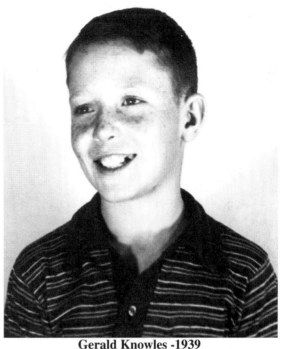

Gerald Knowles -1939

which in those days were called "auto courts." Flynn and Hopkins took up residence in Cameron during

CameronTradilng Post

the final days of the filming. Over the years, the Monte Vista housed a long list of other stars, and many of the rooms now bear their names.

In a letter mailed on November 22, 1939 Errol Flynn describes the impact the VIRGINIA CITY film cast and crew was having on "the little town of Flagstaff with a population less than half of its altitude of 6900." He went on to say that the movie troupe was spread out over more landscape than anyone could have

Search For Bruce Crozier Continues In Rugged Country Near Promontory Butte

Coconino Sun - November 3, 1939

thought possible. In his letter, he shares personal information about the other cast members such as, "Our pet name for Miriam Hopkins is 'Hoppy." He goes on to state that 'Scotty' (Randolph Scott) and 'Bogey' (Humphrey Bogart) are 55 miles from central headquarters at the Cameron Trading Post. The Post hangs on the Canyon wall overlooking the Little Colorado in the heart of the Navajo country — among a few mud hogans which look like upside down salad bowls."

Warner Brothers officials commented that the people of Flagstaff were very helpful, noting as well the fine cooperation offered by the hotels. Glowing compliments were relayed about Lee Doyle, a man who for many years played a significant role in coordinating locations and film sites in the Flagstaff area. Flynn stated in his letter that many Flagstaff children appeared in the picture, boys and girls personally chosen and screened by director Mike Curtiz. A Miss Horn tutored the kids, using a studio bus as classroom. The filming of VIRGINIA CITY was to be completed in three weeks.

Flynn commented on the grueling production schedule. He said that the day began at 5:30am with breakfast having been "bolted down," after which the crew would shiver "in the cold dark morn of November." The production crew left at 6:00am along with "equipment" consisting of 12 limousines, 35 passenger buses, 3 ten-ton trucks, 17 eight-ton trucks, 2 sound trucks, 2 station wagons, 2 camera cars and 1 large generator truck. Forty-eight valuable front horses from the studio — action horses used by the company for special action or stunts — were used along with 250 horses procured from locals in

Flagstaff. The caravan headed out from Flagstaff for various locations — Oak Creek, Schnebly Hill above Sedona, Lake Mary — near Cameron, in the cinder hills east of Flagstaff, areas northeast of Cameron near Luepp, or to the Painted Desert. Flynn speaks of shooting at the Grand Canyon, but the Canyon does not appear in any of the movie's scenes. (Ref: Flynn letter)

Bruce Crozier To Be On Radio Next Tuesday

R. E. Crozier of Winslow, father of Bruce, the boy who gamely

Bruce Crozier becomes a hero

Bruce Crozier center with Errol Flynn, brother Bob and mother,

Flynn further comments on how the locations changed daily, moving to sites within a radius of sixty miles where the scenery resembled Kansas, Colorado, Nevada or Arizona. "One day we are at Schnebly Hill, looking deep down into the depths of glorious Oak Creek Canyon, resembling Colorado. The next we are ninety miles away at Round Hills, starving in a wagon train as it staggers through a Nevada sandstorm (produced in Arizona by Hollywood wind machines). Most of us are traveling between fifty and one-hundred and twenty miles each day going to and from the various location sites. All in all, it's quite a grind. Ordinarily we stay on the job until sunset, which is about 5:30pm. By the time we get back to our respective places of lodging, it's 7 or 7:30. A shower before dinner gets us to the hotel dining room or to one the town's three cafes about 8pm. Most of us are ready to turn in at 9 or 9:30, with that 5 o'clock call staring us in the face next morning."

Early in the movie, Flynn and the "boys" appear with Bogart in a scene shot in the Oak Creek/Sedona

area inside a stagecoach bound for Virginia City. The gorgeous panorama of Oak Creek at the classic "Red Rock Crossing" is captured when the stagecoach gets stuck in the creek. Director Mike Curtiz, obsessed by the beauty of Oak Creek and Sedona, shot yet more film there. The event was cited by the local the Coconino Sun, which newspaper reported on November 10th that Hopkins and Flynn were filming what was to be "the romance scene" at the Schnebly Hill overlook of Sedona the next day — Thursday, November 11th (the day before the author's 7th birthday). Thirty minutes into the movie Flynn and Hopkins do in fact appear exchanging love vows atop Schnebly Hill, the two of them silhouetted against the beautiful, panoramic backdrop of lower Oak Creek and Sedona.

Sitting in the Orpheum Theater a year later, viewing the scene at the film's debut in Flagstaff, the author's father identified smoke from the copper ore smelter at Clarkdale, a town located thirty miles across the Verde Valley below the hamlet of Jerome. In this scene especially, as well as in many other noire scenes in Virginia City, the awesome beauty of northern Arizona's varied topography is captured even in black and white — a credit to the beauty of the land.

Technicolor would have made Virginia City spectacular but would have effected an entirely different mood. Imagine, for example, tinting an Ansel Adams landscape, or coloring the movie Casa Blanca. Black and white film imparted a certain adventure and mystery, whereas color may well have intruded upon atmosphere seen as essential by the artist. The stellar panoramas seen in Virginia City are surpassed only by some in the movie Stagecoach, shot at Monument Valley.

The "rounded hills," as Flynn called them — a series of black, volcanic cinder hills — lay east of Flagstaff and were used as the backdrop for a Nevada sandstorm. Ten covered wagons, full of gold bars and on their way to Richmond via a torturous southern route, were used in the sandstorm scene. Four wind machines manufactured "the storm." Tumbleweeds thrown into fans and Fuller's Earth shipped from the west coast comprised the very fake but absolutely safe blowing sands. Thirty outriders on horseback were lead by Scott; a captive, hand-bound Flynn accompanied the train. The storm segment depicts the plight of the wagon train as it enters the barren, waterless Nevada desert, with one scene featuring the dry bed of the Little Colorado River. At this point, the wagon train sojourners were desperate for water and lapsed into deep despair at the sight of the baked river bottom.

The Painted Desert on the north side of the Little Colorado River, east of Cameron, is also used as a backdrop for the crossing wagon train. It is down one of these Triassic clay hills that one of the most spectacular movie stunts ever filmed was shot. Famed stuntman Yakima Canute, mounted on horseback and doubling for an escaping Flynn, cartwheels down a Painted Desert hill at high speed and, miraculously, was neither injured nor killed. Viewing the episode from atop a desert knoll, Scott and the southerners said something to the effect that "Captain Kerry would no longer bother them."

Privately, they wondered whether they would ever see Yakima Canute alive again. The script line was near prophetic. The tumbling horse scene previewed a near tragic accident that occurred several days later in which Canute was almost killed.

Yakima, again playing Flynn and inspired by a stunt he pulled off in the movie Stagecoach, repeated the leap from a buckboard onto a pair of stampeding horses, leap-frogging over several other pairs of horses until he reached the lead pair as planned. He continued the stunt by falling between the lead horses, hanging onto the coach tongue and dropping to the ground. However, this time pounding hooves and heavy coach wheels barely cleared his body. Nonetheless, Yakima completed the stunt by catching hold of the rear axle and pulling himself up on to the coach. The stunt was exciting to see on film, but chilling in reality.

In the execution of yet another stunt, a child actor luckily escaped calamity. Eleven-year-old Dickie Jones, who plays "Cobby" in the movie, was supposed to be bounced off the buckboard of a stampeding wagon and be seriously hurt. His injury was to become a featured part of the plot dynamic. On the day when the stunt was to be filmed, schoolteacher Virginia Beard and forty-three Navajo children from nearby Luepp Boarding School, Bureau of Indian Affairs, visited the set. One of the Navajo children was wearing a silver concho belt with turquoise settings. Dickie saw this belt and wanted it. The Navajo student told Dickie that he'd sell him the belt for $35.

The stunt had been planned so that Dickie's double would fall from the lofty buckboard of the covered wagon — making $35 for the stunt. Dickie pleaded with his mother until she agreed that Dickie could do the stunt himself. Viewing the scene in which Dickie falls off the buckboard, it's a miracle that the child actor didn't break his neck. It was a hard fall. Dickie's head was bent 90 degrees under his chest and the tumble knocked him unconscious for half an hour. But, he lived through it, got the $35 and bought the concho belt.

Navajo Concho Belt

Eleven years later, in 1950, a grown-up Dickie — by then known as Dick Jones — starred with Flynn in ROCKY MOUNTAIN, filmed in the red rocks near Gallup, New Mexico. Many local Navajo people participated in the movie production. Two newly born babies were used in one scene and, when the paymaster required a name for each, the Navajo parents promptly named the girl Miriam Hopkins and the boy Errol Flynn. (There are many Navajo people in the Kayenta area named *Grey* for author Zane Grey).

The presence of the movie company thrilled Navajos living near Cameron and Luepp. Families came in their wagons from the deep recesses of the Navajo reservation to watch scenes being shot in the canyons and atop Painted Desert hills. Dickie Jones, who was apparently quite a bon vivant, impersonated Donald Duck to roars of laughter from the Navajos. Flynn describes in one letter the story of a Navajo gentleman who requested payment in silver for a one day's use of his entire family, his wagon, his horses and his sheep. He placed the ninety-six silver dollars in his pants, his hat and inside his shirt and waddled to his horse, but he was so weighted down he could not mount the creature. Still, he refused to exchange the silver for paper. In those days, Navajo people did not trust paper money. They wanted hard silver. Finally, according to Flynn, "he was boosted atop a boulder and oozed into the saddle," and the Navajo, along with his silver dollars, sheep, horses and family "jogged into the sunset of the Painted Desert."

The presence of such a large troupe of movie makers and stars in a small community such as Flagstaff always produced exciting, humorous and touching personal episodes. The swashbuckling, notorious persona of Flynn set the town ablaze. The author was in the old Orpheum Theater on a chilly November evening when Flynn walked from behind the curtains onto the stage — causing utter pandemonium and near riot with popcorn boxes and screams flying through the air.

During that same week, both Scott and Flynn attended a carnival at the Arizona State Teacher's College campus. Flynn selected and crowned the Queen of the Annual Ball, "The Questa," in recognition and support of the College yearbook. Miriam Hopkins went out on the town to find Mexican food. She ended up cooking enchiladas in the kitchen of a family style restaurant on south San Francisco Street called the El Charro Cafe. One can still eat Mexican food at the El Charro Cafe to the accompaniment of a Mariachi Band.

The author and his buddies spent most evenings people-watching on Front Street, Route 66. Hanging out in downtown Flagstaff was a prime diversion in the 30's. The Flagstaff Pharmacy, managed by the author's father, was on the corner in the center of town, and its fountain was the social headquarters of the community. The Black Cat Cafe was next door to the Flagstaff Pharmacy. One night in November of 1939, Alan Hale and "Big Boy" Williams and about ten other members of the film troupe were spied sitting in a corner booth in the front window of the Black Cat. The author and his gang of seven-year-olds began making faces, using fingers to distort mouths and eyes, hoping to capture the attention of anyone in the troupe who might happen to look their way. The troupe, obviously aware of them, feigned oblivion.

Determined to gain everlasting fame through notice by the famous, several gang members began tapping on the window, pressing their faces against the freezing glass. Suddenly, Alan Hale's face waxed monster-like, turned purple and emitted a deep roar. The gang jumped back in alarm as Hale hurled the contents of a glass of milk on the window. The episode would have been much more interesting if Bogart had been in the group, but he'd stayed that night with his wife at the Cameron Trading Post Lodge.

Returning back to Flagstaff one afternoon after a day's shooting at Cameron, Scott and Flynn came upon a broken down tour bus on Route 89. Billy Rose's famous San Francisco troupe, the "Aquacade Nymphs" were on their way to back to the coast when their vehicle suffered a flat tire. The two actors were happy to assist, and put on a spare. Flynn later commented in a letter that he and Scott enticed them to stay a week to "see how movies were made." Rumor has it that their education far exceeded mere cinemagraphic information.

Tales about the VIRGINIA CITY film troupe still make up cafe and bar chat in Flagstaff. One of the more humorous stories that continues to circulate among the old timers occurred one afternoon when tourists, traveling northward on Highway 89 on their way to the Grand Canyon, were treated to an utterly unexpected sight. In fact, they were dumfounded to see four Confederate soldiers, side by side with three Union soldiers, pushing a car up a hill just outside of Cameron.

One of the most poignant episodes that occurred within the local community and the film troupe involved a little boy named Bruce Crozier from Winslow, Arizona. He had accompanied his family on a hunting trip along the Mogollon Rim that separates northern from southern Arizona. And, children are sometimes wont to do, he wandered away and became lost in the wilds. The November nights of '39 were bitter cold, and as days passed without locating Bruce, hope began to fade.

Amazingly, after a week, Bruce suddenly appeared in a hunting camp, setting off cheers across all of northern Arizona. Only seven years old, he had survived the wilderness not by pure, dumb luck, but with courage and wit. He had procured his own food, fended off wild animals with a club and even contemplated sleeping with a bear. Bruce journeyed to Flagstaff to thank Sheriff Vendevier and the Coconino County deputies who had tirelessly searched for him for seven long days and nights. When Sheriff Vendevier contacted Warner Brothers, the cast and crew invited Bruce to the movie set near Cameron. (94)

When Bruce arrived on the set, director Mike Curtiz was filming Randolph Scott leading a wagon train through the Nevada desert. Curtiz, a hard taskmaster who rarely allowed interruptions, stopped all filming in honor of the boy and the afternoon was spent asking Bruce questions. The cast and crew were spellbound by the manner and means whereby Bruce kept up his courage and successfully coped with being lost for seven days. Miriam Hopkins, who had a son just Bruce's age, was especially captivated with Bruce's story. Guinn "Big Boy" Williams, who also had a son, was fascinated with Bruce, letting him ride his horse and hold a gun used as a prop in the movie. Before the day was over Bruce's picture was taken with all the actors. The boy later commented that Errol Flynn spent most of that day in his tent, working on a book, and he remembered Humphrey Bogart as being grumpy about any picture taking activities.

The company was rushing to finish the film so they could make it back to the coast before Thanksgiving, and soon left Flagstaff behind. After six weeks of passion and involvement with the cast and crew of VIRGINIA CITY, a deep sadness set in when the red light of the Santa Fe Chief disappeared in the west. The author and his father sat in the Black Cat that night, methodically eating sirloin steaks, hoping to ward off the lonely, empty feeling in their stomachs and on the streets of Flagstaff. Making matters worse, tragedy struck the day that the Warner Brothers' Special Santa Fe train was scheduled to go back to Burbank. An eastbound freight hit a truck carrying some of the Warner Brothers prize horses, killing nine of them and one of their handlers.

VIRGINIA CITY boasted not only a more engaging but also a more plausible and historically accurate plot than the Technicolor film that preceded it — DODGE CITY and THE SANTA FE TRAIL. Although shot in black and white, VIRGINIA CITY appeared to artistically out-do the Technicolor movie. Maltin's review stated that VIRGINIA CITY was a "follow-up to DODGE CITY; which has big cast in a lush a Civil War Western — but the tale of a rebel dance hall girl doesn't live up to expectations. Bogart is miscast as a slimy bandito." Reviewers have also questioned the plausibility of Miriam Hopkins' role, but not her acting. It has been accepted however that Bogart's role as a bandito was indeed a huge miscasting error, one magnified by his weak Mexican accent.

The persona of Errol Flynn, both on-screen and in private life, still lives in the canyons of the Little Colorado. The "In Like Flynn" legacy imposed by society on Errol Flynn would seem to reflect little of the real-life person. Flynn was always seemed to play the role of the quintessential hero — a man undaunted and intelligent, energetic and courageous in the face of overwhelming odds. Yet, rather than glory in this legend, Flynn would have preferred more serious roles and often complained that Warner Brothers typecast him.

"Putting me in cowboy pictures, seemed to me, the most ridiculous miscasting. Dialogue would go like this, 'Where you from, pardner?' "I happen to come from Ireland, but I am as American as you are." (Flynn, 1948-Web Page) In 1947, Flynn stated that "I am not denying that westerns are wonderful entertainment. I love to look at them as well as anyone. I just wanted to act. To have a chance to play a character, to say good-bye to the swashbuckler rolls, to get swords and horses the hell out of my life. I itched to turn in a prize winning job — but they held to make money, box office, box office." (Flynn, 1947-Web Page) "I despise mediocrity above all things. I fear it, yet I know some of my performances have been mediocre. I also know that I have turned in half a dozen good performances. I call myself a bum, but I have been working hard most of the days of my adult life." (Flynn, 1938 -Web Page)

Flynn made fifty-three films, most of them with Jack Warner. His leading ladies included Olivia De Haviland, Maureen O'Hara, Bette Davis and Greer Garson. In 1950, he starred opposite Patrice Wymore in ROCKY MOUNTAIN, filmed near Gallup, New Mexico. This co-starring experience culminated in a real-life marriage. Wymore still lives on Flynn's cattle ranch in Jamaica.

Carefree and adventurous, Errol Flynn had many detractors and made more than a few enemies. He was identified in one book as a Nazi spy. The supportive evidence for this charge has been shown to be flawed (THE SPY THAT NEVER WAS - Thomas). The charge of rape for which Flynn was acquitted in the 1940's was subsequently uncovered as a general extortion scheme aimed not only at Flynn, but also at many other Hollywood notables.

Greer Garson, one of the brightest and most respected stars of Flynn's day, remarked, "I found Errol much more objective and modest than many performers. He was satirically deprecating about himself as a screen idol and as the target of scandal journals and nightclub comedians. If he had lived longer and more temperately, he would probably have emerged as the serious actor he longed to be, although I think eventually he would have preferred to earn a reputation as a writer."(Ref: Thomas)

A family sponsored website now petitions to give Flynn the recognition that he deserves. The "Greatest Swashbuckler" site states that "In his lifetime, Errol Flynn received no recognition from his peers at the Academy of Motion Picture Arts and Sciences. He never attended a ceremony in his honor and was not

nominated. Could it be that his screen persona, the swashbuckler, the rake, stuck to him too well? Yet in his career he defined a male archetype and forever set his mark on movie maleness, in fact, he created a constellation of manly virtues that even today is the stuff of dreams. Long regarded as the prodigal son of Hollywood, with his real-life adventures, scrapes and insubordination, Errol Flynn lived every man's dream of a full life and found himself typecast. As an actor, Flynn built the foundation for characters later elaborated by Mel Gibson, Arnold Schwarznegger, Harrison Ford or Kevin Costner. Flynn made movies, did his own stunts, lived his life, thumbed his nose at studio rules, left Jack Warner fuming in his Burbank office suite and went off to sea."

Flynn had many interests, including writing and politics, which toward the end of his life in the late

1950s had him filming in Cuba, making him persona non grata in conservative Hollywood. Careers in the film business ebb and flow, but unfortunately, Flynn did not have a chance to make a comeback late in his career. He died at the age 50 of a heart attack. (Official Errol Flynn website: "You Are In Like Flynn" — http://www.inlikeflynn.com/index.html December 5, 2000)

A year before the premature ending of his life in 1959, Flynn remarked: "I wonder if you can imagine what it might mean to be one who believes that, given the chance at good and great roles, he might be able to act, say, like a Barrymore. I was only offered those sure-fire box office attractions — entertainment pictures that often didn't entertain — action, action, action." (Ref: Flynn 1957) Flynn expressed his concept of happiness as being "A quiet spot by the Jamaican seashore looking out at the

El Rancho Hotel in Gallup

activity in the ocean, hearing the wind sob with the beauty and the tragedy of everything." (Ref: Flynn 1938).

New Mexico

Stars on El Rancho walls

ROCKY MOUNTAIN

Errol FLYNN
Patrice WYMORE

Warner Brothers movies among the red rocks near Gallup, New Mexico

Massive, round red rock cliffs rise up hundreds of feet just east of Old Route 66, extending from the Arizona and New Mexico state lines all the way to the Continental Divide. East of Gallup, New Mexico and just north of what is now called Red Rock State Park (home of the Gallup Indian Ceremonials), lies a region known as Church Rock, wherein scores of movies were filmed. Beginning in the 1930's, Director King Vidor featured the site in the film BILLY THE KID, and as late as the 1970's Christopher Reeves was there filming the flight of Superman through the canyon walls. Formations in that area feature beautiful white and golden spires as well as the famous cave of Kit Carson.

Used as powerful backdrops for western scenes, the stunning red rock cliffs inspired R.E. Griffith in 1937 to build Gallup's Hotel El Rancho as a haven for Hollywood's famous. R.E. was the brother of D.W. Griffith, director of BIRTH OF A NATION. R.E. encouraged the use of the El Rancho as an operation base for crews and stars on location. The rustic elegance of the hotel and its easy access to the magnificent red rock country made it a perfect headquarters for movie idols of the day. The El Rancho captured the essence of the old West while offering the food and superior service of Fred Harvey trained personnel. The Hotel's accommodation provided the stars and film crews with a way to "rough it" in comfort, and included amenities such as gambling tables and liquor.

The long-standing identification of the El Rancho with the stars of the 30's, 40's and 50's is evidenced by the building decor of today. The lobby of the El

Rancho is adorned with signed photographs of the parade of stars who stayed there over the years, some with their famous names above guest room doors, others with autographed glamour photos lining the lobby balcony. The film crews came to Gallup on the Santa Fe Railroad and were taken to the El Rancho by wagons, carriages or buggies. Yet, when it came to the early morning trip to filming locations, cast and crew often road in limousines.

Hollywood idols had natural contact with locals similar to the associations forged during the making of VIRGINIA CITY in Flagstaff. According to Sallie Noe,

The Desert Song
Dennis Morgan
Irene Manning

The DESERT SONG ~ Warner Brothers

many locals acted as stand-ins, extras, and location employees. A large number local citizens worked as delivery boys, guides, stock suppliers, and Navajo/English interpreters. Trading companies like Richardson's sold everything from cowboy hats to Navajo jewelry as movie props. Gallup became a working getaway away from the Hollywood limelight. Its remote location placed it way beyond the grasp of gossip columnists of the day like Walter Winchell. Many stars and crew drank a lot. "Errol Flynn drank all night and worked all day," Noe recounts. He patronized the bars on the north side of the Santa Fe Railroad tracks in Gallup. John Wayne never tarried in Gallup, but headed straight for Monument Valley via Shiprock and Bluff, Utah.

Robert Mitchum starred with Teresa Wright in the movie PURSUED. The Gallup Independent local newspaper ads announcing the film's debut hyped the fact that it was made locally. In those days newspapers published a five or six part abridged versions of the story. The Independent ran these episodes for six weeks preceding the debut of PURSUED.

The first and most famous stunt in PURSUED involved a jump from a stagecoach buckboard followed by a climb to the lead pair of galloping horses and ended with a fall under the horses and the stagecoach to catch the rear axle of the coach. The stunt was done along the banks of the Rio Puerco River. It was repeated by Canute in the Painted Desert during the making of VIRGINIA CITY, and was for the famed stuntman a near-fatal episode.

A large number of movies were filmed in Gallup –

1940 THE BAD MAN – Wallace Berry, Ronald Reagan
1941 SUNDOWN – Gene Tierney ad Bruce Cabot
1942 THE DESERT SONG – Dennis Morgan
1944 SONG OF THE NILE – Maria Montez, Jon Hall
1946 PURSUED – Robert Mitchum and Teresa Wright
1947 FOUR FACES WEST – Joel McCrea
1948 COLORADO TERRITORY – Joel McCrea, Virginia Mayo, Dorothy Malone
1948 STREETS OF LOREDO – William Holden and William Bendix
1950 ROCKY MOUNTAIN – Errol Flynn
1950 BIG CARNIVAL – Kirk Douglas
1950 ONLY THE VALIANT – Gregory Peck
1950 QUANTRILL'S RAIDERS – Allan Ladd
1951 RATON PASS – Dennis Morgan
1951 NEW MEXICO – Marilyn Maxwell and Lew Ayers
1951 FORT DEFIANCE – Dane Clark
1957 FORT MASSACRE – McCrea and Forest Tucker
1964 A DISTANT TRUMPET – Troy Donahue and Susan Pleshette
1964 THE HALLELUJAH TRAIL – Burt Lancaster
1978 SUPERMAN – Christopher Reeves and Marlon Brando
In his book about Flynn's pictures, Thomas notes that the film ROCKY MOUNTAIN depicts a true inci-

dent occurring during the Civil War but suggests that the superficiality of the characters and a dull script marred its quality. ROCKY MOUNTAIN was Flynn's

Douglas Fairbanks and Mary Picford

last western, and he played his role in a straight and convincing manner. While on location, Flynn became interested in the leading lady, Patrice Wymore, who had appeared before in only one film. Thomas notes that the "the role did little for her as actress, but she looked pretty and moved with a dancer's grace." (Thomas, 168) In 1951, Wymore became Flynn's third wife.

Flagstaff, Gallup and Monument Valley stand as the most frequently favored settings for moviemakers. In the 20's, Albuquerque was also used by a number of studios. The appearances of Douglas Fairbanks, Jean Harlow and Jackie Coogan on the station platform in front of the Alavarado brought out the whole town. Winslowites were privy to a gigantic explosion downtown at the Old 66 Diner in a scene filmed for NATURAL BORN KILLERS. The exquisite and unique rock formations at Lake Powell provided terrain for the construction of a biblical city in the filming of THE GREATEST STORY EVER TOLD.

Scenes captured on film at Oak Creek, at the red cliffs near Gallup and amid the massive buttes of Monument Valley serve to cement our fantasies about the legends of the West. They are priceless records of times past, archives of primitive beauty showing us what the land was like prior to the onslaught of condos, houses and pavement. Be it sunset at Red Rock Crossing, dawn in the painted hills near Cameron or nighttime deep in a canyon inside Monument Valley, one can hear the eternal echoes of the Old West.

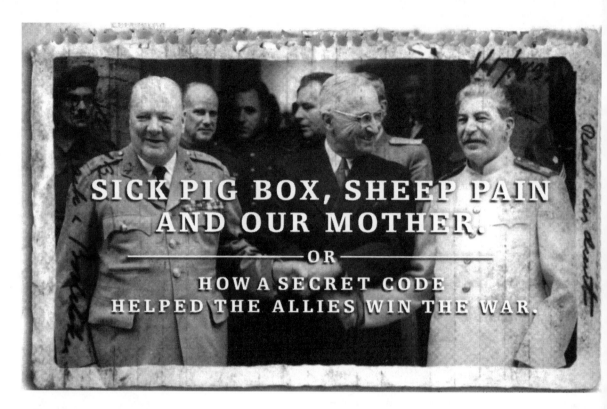

SICK PIG BOX, SHEEP PAIN AND OUR MOTHER.

— OR —

HOW A SECRET CODE HELPED THE ALLIES WIN THE WAR.

TWELVE
The Navajo Code Talkers
America's Secret Weapon in Defeating the Japanese in World War Two

His body sunk into a wet, black Iwo Jima beach, the Marine pushed his hand slowly into hot sand. He felt cold steel several inches below the surface and froze with fear, knowing that few of his fellow marines had survived blasts from the dreaded Japanese land mines. Corporal Teddy Draper, a Navajo from the towering red canyons of Chinle, Arizona, was a long way from home. Yet his presence and that of other Navajo Americans on Iwo Jima and other islands on the road to Japan played a key role in the ultimate victory of U.S. forces in the Pacific theater of World War Two. (26)

The war in the Pacific had just begun. American forces were having a hard time preventing the Japanese from anticipating their every move. The combination of Japanese obstinacy and countless physical challenges posed almost insurmountable

difficulties in retaking the islands critical to allied victory. The enemy had broken every communications code set up by the Marines and defeat seemed only a matter of time. Most radio communications essential to critical combat operations were intercepted, as many of the Japanese not only understood English but also sounded like American Marines.

Japanese land mines at Iwo Jima

Just as the concerns and frustration of the American command approached critical mass, in walked a gentleman named Philip Johnson. As a boy, Philip had gone to Washington as a translator with Navajo and Hopi groups to petition President Theodore Roosevelt for improved tribal resources. In early 1942 he met with high-ranking Marines at Camp Eliot in San Diego to present his idea of using the

Phillip Johnson lived at Tochaco Mission

Navajo language as a code. The American officers gave the project only a skeptical go-ahead, feeling that two soldiers communicating with each other in a strange tongue was a concept too simple to be worthwhile. Nonetheless, the idea was pursued.

The initial reaction to recruiters circulating within one of the largest and most remote Indian nations in the United States was one of suspicion. It was up to the Chairman of the Navajo Nation, Chee Dodge, to get the word out, to alert tribal members about the

Navajo Nation Council Chambers

proposed mission — that of employing Navajo marines as Special Communication Agents to assist the war effort.

Notices were put up in trading posts all over the Navajo Reservation. In time, the objective was understood, and Navajo men, some of them only fifteen years old, rose to the occasion in defense of their country. Thirty recruits were selected. They arrived from all directions in faded jeans and dusty boots, some by horseback, some on wagons. Carl Gorman, Sr., the father of famous Navajo artist R.C. Gorman of Taos, New Mexico, was the oldest of the chosen Code Talkers. The men boarded trains at

Flagstaff, Arizona, and Gallup, New Mexico, and headed for Marine base training camp in California. In all, 191 Navajo Code Talkers joined the service in 1943. Eventually, 450 Code Talkers would serve in World War Two in the Pacific.

Great Seal of the Navajo Nation

The Navajo Marine recruits distinguished themselves in boot camp with their superior agility, endurance and marksmanship. Trained initially as runners, they were responsible for carrying messages from one position to another. Top intelligence officers were doubtful, however, about the value and security of Navajo soldiers talking back and forth in thick of battle. Fortunately for the United States war effort in the Pacific, the officers' misconceptions were to be abruptly reversed. The Navajo prevailed, their command of the situation expressed in part by their remarkably skilled night maneuvers and uncanny ability to operate behind enemy lines.

Even today, after fifty years, there remain misconceptions about the use of the Navajo language as a code. While the agility, endurance and courage of Navajo soldiers in the Pacific campaigns are legendary, only a passing notion of the use of the Navajo language as a code is understood.

The code was mistakenly construed as the superficial process of two Navajos talking to each other in their native tongue. In actual fact, their conversations were cerebral to the degree that the words were unintelligible to the anyone. They quite literally created an alternative Navajo language. Words were

Navajo Codetalker Marines at Camp Pendelton, California

substituted, disguised and changed around, the result being an almost incomprehensible, highly effective, mixed-up Navajo.

Not even native Navajo speakers tested with the new code talk knew what the Navajo marines were say-

Navajo Code Talker King Mike

ing. 'That's crazy Navajo,' one remarked. Amazingly, none of the code was written down. It was all committed to memory! Navajo Code Talk had been born and ultimately became one of the most potent weapons used by the United States in the Pacific campaign.

Military intelligence, still skeptical, demanded a demonstration. Two top officers, specialists in breaking codes, were called in to test the Navajo Code Talk. They couldn't begin to transcribe the sounds they were hearing, much less decipher the meanings. Their failure firmly established the potency and practicality of the code. When the Japanese first heard Navajo Code Talk they were completely confused. It was not until decades after the war that the code source was revealed.

A man named King Mike went off to boot camp with the original group of Navajo Code Talkers. King was living in the Monument Valley region because his wife's family's sheep camp was located near there. The region was one of the most remote communities in the Navajo Nation and could only be

6th Marine Division landing on Okinowa

reached by a dirt road, sixty miles off pavement. It was from this point that King Mike made his trek toward the vast Pacific Ocean to play a decisive role in one of the bloodiest battles of World War II. King

Yontan Airstrip

Mike was reassigned to the 6th Division of the 22nd Regiment before the invasion of Okinowa, and was the lone survivor of the1st Provisional Brigade on Guam. (55)

Navajo Code Talkers were assigned to one of two teams. One was a ship assault team, the other regimental intelligence. King was the member of a five-man regimental intelligence team composed of a demolition specialist, a Japanese speaker, a communications expert, a technician, and a Navajo Code Talker.

King Mike and personnel carrier

The team would land on a beach and infiltrate inward behind enemy lines, sometimes moving in immediately after naval bombardment of the shore. Their job was to radio back information on fortification layouts, the concentration of enemy forces and likely invasion routes. Intelligence information was radioed , not sent by runner, as capture and death were always possible. Code Talkers arrived after the bombardments to assess damage while the Japanese were still in hiding. This intelligence was critical to the success of American forces as it provided information about when and where to attack.

King Mike with natives

Code talkers who were part of the assault teams prevented the Japanese from monitoring battlefield communications. As troops rapidly advanced on Saipan, shells hit so close to the marines that they radioed headquarters to redirect fire. Headquarters felt that no Americans could have advanced that far inland and decided they were Japanese soldiers, many of whom sounded like Iowa farmers. It wasn't until a Code Talker monitored the radio that command post officers were convinced troops at the advanced position were truly Americans.

Richard Mike, co-owner of the Kayenta Burger King and three other Burger Kings at Page, Chinle and Shiprock, is King Mike's son. He relates that his father experienced recurrent nightmares of being chased by a Japanese soldier with a bayonet. There had been constant close encounters at night along with hand to hand combat behind enemy lines, and many of King's buddies were killed. King Mike's first regiment was wiped out on Guam; what men remained were incorporated into the 6th Division, 22nd Regiment.

Code Talker Teddy Draper, Sr. also had nightmares — he dreamed of setting off one of the dreadful

Japanese land mines. Many of Draper and Mike's friends died in the pitch-black darkness behind enemy lines. Draper tells of the front line battle at Iwo Jima, which he referred to as Hell Island. The thirty-six day ordeal was characterized by hand to

Japanese tank

hand combat and a constant stream of hand grenades, mortars and bayonet duels as well as the deployment of flame throwers by American forces. Comrades were left dead in the hot tropic sun because rescue often meant death to those who

Japanese bandanna

attempted it. As time wore on the marines wearied, feeling that only death would remove them from the hellish struggle.

King Mike forwarded a postcard home depicting Okinowa's Sugar Loaf Hill, saying, "the bloodiest and dirtiest fight in the South Pacific was fought on this hill." The Japanese had taken the hill ten times Finally, with King directing naval gunfire, the marines triumphed and the hill was secured on the tenth go-round.

More marines died in the assault on Sugar Loaf Hill than in any battle in the history of the Marine Corps. A total of 2,662 marines lost their lives and 1,289 suffered combat fatigue. Yet few remember that April devastation because President Roosevelt died the same day.

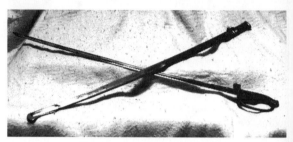

Japanese officer's sword

When the Code Talkers finally came home, they participated in a special Navajo ceremony called the "Enemy Way" to exorcise themselves of the painful memories, the harrowing encounters, the ghosts of the dead.

The Navajo Code Talk may have been the only unbreakable code in the history of warfare. It was so top secret that it was not declassified until 1968 — a time when the country's attitude toward war thwarted any public recognition of the significance of the Code Talk as a major weapon in the defeat of the Japanese. No Navajo Code Talker was awarded a Medal of Honor. No parades were held to recognize them.

In December of 1981, President Ronald Regean recognized the Navajo Code Talkers for their "dedicated

Japanses post card to troops

Navajo Codetalkers honored by the Navajo Nation Council

service, unique achievement, patriotism, resourcefulness and courage." Through the efforts of then

King Mike on the right at War's end

Senator Dennis D. Concini, April 14, 1983, was proclaimed as the first Navajo Code Talker Day.

The torturous climate and terrain of the battle area combined with the tenacity and defense of the Japanese soldiers could well have combined to stop the essential U.S. capture of the Pacific Islands. Many believe that the Navajo Code Talkers tipped the balance, securing victory for the American forces. Major Howard Connor was to remark after the war that "without the Navajo (Code Talkers), the marines would never have taken Iwo Jima."

When General Setzo Avisue, head of Japanese intelligence, was told about the Code Talkers after the war, he sighed and said "Thank you. That is a puzzle I thought would never be solved."

At the time of this writing, two major Hollywood films of the Navajo Code Talkers are being planned.

Other Native American tribes also participated in code talking. There were three Hopi Code Talkers, and rumor has it that three Kiowa Code Talkers were part of the Army Paratroopers. (93)

In July of 2001 the orignal 29 Navajo Code Talkers were awarded the Congressional Gold Medal by President George W. Bush. Over 400 Code Talkers were awarded Silver Medals in November of 2001.

Ironically, the Navajo language may have saved the very country that attempted to stamp it out.

Indian-detour

Santa Fe

F. J. Hinchman

THIRTEEN
The Harvey Houses and Girls

They Civilized the West

For many, that famous highway, Route 66, evokes more than anything else fond memories of places to eat and places to sleep. It's true that anticipation of cuisine such as that served by the elegant La Posada in Winslow greatly relieved the road monotony associated with the long sojourn from Gallup or the endless trek from the Midwest to the Southwest. Emerging from the dark of the wilderness into the lights of La Fonda is as reassuring today as it was to the travelers of the old Santa Fe Trail. Further south in New Mexico, the Indian Room of the Alvarado in Albuquerque brought not only rest and relaxation, but also a certain solace to meandering urbanites that wished to connect with the ancient history of the region. Route 66 was more than a just a road — it was a motherlode of new realities, a highway of dreams.

Much of the memorable ambiance that has come to be associated with the southwestern segment of Route 66 can be traced directly to Fred Harvey's restaurants and hotels. The Fred Harvey institutions have been hailed as "civilizers" of the Southwest. "Harvey imposed a rule of culinary benevolence over a region larger than a Roman province and richer than any single British dominion save Indian." (Marshall). That the architecturally intriguing western, Spanish and Mexican styled buildings dotting the country came to the Road through the creativity of a woman from Minnesota makes for a wonderful 'only in America' tale.

Passages to the West

The Route 66 path across the Southwest to the Pacific Ocean follows trails that go back deep in time, to an era when portions of the future highway were used by the Navajo, the Pueblos and the Plains Indians. The Spanish Conquistadors led into the Southwest by Coronado followed many of the same streams, valleys and mountain passes that mark the route today. The old fur trappers ferreted out every possible nook and cranny along the way, and the Pathfinders of the West, particularly Ned Beale, formally charted what has become the route followed to our present time. One can say with some certainty that the Grand Mother Road across the Southwest, the harbinger of Route 66, had to have been the Old Santa Fe Trail.

Coronado first used the Santa Fe Trail route, followed by the Americans in the 1800's. Zebulon Pike persevered along the Trail all the way to the

Purgatory River and his namesake, Pikes Peak, and even took it upon himself to build a fort in the San Luis Valley of Colorado. It was Pike's account of his legendary journey that inspired traders and explorers

Wagon swales of the Santa Fe Trail

from near and far to investigate the Santa Fe Trail, and in 1812, the first wagon train made its bumpy way west. In 1825 the U.S. government surveyed two of the Trail routes — the desert route, and the mountain route that snaked through the pass at Raton, New Mexico. The Santa Fe Trail allowed a gentleman named La Lande to access Spanish social customs and lifestyles in the Southwest and he fell in love with the charm and hospitality he encountered. He became an ambassador of the Southwest, promoting it throughout the rest of the United States. (66)

Fort Union on the Santa Fe Trail

Abuse by American invaders of both the southwestern land and its huge herds of buffalo angered the Indians, and they attacked with a vengeance. In 1847, a bloody massacre forced the U.S. government to ask Kit Carson and Richard "Uncle Dick" Wooten to work as scouts and guides on the Trail. By the

The Plaza in old Santa Fe ~ end of the Santa Fe Trail

year 1865, Wooten had opened a toll road, an inn and a supply store at Raton Pass. Havens on the Trail such as Wooten's establishments, Bent's Fort near La Junta, Colorado and, sometime later, the stagecoach stations became the precursors to roadside services for travelers across the west. In 1850, stagecoaches appeared on the Santa Fe Trail, each coach carrying all of nine passengers. A stagecoach journey from Missouri to Santa Fe took two weeks at a rate of eighty miles per day.

Recognizing the accelerating fascination with and the promotional possibilities of the southwestern lifestyle, another railroad, calling itself the Santa Fe, started up in 1850. In 1868 the Santa Fe Railroad completed its first seven miles out of Topeka, Kansas, and by 1872 it had reached Dodge City. Its ultimate goal was to reach the Pacific Ocean, connecting Chicago to Los Angeles. By 1879 the train had reached Willow Springs in Raton Pass. There, its progression was briefly delayed due to an altercation with the Denver and Rio Grande Railroad over control of the Pass.

In the final analysis, the Santa Fe Railroad certainly manifested the dreams of its founder, Cyrus K. Holliday. Holliday envisioned a railroad that would cross the Rockies to the Pacific Ocean and touch the Gulf of Mexico, linking Indian territories, buffalo prairies, old roads and open desert to the Midwest.

He foresaw the interest of future generations in the mystery and splendor of the great Southwest and opted to encourage it.

On a Man's Stomach

Food and lodging throughout the Southwest has come full circle. The fare of the ancient ones, the Anazasi — dried, roasted corn and beans — is now served in the fashionable cafes of Santa Fe as "Chicos" and "Anazasi Beans." Back in time, however, the food of those who came after the Anazasi had gone from bad to worse. Old fur trappers were known to cut a mule's throat for its blood, to eat the mules and even eat their saddles. Trail food was simple and monotonous except when fresh buffalo or deer were available. The stagecoach stops were so brief, the hard biscuit and fatback fare so plain, that the two-week journey easily became a gastronomic torture.

The railroad crossed hundreds of miles of open prairies, zigzagged through mountain snows and operated during the summer across endless deserts. Those riding the rails suffered dismal stops at small boomtowns, mining camps, cattle pens and government outposts. Clean hotels didn't exist — only shacks or public rooms. The early railroad passenger had to have a sense of humor and an iron stomach. Joseph Jefferson O'Neill aptly described the travel

Iron Horse on the new Santa Fe Trail

conditions of the day when he stated that "West of Kansas City, there is no Sunday. West of Dodge City, there is no God." ("Dodge City in Technicolor," SANTA FE MAGAZINE, May 1939)

Mary Colter charms and enraptures

Indigestion was the rule of day on the westbound trains, and the rides were often referred to as "hell on wheels." Meals were offered at shack towns that were nothing more than a depot and water tower. There was hardly a place fit to eat, much less a place to spend the night. (66) One could expect greasy fried meat, canned beans, rancid bacon, and maybe, with a little luck, fresh coffee — once a week. There would be pie made of dried fruit and crust, biscuits called "sinkers," eggs shipped and preserved in lime and chicken stew, usually made with prairie dog parts. The ambience of these dining stations featured dangerous looking miners (Twain), dirty tables and saucy waitresses. During the 20-minute culinary stopover, passengers probably ate a meal left untouched by previous diners. On the train there

were lunches from Butcher Boy or food brought from home, often spoiled and smelling bad. Some survived the ordeal only by drinking themselves into oblivion.

Fred Harvey Beginnings

Thanks to Santa Fe Railroad President Holliday's promotion of the adventure and romance of the West, America wanted to see what it was all about. The only thing left was to attract the weary traveler by assuring that his passage would boast comfort, style and taste. The stage was therefore set, the opportunity ripe, for the creative synthesis of three

First Harvey House ~ Florence, Kansas

key influences that ultimately shaped the nature of western travel and the soul of Route 66 in the Southwest.

The Bisonte ~Hutchinson, Kansas

The impeccable service and superb cuisine later provided by Fred Harvey made travel stops a delight, and in some cases, a major motivation for transit. The lore associated with the Southwest materialized into dining rooms, curio shops, lobbies, sunken gar-

El Vaquero ~ Dodge City, Kansas

dens and enchanting sleeping quarters thanks to one Mary Colter. Dining today at the La Fonda in Santa Fe, one may surmise that its mystique, its charisma, is the result of the combined talents of these three individuals.

Fred Harvey began working for the Santa Fe in the 1850's. He rode the rails throughout the Midwest, unhappily experiencing unsanitary lodgings and poorly prepared food that made his time away from home an ordeal of discomfort, and he realized the great risk of illness from either of these intolerable situations. Harvey's own bout with yellow fever and typhoid, and the death of his two children from scarlet fever, instilled in him a passionate intolerance of inadequate and sordid services. He acted by opening his first cafe in St. Louis in 1857.

In 1875 Harvey and a partner opened two cafes, one in Kansas and the other in Colorado. Harvey then went to the Burlington Railroad and offered meal service to its passengers. The company officials laughed at his proposal, declaring that expensive food was not any business of the railroads. They sarcastically told him to go to the Atchison, Topeka and Santa Fe, "because they would try anything." Fred Harvey took their suggestion to heart. In 1878, Fred Harvey and Mr. Nickerson, the President of the Santa Fe, became partners in the operation of the first Harvey House at Florence, Kansas. The Santa Fe Railroad and Fred Harvey sealed a formal partnership in 1889.

Suddenly, eating houses, lunch stands and hotel facilities began appearing along the Santa Fe line in a westward march out of Topeka, Kansas. The Topeka lunch counter was soon recognized within the whole region as a most elegant place to eat. The food, efficient service and sparkling clean atmosphere spawned epithets like "travelers declined to go further once they had eaten with Fred Harvey." In order to provide meals for train passengers, a Harvey House was positioned every 100 miles along the Santa Fe line. Although some of the diners were lusterless frame dwellings or even boxcars, the food was fresh and inventive, the linen clean and the silver polished. Passengers making a stop in Arizona

— one hundred miles from the nearest lake or stream — marveled at the near-miracle of filtered spring water, ice, fresh fruit and everything else that might be found in New York or Chicago.

The cliché that the Harvey Houses and the Santa Fe Railroad brought civilization to the West was clearly evidenced in the early efforts across Kansas. The Clifton House at Florence was built to resemble a fine English home, with fountains in its yard and candelabras in its dining room. It provided luxurious guest accommodation, and stood in 1879 as largest building in Central Kansas. For the locals in Hutchinson, whose environment was restricted to several streets that all ended at open prairie, the Bisonte Hotel was elegance personified; to the weary traveler, it offered a quiet, restful reprieve from the rigors of early cross-country travel. The availability of cranberries at Bisonte's kitchen was so unique that it was impossible to keep the waiters from pillaging them. One night, as a trap to shock and discourage, the cooks put a dead rat in the bottom of the cranberry crock. It was removed the next day, but the ploy worked. The cranberries were left alone after that.

The Santa Fe reached Dodge City in 1872. Dodge had been a Mecca for buffalo hunters because of its location near the Great Plains. The first winter the railroad was there, 200,000 buffalo hides were shipped, but soon the scent of buffalo hides was replaced by the smell of cattle dung. The construction of the El Vaquero in Dodge City in 1900 eliminated a boxcar, the first eating station set up in 1896. However, the El Vaquero was the least favorite station among Harvey employees because of the overwhelming odor of cattle dung and the masses of cowboys and noisy cows that cluttered the community.

Later on, both Newton and Dodge City challenged the Harvey system and its ability to bring gentility to a railroad community. At stations like the one in Emporia, the dedication of a Harvey House often produced the almost unbelievable — fresh fruit and home made ice cream, sherbet, rolls, breads and pastries and home made thousand island dressing. The Sequoia in Syracuse, which was opened in 1908, featured Spanish Mission style architecture with stuccoed arches and shaded walkways, and was considered to be an oasis in the high plains of western Kansas. It attracted celebrities like Will Rogers, Herbert Hoover, Clara Bow, Ann Sheridan and Leo Carillo and Franklin Roosevelt. It closed in 1936. The Union Station Harvey House in Kansas City highlighted the downtown area for both locals and visitors. Harvey's diner was the take-off point for the author and his friends during Christmas recesses and summer vacations from college in northwest Missouri.

Food Fare and Fare Maidens

Fred Harvey's girls, their service and the Harvey House menus were like a breath of fresh air to North American food service, totally transforming what railroad travelers had come to know. To provide systematic dining opportunities to all Santa Fe Passengers, Harvey Houses were established every 100 miles. The Houses brought a brand new dimension to those frontier towns, and their reputation varied from being celebrated as the "toast of town" to denigration as houses of prostitution.

One of the first Harvey Houses was set up in Holbrook, Arizona, of all places. In 1884, a Harvey

Mrs. Severson, La Posada Manager ~circa 1947

House was constructed inside the shell of five boxcars. The structure was painted red and decorated with large geometric designs. This bright innovation was quite the thing in a town full of the wildest bunch of cowhands the West had ever known — the Hashknife Outfit. Harvey House décor included Irish linen, Sheffield silver and china from France and fresh cut flowers from California. Great pitchers of ice water graced the tables. The menu featured the exotic terrapin as well as antelope, quail, and blue point oysters. A steak dinner could be had for seventy-five cents, and was served with a choice of five different wines. Harvey used refrigerated boxcars to bring in the best grade of meat from Kansas and the finest fresh fruit and vegetables from California. It is difficult to imagine such late 1800's largess being

Harvey Girls at work

offered to a group of Holbrook, Arizona Hashknife cowboys who rode their horses into saloons and tied them up at the bar.

The Albuquerque Morning Journal of July 29, 1911 provided a fine description of the Fred Harvey system: "….a management which allows a traveler to dine on brook trout in the middle of the desert and on the rarest fruits in vast reaches of country where nothing is raised but cactus and sagebrush. The Castaneda at Las Vegas, a great building of dark red brick in the Mission style; the Alvarado at Albuquerque, fronted by long colonnades and well proportioned arches; the Cardenas at Trinidad; the Fray Marcos at Williams; the Escanlante at Ash Fork; the El Garces at Needles — all these and many

Kitchen staff

others are…worthy of the study of the artist, the epicure, the student of Indian life. Of the many men in the United States who laid claim to the title of hotel manager, Fred Harvey was the Napoleon of hotel managers."

Harvey faced a serious problem in staffing. Waitresses were viewed as coarse, and waitressing was at the bottom of social scale. How then was Harvey able to get such wonderful women to do the job? The impeccable standards of service that Harvey would establish and maintain over the years required him to advertise in all of the Midwestern papers for the finest, most educated young women

La Fonda Lounge ~ Mary Colter

available. Harvey was able to draw and keep his female staff because he ignored the social stigma of waitressing, caring little for that popular concept.

He truly "did it his way." The original "Harvey Girls" were motivated by economics, adventure, a change of scene and life in a new territory. Harvey insisted on good manners, clear speech and absolute neatness. A Harvey Girl had to agree in her contract to follow the Harvey system to the letter, to obey supervisors without question and to accept any assigned location. Being a Harvey Girl was a way of life. Since most Harvey Girls were from small town America, often farmer's daughters from rural areas, what Harvey offered them was in essence a form of a higher education. Before long, the naïve country girls waxed urbane, changing from their somewhat dowdy selves into worldly, well-traveled, sophisticated women. They could move easily from one Harvey House to the next, going from state to state, from deserts to mountains, from city to outpost. The first "Girls" were hired at Raton, New Mexico in 1883.

The Harvey system was highly regimented, and there was little or no deviation allowed. Codes for hair, uniform and makeup were set up in 1883 and changed little for over 50 years. The only exceptions to the rules were found at the Grand Canyon, Winslow's La Posada, the Santa Fe La Fonda and the Alvarado in Albuquerque, where full Mexican style skirts and blouses were worn.

The service routine was precisely defined and of the highest quality. When a train pulled in and the pas-

Navajo rug

sengers gathered on the platform, a gong was sounded and a bellboy showed the way to the dining room. The Harvey Girls stood silent with fruit or salad at the ready and immediately asked the customer what they wished to drink. "You could be fired for carry-

Navajo jewlry ~ Fred Harvey patterned

ing a glass of water in your hand — there were no ifs, and, or buts — you minded or you lost your job." (ALBUQUERQUE MORNING JOURNAL, July 29, 1911)

Orders had to be memorized. Training was nerve-wracking and exhausting, and required 30 days of full time duty. There was no pay — only room, board and uniforms. The dorm rules were very strict.

Harvey tour bus

Trainees were subjected to the pressures of passengers operating within a definite time frame. Total adherence to serving rules and codes of behavior — to both customers and fellow employees — was demanded. For many of the girls, this required some adjustment. The rigors of training were designed to scare off the unstable and flush out those who could not carry their weight. The Harvey system controlled all.

Harvey maintained a large staff, no matter where the location. The staff configuration included a manager, a chef, a head waitress, 15 to 30 Harvey girls, a baker, a butcher, an assistant housemaid and team of

Harvey tour group

busboys. The entire operation was inspected on a regular basis. Chefs and managers were highly paid, with the chefs being the most respected and the highest paid. There were French, German and Italian chefs. The bakers, cooks and head chefs were prominent and well schooled. Badges were used to indicate status in the team, and one progressed up the hierarchy by hard work.

Afro-American, Hispanic, and Native American women were never recruited as waitresses, but minority workers dominated the kitchens. The

Harvey system was a friendly, familial community, and the large extended family of individuals who worked long, hard hours and shared dorm life and days off together. Social contact with customers was discouraged, and any intra-staff romance was carried on discretely. But, the Harvey system was in the end flexible and individualized enough to accommodate and retain long term employees. It has been said that the Harvey staff became the future aristocracy of the West.

The mystique surrounding Fred Harvey's success has been summarized by the simple statement he made on the occasion of his death in 1901: "Don't cut the ham too thin." The Dare Greatly motto fit Harvey to a T. He dared to put his theories of good service into practice, and would fire a manager for cutting corners on quality. Harvey gave out more in food and service than he took in. He fired one manager for creating a profit, replacing him with one who would assure the $1000 monthly loss the chain was experiencing at the time. In fact, many considered Harvey's operation to be a form of economic suicide. In 1930, Fred Harvey's restaurants served 15 million meals.

Many wealthy Americans preferred Harvey's cuisine to that of Europe. A Harvey menu in a diner in the middle of a barren desert might list the following choices—bluepoint oysters on the half shell, English pea soup au gratin, roast sirloin of beef au jus, pork with apple sauce, salami of duck, queen olives, New York ice cream, bananas, grapes, oranges, Edam and Roquefort cheese, French coffee and homemade pies. Quarter-size Whitefish from the Great Lakes were consumed in Winslow, Arizona, while sea turtles and sea celery were standard at the Montezuma in Las Vegas. Menu offerings were rotated along the line to avoid repetition. The Harvey kitchens made their own mayonnaise and their own ice cream. Women relished the opportunity to dress. Male diners were required to wear jackets.

From the turn of century up to World War I, the Santa Fe Railroad and Fred Harvey opened the West to America and in doing so tamed a wilderness. Upper-class American and Europeans sought adventurous excursions and leisurely vacations, desiring to see as much of the west as possible via excursion trains and tours. The Harvey Houses throughout New Mexico, Arizona and California complimented this exciting exposure by offering elegant dining, enchanting architecture and environmental immersion, all part and parcel of the rich Southwestern heritage. The Santa Fe Railroad made real that blissful California dream — the sun-drenched orange groves, Spanish missions, salt air and sandy beaches, banks of exotic, colorful flowers, palm trees and cactus and, of course, the mystique and romance of Hollywood.

It was Mary Elizabeth Jane Colter, a Minnesotan, who gave the extra special touches to Harvey Houses that rendered them more than railroad hotels. Colter was the chief architect and designer for Fred Harvey from 1902 to1948. Before Colter began her work, the Victorian gingerbread style, the classic Roman columns and Renaissance models were the major highlights of Harvey architecture. (36)

Thomas O'Mara ~ Trinidad, Colorado
Santa Fe Supervisor - Great Great Grandfather

Colter changed all that by working with the land and the materials at hand. She created buildings in harmony with the environment. Her use of soft lighting produced a restful atmosphere and recreated a bygone era, a more serene age when time seemed to stand still. Hispanic Americans brought with them Spanish culture and tradition, shaping the edifices in their New World to reflect visions of old Spain. Colter emphasized the same simplicity of that early architecture, capturing the charm and dignity of the rustic Southwest in a rediscovery of cultural heritage and style. She insisted that designs correspond to a building's purpose and the setting in which it was to function.

Outstanding examples of her artistry are seen at the Grand Canyon, in the south rim Watchtower patterned after authentic ruins of southwestern Indian towers and dwellings. Her deft touch can be seen in the Hopi House modeled after the Hopi dwellings at Oraibi, and is exemplified in the Bright Angel lodge, fashioned in the style of early pioneer buildings at the Grand Canyon. The La Posada in Winslow, a

romantic interpretation of the Spanish ranch style of early Mexican settlers in the Southwest, is a superb example of Colter's work.

Harvey paid homage to Indian art, using the finest example of weaving, painting and pottery in his hotels. The Mesa Verde artifact display at the 1892 World's Colombian Exposition in Chicago intrigued him, and he began to contact museum curators and private collectors in a search for similar items. He is credited for saving from destruction thousands of worthy old specimens of Navajo weaving. Those same Navajo Chief rugs might sell today for over $60,000 each.

Fred Harvey incorporated an Indian motif in all the company's advertising. Exotic paintings of Navajo and Hopi lands and people decorated the Fred Harvey brochures. In 1930, Mary Colter created an exclusive line of china for the Santa Fe Super Chief. She decorated the plates with thirty-seven different Mimbres designs found on thousand-year-old pottery found in southern New Mexico's Mimbres sites. Such plates are now highly valued collector's items.

The first Harvey House to sell pottery, jewelry and weaving was located at Coolidge, Kansas. The manager there, Herman Schweizer, commissioned Navajos to create new work using authentic "pawn" silver designs. Schweizer only produced the very best replicas, demanding that they personify collector quality.

In the 1920's, the Santa Fe Railroad brought travelers to the Indian country, but they were afforded only a fleeting glimpse of the southwestern terrain and Indian lifestyles and were offered little or no explanation of what they were seeing from the windows. Automobile trips on rough, challenging roads were the only way to get a more intimate look these scenic attractions.

The desert climate, the Indian festivals and the incredible natural wonders called to travelers from all over the globe. Recognizing this, Fred Harvey built a chain of Santa Fe station hotels across the Southwest that were used as jumping off points for motor tours to the hinterlands. Harvey's Pullmans and stopover hotels were located within sightseeing distance of some major attractions — national parks like the Grand Canyon, the Petrified Forest and the picturesque Indian pueblos of New Mexico and Arizona.

The Santa Fe Transportation Company ferried tourists from Santa Fe to the Rio Grand Pueblo communities, Chaco Canyon and other destinations.

Gallup was used as a base of operations for trips to Canyon de Chelly, Mesa Verde, Zuni Pueblo and Inscription Rock. La Posada in Winslow was a headquarters for trips to the Petrified Forest, Hopi Villages, Painted Desert, Meteor Crater and the White Mountain Country. At the Williams, Arizona junction, side tours left for the Grand Canyon. These tours became known as Harvey's Indian Detours and were operated by Yellow Cab of Chicago. They conducted one to three daily trips from Winslow, Santa Fe and Albuquerque. The promotional flyers claimed that taking the tours would be a way to "access buried cities that flourished when Britons crouched in caves," and to see the vestiges of medieval Spain hidden away for centuries in the mountains of America. (pg. 150)

In 1926 the auto detours from Albuquerque to Santa Fe and Las Vegas, New Mexico, were long, difficult journeys run on terrible roads. The rough ride was worth it because of what awaited travelers at the end of the trip. The food and accommodation at places like the Alvarado and La Fonda more than compensated for any inconvenience. Cross-country travel on the Santa Fe Railroad to and from the west coast included stopovers in Albuquerque, the Grand Canyon, Gallup and Santa Fe.

Writer Erna Fergusson organized a courier corps of women, Indian Detour Couriers, to accompany the Detour passengers. The group consisted of 25-year-old college graduates who functioned as hostesses and guides on the Harveycars. They received crash courses in southwestern art, geology, sociology, architecture and history. Some recall their experience escorting the rich, famous and adventurous. For example, courier Margaret Moses, a German native, was assigned to Einstein. She remembers the remark he made at the Petrified Forest about a sign citing it as being 6 million years old. Einstein corrected the figure to 60 million years.

Road Harbors of Pleasure and Repose

The Harvey Houses established in towns along the New Mexico, Arizona, and California segments of Route 66 were highly instrumental in creating romance of the road. The Houses were exemplary standards of decor, architecture and cuisine and displayed the best in southwestern art. They were resort destinations, veritable oases in the desert and launching points for excursions ferrying delighted travelers to the natural wonders of the Southwest. For some communities, the Harvey House was a vortex , the core of all social activity. Some people even referred to Harvey Houses in the deserts as "Branches of Heaven." What Fred Harvey was able to accomplish from 1920's through the 1950's was never done before and has not been done since.

Each Harvey House was unique. From Lamy to Barstow, the houses had their own history, their own special stories, their own atmosphere and design. The impact that these Houses had on travelers and locals who frequented them was so powerful that restoration plans have been initiated in communities from Kansas to California.

The New Mexico Harvey Houses

In 1880, the Santa Fe Railroad, in order to avoid conflict with the Denver and Rio Grande Railroad and the expense of forging a difficult mountainous route, built a spur from Santa Fe to a station stop at Lamy, New Mexico. Louis Curtis of St. Louis designed the El Ortiz Harvey House in that tiny town. Curtis fancied a Spanish-Pueblo style design, one patterned after early New Mexico adobe buildings and the University of New Mexico's restoration of Governor's Palace in Santa Fe.

La Fonda ~ Santa Fe, New Mexico

The Alvarado ~ Albuquerque, New Mexico

The El Ortiz had a viga (log) ceiling and a huge fireplace. In the center of the lounge area was a heavy carved Mexican table surrounded by brass studded straight-backed chairs. Owen Wister (The Virginian) described the lobby as "a private house of someone who had lavished thought and care upon every nook. This little oasis among the desert hills is a wonder of taste to be looked back upon by the traveler who is going to stop there." Wister also shared his temptation to forego future plans and stay there a week, simply for the pleasure of living and resting in such a place. (36)

Wister aptly expressed how the ambience of Lamy and other Harvey Houses charmed their guests. "A cold wind had come up with the rain, and the glow of a log fire in the open fireplace of the large hotel living room gave a cordial welcome that caused the rain and the hours of waiting to be forgotten."

One Harvey Girl, a woman from the fertile farmlands of Texas named Ruthana Walz, came to Lamy to take a bus to Santa Fe. Upon her arrival, she thought she was abandoned in the desert, that she had come to "the ends of the earth." She wondered what she was doing there. Happily, she made it to Santa Fe, found employment as a waitress at La Fonda and was rewarded with three hundred dollars a month in tips.

THE LA FONDA AT SANTA FE

Established in 1610, Santa Fe is the oldest European community west of the Mississippi River. Santa Fe has several distinctive names — The City Different, the Crossroads of the Centuries, the Royal City, the Ancient Capital and the Athens of America. For three centuries Santa Fe has been conscious of itself as being something extraordinary and in fact it always was. It sat right at the very end of the Old Santa Fe Trail. The historic adobe inn named "La Fonda" was in existence as early as 1609 and was quite literally "the inn at the end of the trail."

The La Fonda opened in 1827 and became a rendezvous for all manner of types — trappers, gamblers, pioneers, miners, soldiers, merchants, and politicians. A Confederate General and his staff lived there. A chief justice was shot near the front desk and a lynching was carried out in the back yard. Kearney held victory ball, and Grant entertained. At the annual Santa Fe Fiesta, a girl would ride a horse into the lobby. The La Fonda has had several names over the years — the Inn, the U.S. Hotel and The Exchange. The earlier version of the hotel was torn down in 1910 and replaced by the building that was to bear the official title of "The La Fonda."

The La Fonda was constructed in Spanish-Pueblo style reminiscent of Indian pueblo dwellings. The design of the original building blended Moorish elements with that of Native American. Natural materials, such as pine logs and adobe mud, were used in construction. The "new" La Fonda was designed in 1920 and was accented by massive rounded bulks, terraced roofs, open towers, wooden balconies and rows of projecting vigas constructed around an open courtyard.

In 1926, La Fonda was bought by the Santa Fe Railroad and assigned as a Harvey House. The hotel was enlarged, and deluxe rooms were added on the fifth floor. Mary Colter was asked to decorate the hotel to Harvey standards. Colter refurbished the guestrooms, lounges and dinning area, using warm, informal Mexican furnishings. Waitresses wore colorful Mexican skirts and blouses. Colter filled La Fonda with Mexican furniture custom made to her specifications, and painted to fit the color scheme of each room.

She hired artists to paint 798 pieces of art, each piece created to accent 156 unique rooms. Interior doors contained glass panels painted in a rainbow of colors. Traditional Mexican light fixtures were hung throughout, and the top floors contained antique beds from Spain. Just before her retirement, Colter redecorated the La Cantina bar as an old Mexican kitchen, the room featuring pots and pans and huge old copper kettles.

The La Fonda was the headquarters of The Harvey Indian Detours and became a Mecca for tourists traveling to the Southwest. The wall of the lounge had an immense map of the Southwest pinpointing all the tourist sights – the Grand Canyon, Rainbow Bridge, Canyon de Chelly, the Painted Desert, the Hopi mesas, Mesa Verde, Carlsbad Caverns and Acoma Pueblo.

La Fonda was a haunt for Santa Feans and a social center for Hispanics, Indians, Anglos and tourists. In fact, segregation was less noticeable and often nonexistent in local restaurants and hotels. The La Fonda and the Alvarado in Albuquerque served everyone who walked through their doors. In the 1930's, fifteen thousand people visited La Fonda, including 150 artists and writers. Ernie Pyle, the famous corespondent of World War II, observed that Santa Fe contained an "Awful gob of genius." He noted that life among the upper crust centered at the La Fonda: "You could go there any time of the day and see a few artists in the bar, or an Indian that some white woman loved, or a goateed nobleman from Austria, or a maharajah from India, a New York broker, or an archaeologist, or some local light in overalls and cowboy boots." (66)

Castaneda ~ West Las Vegas, New Mexico

THE LAS VEGAS Casteneda

There were two major Harvey Houses in Las Vegas — the Castenada and the Montezuma.

The Castaneda was constructed 1899 next to the railroad tracks in what is known as East Las Vegas. West Las Vegas contained the old plaza, a station stop of the Santa Fe Trail. The Castaneda was constructed facing the Great Plains of New Mexico, and from its front porch one could go all the way to the Mississippi without running into mountains. The silver service in its restaurant was valued at $200,000 and was set out only on special occasions.

The Castenada is best known for hosting the annual Roosevelt's Rough Rider Reunion. Roosevelt's Rough Riders attained renown by distinguishing themselves in their campaign during the Spanish-American War. Twenty Las Vegans had signed up for the Rough Riders. On June 24, 1899, the Roosevelt's Rough Rider Reunion was initiated and consisted of several days of parades, speeches, bands, dances and rodeos. Roosevelt himself stayed in the Castaneda at night, spending the rest of his time with his riders. After the Rough Rider Reunion the hotel lapsed into a sad state of disrepair, the furniture scarred and dirtied from parties and free balls held for local citizens. The Castaneda, although rough and tumble, was a favorite of Harvey employees.

The Montezuma OF LAS VEGAS

The Montezuma Harvey House was built in 1882 up a canyon at the end of a spur, six miles west from the main line in Las Vegas. It was constructed at the point where hot mineral springs bubbled out the side of the canyon and attracted health seekers from the east. It was made completely of wood, four stories high, with a tower that extended upward to eight stories. Each of the 270 rooms had its own balcony that opened out onto the big skies of New Mexico. It boasted huge bathhouses, and could accommodate 500 guests per day!

Harvey girls walked the streets of Las Vegas with the likes of Billy the Kid, Doc Holliday, Pat Garrett and Jesse James. John Carson, the son of Kit Carson who at the time worked at the OK Barber shop, raised a $1,200 reward for the finding of Pat Garrett after he shot Billy the Kid.

The Montezuma was later acquired by Armand Hammer and made into an upscale, avant guard

The Montezuma ~ Las Vegas, New Mexico

International College. At the onset of the millennium, the Montezuma was still in operation and its wooden frame was being refurbished and repaired.

The Albuquerque ALVARADO
The Alvarado Hotel was constructed in 1902 beside the tracks in New Town Albuquerque. Charles F. Whittlesey decorated the hotel with Spanish arches patterned after the old mission-way stations used by wagon trains on their way to California. It was the first building in New Mexico to revive this Spanish tradition in building design, and it raised the historical consciousness of the entire Southwest. The hotel was ahead of the times in its use of electric lighting and thermostatically controlled steam heat. It featured a two hundred-foot long arcade, a clubroom, 75 guestrooms, brick walkways and a private courtyard. It contained barbershops, parlors, reading rooms and dining rooms.

Locals walked along the arcade, enjoyed lavish lunches and hung out, hoping to sight famous people and movie stars. The Alvarado's Old World charm, fountains and lily ponds intrigued the famous and they made a point of stopping there. When the train pulled in, both the locals and the passengers kept their eyes peeled. They often saw celebrities disembark, and they crowded around them for autographs.

Douglas Fairbanks, Jr. and Mary Pickford stopped on occasion, and Lindbergh, Shirley Temple, Jackie Coogan, Albert Einstein, Don Ameche, and Bob Hope all decked the halls of the Alvarado.

Everyone knew the Alvarado to be the classiest, most romantic, elegant and authentically furnished New Mexican hotel ever to grace the Rio Grande Valley. The Alvarado became known as the best railroad hotel in the world. New Yorkers who frequented Europe claimed that nothing there could compare with the Alvarado. In 1941, when the author lived in Albuquerque, the Alvarado was considered the social center of the town. Cross country travelers, Anglo customers, Hispanic and Indian natives and fellows of both the frontier and modern America considered the hotel's cuisine to be the best in the region. Many of them enjoyed Sunday dinner at Alvarado on a regular basis. Ernie Pyle declared that he "always went

Busy platform at the Alvarado

to the Alvarado Hotel's swell Concina Cantina in his overalls and added that nobody raised an eyebrow."(66)

The Indian Room at the Alvarado was designed and decorated by Mary Colter. She was commissioned as well to set up the museum and sales shop to launch the Harvey Company's full scale involvement in the promotion and sale of Indian arts and crafts. A section of the room was designed as a museum to display North American Indian arts and crafts, ancient and modern Eskimo crafts and artifacts from the South Seas. Schweizer spent five years gathering artifacts. Colter's decor for the salesroom included Indian pots and baskets, stacks of Indian blankets and a replica of a Hopi religious altar. It was later claimed that the Hopi builder of the altar experienced some unusual and debilitating physical reactions. Locals, visitors and tourists could observe artisans at work — Navajo weavers and silver smiths, and Acoma and Laguna potters. When the trains stopped, visitors were immediately drawn to Museum.

Across the street from the Alvarado in 1941 was a Class B movie theater. After the Saturday afternoon matinee, the author would spend hours walking around the Alvarado, admiring the decor and standing in the Indian Room watching the artisans work. On the author's way home for Christmas in 1951 and 1952, the Santa Fe's Grand Canyon Limited would stop for an hour beside the Alvarado. A carol, "SILVER BELLS," would boom over the loud speakers. The author and several companions dined on thick, juicy Fred Harvey roast beef, excellent coffee and delicious peach cobbler.

The El Navajo of Gallup

When the railroad arrived in 1881, Gallup, New Mexico was still an old Pony Express station. By the early 1900's, the Gallup station had become a jumping-off spot for tourists wanting to visit Indian country. INDIAN DETOURS took groups to Enchanted Mesa, Chaco Canyon, Zuni and Acoma Pueblos, Navajo land, the Painted Desert, the Petrified Forest, and Inscription Rock.

The El Navajo was constructed in Gallup in 1921, but not in Spanish or California Mission revival style. This particular Harvey House was a unique tribute to the American Indian, a place in which Mary Colter had brilliantly blended modern architecture and ancient art. Colter forged a close relationship with Indian artists in order to be able to create authentic designs, and in addition, she had received approval from the Navajos to use Indian sand paintings as a motif throughout the building. Very few non-Indians had seen sand paintings as they were sacred and always erased after ceremonies. Sand paintings were only executed for the healing of sickness, the dispelling of evil and the bestowing of blessings. With its long low arches, black and red batik drapes, red tile floor and bright Navajo rugs, the El Navajo presented the traveler with a warm, spacious and restful haven (36)

The El Navajo was opened with an impressive ceremony on May 26, 1923. Thirty medicine men carried out a "Blessing of the House - A Ritual to Make Perfect." Two thousand Native Americans attended, along with an associate of Kit Carson's.

Gallup's Annual Inter-Tribal Indian Ceremonial in the 1920's used the El Navajo as its natural center for activities. Harvey Girls wore festive dresses and skirts for the Ceremonial instead of their standard black and white. Gallup eventually became one of the most popular tourist attractions in the Southwest. The author's father and mother lived in Gallup in 1930 and experienced the Annual Inter-Tribal Indian

Albert Einstein ~ Harvey Indian Detours

The dining room

La Posada became a winter resort for wealthy Easterners and an oasis in the hot Arizona summers of the 1930' and 1940's. One parched soul, after hours of viewing little but cactus and dry, cracked earth, described the entry into the La Posada lunchroom as "a sudden paradise." Travelers even changed their itinerary to stay a couple of nights after dining at La Posada.

Many celebrities crossed the portals of La Posada. Charles Lindbergh had a suite at La Posada that is

News stand

Ceremonial. Gallup was a training site for Harvey Girls as most of the staff, many from Kansas, were older and more experienced.

The LA POSADA of Winslow

Colter's favorite building, La Posada, was built in Winslow, Arizona in 1929. The cost of construction exceeded one million dollars. Since Winslow was surrounded by favored tourist destinations, the cost of the hotel was an easily justifiable extravagance. "The Resting Place" was a rendition of the great ranchos built by the Spanish dons in the1700 and 1800's. It was built on 8 acres, and featured archways, great portals, tiled roofs, smooth pink plastered walls and wrought-iron grills reminiscent of Spanish Mediterranean architecture. There were seventy guestrooms, five suites, and a lunchroom designed with Spanish tile that seated 120 people. There was also a large dining room, as well as numerous corridors and lounges.

Walking into La Posada gave one the feeling of being in a great ranch house. Colter had chosen rough-hewn pieces of furniture in combination with imported and rare furnishings and Navajo rugs for the floors in the rooms. Outside, there were horse stables, tennis courts and a sunken garden. The complex was considered a work of art, inside and out.

Jack Mullen captures the flavor of La Posada:"There were hand-hewn benches next to a two-hundred year old antique chest that had once hauled grain from Spain to the New World. Rare old Spanish plates and Chinese copper jars inside a primitive Mexican trastero — blue and white Chinese Chippendale jars in the lobby and fine old samovar in the dining room — lampshades made from a cardinal's umbrella." {100, pg. 3}

still there — the Lindbergh Suite is available for a one-night stay. John Wayne and Bing Crosby were guests, and Carol Lombard, the wife of Clark Gable, spent her last night at the hotel prior to her tragic death in a plane accident. The author's close friend and football team member, Aurthur Rubi, was a bellboy at La Posada in the 1940s and carried baggage for Charles Lindbergh . The author stood on the platform in front of the La Posada in 1945 when Harry Truman campaigned off the back of his special Pullman car. The whole town came out to see him.

Dances for teenagers were held on the tennis courts at La Posada in the mid-1940's. The scene remains vivid in the author's memory — a green enameled lamp shades casting a dim light out over the courts…the moon shining bright…the balmy summer breeze of the Winslow night on the Little Colorado River Valley undulating with the rhythm of the music…"It was only a paper moon, shining over a cardboard screen – but it wouldn't be make believe if you believed in me." Pre-pubescence was over, along with World War II, and the world seemed like a magic, mysterious and wonderful paradise. It was easy then to believe in "that old black magic called love."

In December of 1947, the Winslow Bulldog football banquet was held at La Posada in Winslow. As always, the service and the food were exceptional, nothing better to be had in the entire state of Arizona.

In 1945 the author stood in the snow in front of La Posada watching each train go by and waiting for a girlfriend to come back from San Bernadino. In doing so, he had missed a hiking trip to a favorite haunt at Tucker Spring where his friends had weathered out a blizzard.

Meandering through the halls of La Posada was a delightful, aesthetic experience. The hotel brought such beauty, such elegance to that small western town. It was pure enchantment, a different world — like walking through the set of a western movie. It was warm and lovely, it smelled of fresh rolls and roast beef and flowers, and the magnificent pictures, sculptures and Navajo rugs were a feast for the eyes.

Grand Canyon's EL TOVAR
The Grand Canyon was largely unknown in the United States in the 1880's. The only means of seeing the Canyon was by stagecoach from either Williams or Flagstaff. The Santa Fe Railroad built a

Lobby

spur line to the rim of the Canyon in 1901, launching its reputation as the greatest natural wonder in the world. However, the Canyon needed comfortable facilities and a public relations campaign. Ripley, President of the Santa Fe Railroad, began the promotion of the Canyon through brochures and the commissioning of a spectacular painting by Thomas Morgan. Several thousand full-color lithographs of Moran's painting were given to schools, hotels and railroad stations.

La Posada - train platform side

Fred Harvey and the Santa Fe Railroad were guided in creating facilities that both protected and enhanced the Canyon's natural beauty. Thus, El Tovar, designed by Whittlesey, was constructed with care in 1903. The resort hotel was named for Don Pedro de Tovar, the Spanish Conquistador and "conqueror" of Tusayan (The Hopi Pueblo). Douglas fir

Hall and staircase

from Oregon and local stone were combined into an impressive four-story log and boulder structure with a Swiss chalet motif in the tradition of the great resorts of Europe. El Tovar contained one hundred rooms, a public bath on each floor and electric lights powered by a steam generator.

The dining room had a 15th century feel, and inside the hotel were galleries that offered the works of great landscape painters like Moran. The complex contained a solarium, a music room, a clubroom, an amusement room and a roof garden. Overall, the hotel resembled a village. It had its own greenhouse, a herd of cows for milk and numerous chickens. Water was hauled from Del Rio at a distance of one hundred miles. The lobby was decorated with hunting trophies and Indian pottery. Sight-seeing tours in horse drawn carriages came and went from the entryway.

Nearly a block long, El Tovar was jokingly called the most expensive log house in America. It soon rivaled the great resort hotels of Europe and became a favorite destination for travelers from all over the world. The kitchen, bakery, and butcher shop had the finest baked goods and meats in the United States — salmon from San Francisco, celery from Michigan, honeydew and Persian melons, apples, pears and oranges from California, French and Portuguese sardines, Kansas beef, Camembert cheeses and raw milk from a dairy at Del Rio.

Grand Canyon Village, established to support the Harvey operations, required the services of no less than 500 employees. The Harvey staff at the Grand Canyon hiked, danced, worked, and partied together. The isolation at the Canyon made it necessary to suspend rules forbidding fraternizing.

Creations of Mary Colter at the Canyon

El Tovar was soon overwhelmed by the tourist trade. Wishing to expand services and facilities at the Canyon, Fred Harvey called once again on the genius of Mary Colter. Soon, the Grand Canyon would become a showplace for Colter's art. She would fashion stone buildings on the Canyon's South Rim that looked as old as the Canyon itself and which resembled the ancient structures left by the tribes that inhabited them. In 1934, Colter designed and supervised the construction of Bright Angel

The late Jim Curtis ~ coach and administrator

Lodge to meet accelerating tourism demands. The hotel served several hundred people after sunrise services. It was a glamorous place.

Colter then turned her attention to the construction of the Hopi House, patterned after Hopi dwellings at Oraibi and featuring such elements as terraces, steps and porches. The inside of the structure contained massive adobe-like walls of rough plaster with ceilings constructed of log beams with small branches lying across them. The rooms were decorated with huge baskets, the floors covered with Navajo rugs. One room contained a caballero's saddle, spurs, sombreros, and rifles. The Totem Room was filled with artifacts of the Northwest Tribes. Another room contained a Hopi altar and sand paintings.

The Grand Canyon of the Colorado River

The Fred Harvey Fine Arts Collection, consisting of five thousand pieces, was displayed in the Hopi House. The collection, which garnered a grand prize at the 1904 St. Louis Exposition, contained ancient Pueblo pottery, baskets, beadwork, Kachina dolls, jewelry, costumes and buffalo-hide shields. Harvey and Colter wished to re-create the distinctive dwellings of an ancient culture and acquaint the public with the richness and beauty of Native American art, and they succeeded. The Hopi House, like the Alvarado, had Native craftsman working throughout the building. Hopi House was the main sales facility for Harvey. Of an evening the tourist could experience traditional Hopi songs and dances.

Another outstanding achievement of Colter's was the building of Hermit's Rest, a spot for tour groups to stop and refresh. The place was constructed with boulders and natural timber, and looked like a dwelling built by mountain men. The most striking feature of the building was the stone gate with a broken mission bell at its entrance. At first glance, the building looked like a haphazard jumble of stones with a protruding chimney spire. A beautiful porch reached out to the very edge of the canyon.

In the 1930's, Colter continued her creations west of El Tovar with the Watch Tower at Desert View. A massive stone tower, 70-ft high, was modeled after primitive Anasazi watchtowers. This was followed by the Lookout, which was perched right on the edge of the Canyon. Finally, Colter designed and constructed the famous Phantom Ranch on the Colorado River, right at the bottom of the Canyon. Artistic plans were made for a two-story, 3,200 square foot lodge in the Canyon at Indian Gardens, but it was never constructed.

One Harvey Girl, Bertha Parker Maddux, commented that the staff didn't feel isolated at the canyon because of the incredible beauty surrounding them. The staff learned to create their own fun. Many took mule trips down into the Canyon on a trail that went straight down and around big curves. Both fear and fun were experienced when the mules reached out over a precipice to munch on some grass. In addition to the Canyon, there were many sights to see in northern Arizona, right out in the middle of nowhere. Some Harvey Girls quit but most stayed, enraptured by the wild, open nature of the country.

Other Harvey Oases across Arizona

There were a number of other notable Harvey Houses and hotels in Arizona besides La Posada. The Painted Desert Inn outside of Holbrook was a favorite spot for the off road tours called Harvey Indian Detours. The Painted Desert Inn is still in operation as part of the National Park system.

THE FRAY MARCOS

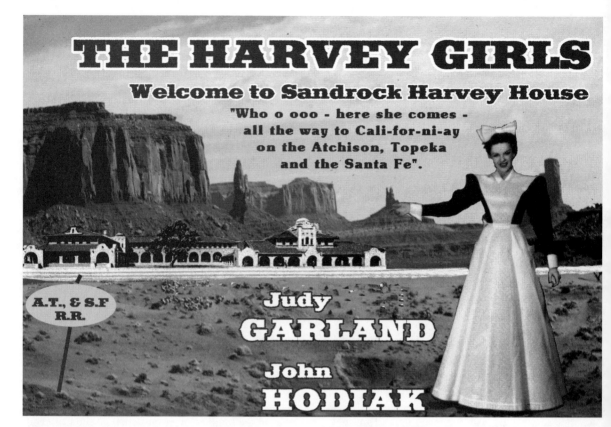

THE HARVEY GIRLS

Welcome to Sandrock Harvey House

"Who o ooo - here she comes -
all the way to Cali-for-ni-ay
on the Atchison, Topeka
and the Santa Fe".

A.T., & S.F
R.R.

Judy
GARLAND

John
HODIAK

The Fray Marcos in Williams, Arizona was established in 1905. The Fray Marcos was named for a Franciscan Monk who enticed the Spanish Conquistador, Coronado, to march from Mexico into north Arizona and New Mexico in search of the famous Cities of Gold — the Seven Cities of Cibola.

THE ESCALANTE

The Escalante, named after the famous Spanish Padre who explored southern Utah and the area around the Grand Canyon, was established in Ashfork, Arizona in 1905.

El Tovar at the Grand Canyon ~ Painting by Judy Schauermann

Tower at the south rim ~ Mary Colter

ater for employees, a laundry, an ice-making and ice-crushing machine, a butchering station and an ice cream plant. The Casa del Desierto made thirty gallons of ice cream daily, which sweet concoction was peddled to passengers on the train platform. The remainder of the ice cream was shipped to Needles, Seligman, Winslow, San Bernadino, Los Angeles and San Diego.

The MGM Movie

In 1940 MGM produced a movie glorifying the Harvey Girls called THE HARVEY GIRLS, based on the novel of the same name by Samuel Hopkins. The film stared Judy Garland, Preston Foster, Ray Bolger, Chill Wills, Angela Lansbury, Marjorie Main, Cyd Charisse, Virginia O'Brien and John Hodiak (Poling-Kempes). The movie was a musical with many romantic songs, including the "The Atchison, Topeka and the Santa Fe."

The setting for the film was an imaginary western railroad town called "Sandrock." It was a fast moving epic set to the repercussions of a fight typical of the west in the 1800's — a battle between the civilizing influences of the Santa Fe Railroad and the lawless rule of outlaws, gamblers and crooked officials of the early west. The squeaky clean image of the Harvey Girl was contrasted with that of western dance hall prostitutes. Publicity men for MGM came to Albuquerque in hopes of finding Harvey Girls who had attained wealth and power as a result of their work.

Although the real Harvey Girls were flattered by the attention given to them, they scoffed at the film, saying that the realities of their work rarely included much singing and dancing.

Kingman Harvey House, built in 1901, operated only as a lunch and dining facility. The largest of its kind west of Kansas City and east of Los Angeles, it was closed in1930's.

CALIFORNIA HARVEY HOUSES
EL GARCES HOTEL

El Garces Hotel was established in Needles, California in the 1900's. Located just across the Arizona line into California on the Colorado River, the town of Needles was very isolated and very hot, with temperatures that sometimes reached 125 degrees. Celebrities like William S. Hart stayed there. One of the Harvey Girls actually died of heat prostration. Harvey Girls were paid a bonus for summer work at Needles

BARSTOW.
THE CASA DEL DESIERTO

The Casa del Desierto was built in Barstow in 1910 and still stands as the final Harvey House constructed in that town. Other Harvey Houses had been built there before 1910, but, made of wood frames, they burned to the ground from careless use of cooking fires and lanterns. Casa del Desierto was a pseudo-Spanish-Moroccan Complex considered to be the jewel of the desert in an otherwise dismal landscape. It was a self-contained village and contained its own bowling alley, a swimming pool, a library and the-

The Beginning and End of the Trail

The author's experience with Fred Harvey and the Santa Fe Railroad began very early in life. The author and his mother took many trips from Flagstaff to Los Angeles and down the coast to San Diego. Boarding the Santa Fe in Flagstaff early in the evening, the trip was an all night event on the sleeper to Los Angeles. There were times when the shade on the Pullman sleeper was raised to reveal the Needles or Barstow lettering the side of the station-house. A vivid image imprinted on the author's mind is of the zigzag red, black and buff tile that covered the floor of the Los Angeles Terminal Restaurant.

Meeting the author's aunt and friend at the station was always followed by lunch in the huge dining room.

The Luxurious Pullman car was decorated in the tradition of Louis XV and was embellished with mahogany, velveteen, antique oak paneling and electric lights. Happily, the ticket included "meals by Fred Harvey." The aroma of coffee is burnt into the author's mind as well as memories of the Corn Flakes with heavy cream and a morning glass of fresh orange juice. The passage down to Los Angeles still seems like some kind of wonderful, other-worldly dream.

During college days in Missouri, the author would stand between the cars on a small platform, watching for the mountains and sniffing the scent of pines as the Grand Canyon limited crept over Ration Pass

Coming home for Christmas vacation from Chicago, the author and his family arrived after the big snow

of 1968 on the first train to enter Flagstaff in two weeks. The author was met at the depot by his father in a four-wheel drive.

Eventually, Fred Harvey's empire and the miracle of train travel reached the end of the trail. With the advent of the automobile and the onset of airplane voyages, the problems faced by railroads in 30's proved to be insurmountable. Scores of Harvey Houses were closed throughout World War II. Mammoth changes in the American lifestyle during that time ended the golden era of the Harvey Houses. However, many are being rebuilt or renovated, most notably La Posada in Winslow and the Alvarado in Albuquerque.

Harvey Indian Detour Room in Ration, New Mexico

Fred Harvey Indian Detour Guides

Hopi House at Grand Canyon

Harvey Detour Guide With Snake

Hidden Mountain

FOURTEEN
Ancient Messages on a Stone
Route 66 Visited in 2500 B.C?

Motoring west out of Albuquerque on Interstate 40, one passes the Los Lunas turnoff connecting to southbound New Mexico Highway 6. Following Highway 6 southward, you cross a section of New

Mexico Highway 6 going through Los Lunas that in days gone by formed a segment of Old Route 66. Peering southward from I-40 into the midnight darkness, the eyes note a red neon beer sign in the window of the Whitehorse Bar located on the now abandoned "New Route 66."

Beyond that point, seventeen miles into the blackness, lies one of the most enigmatic spots on the Mother Road. A mile to the west on "Old 66" is the tall, dark silhouette of Hidden Mountain. For over 75

Canyon location of stone

years now the mountain remains one of New Mexico's deepest mysteries, and, is to this day the focus of intense interest and controversy. Research suggests that the first tourist lodgings were located on Hidden Mountain — 2,500 years ago! Regardless of what one is led to conclude from investigations claiming to penetrate its shroud of secrecy, the very existence of this mystical Stone and its abstruse message send a chill down the spine.

The phenomenon found in the canyon on the east side of Hidden Mountain is generally referred to as the MYSTERY STONE OF NEW MEXICO, or as "Inscription Rock" or "The Los Lunas Mystery Stone." For most of the 20th century and now into the 21st, the origin of the Stone and the meaning of the inscriptions remain an enigma. The 1.5-meter wide inscription contains 216 chiseled characters that resemble ancient Phoenician script, the deciphering of which has challenged amateur archaeologist, historians and epigraphers alike.

Home of an ancient Greek sailor?

Scholars from a wide range of disciplines have offered various inscription interpretations that include a rendering of the Ten Commandments, a 4,000 year old message form Near East relatives of the Navajo, a 2,500 old tale of a Greek exile, a treasure map of the Acoma people, a message from Roman colonists, a Mormon inscription, the 200 year-old carving of a Spaniard who was secretly a Jew, a message left by a lost Tribe of Israel, the coded message of a Hebrew extra-terrestrial and, finally, the dispiriting possibility of a simple hoax by college pranksters. Whatever may have unfolded on the side of Hidden Mountain, the drama of it all has certainly inspired attention and comment.

Hidden Mountain is secluded on three sides — from the east by the highlands rising from the Rio Grande River, from the west by a long Mesa and from the north by a large butte called Lucero Uplift. Below the Mountain, and extending north and south, is a deep arroyo and stream bed known as the Rio Puerco River. From the site of the Mystery Stone, one can see the Sandia Mountains to the east as well as the mesas that mark the edges of the Colorado Plateau.

Hidden Mountain itself is a made up of lava deposits several hundred feet high. Chiseled down its side are canyons and ravines of relatively recent geological origin. On its eastern side is an arroyo that serves as a water drain. At the very top of the Mountain lies an Anasazi pueblo inhabited circa AD 1400; it contains 150 rooms and functioned as a fortified domestic sanctuary. The Mystery Stone lies on the lower right side of a large mound of lava, tucked within a small canyon that dimples the base of what is clearly an extinct volcano. Rocks in the immediate vicinity contain both petroglyphs and graffiti, and an Anasazi inscription of a cat. There is an Anglo carving three meters to the north on top of a flat stone that reads "Hobe and Eva — 3-19-1930." There are also many Euro-American glyphs near the top of the mountain, including an exact replica of "Hobe and Eva — 3-19-1930" and another inscription which reads "Sore Foot Canyon."

Travelers on "old Route 66" passed within a mile of Hidden Mountain, near where Lucero Uplift and the Rio Puerco fault zone come together. (Lucero Mesa rises immediately west and extends as far as the eye can see to the north). From his mountain home, Zakyneros, the alleged ancient visitor, could have seen water gushing through what is now a dry Rio Puerco. The Spaniards found the Rio Puerco dirty, actually "piggish" — but Zakyneros would have found it a fast-flowing fresh water stream. On a day in August when the author visited the site of the Mystery Stone, only the wail of a passing train and

Ancient message?

the whisper of a desert dust devil (a small, tornado-like dust storm) twirling through scrub Juniper broke the silence. The bed of the Rio Puerco lay at the bottom of ten-foot long red banks lined with small Willow trees. Although the river is as dry as a bone, occasionally, a four-foot wall of water may rush through it, a journey of rain runoff on its way to the Gulf of Mexico.

The Mystery Stone of New Mexio

The entrance to the site is located on the road leading to a Solid Waste Station. Immediately across a bridge over the Rio Puerco and on the south side of the road are a pedestrian break in the fence and a sign in the background reading "Hidden Ranch, Isleta Pueblo." Access to the site is controlled by permit from the New Mexico State Land Office.

Approximately one mile into the flatlands, one-half mile westward up the arroyo, is a large lava outcropping. On the lower eastern face of the lava formation is a smooth 8 x 4 x 2-meter surface with carved inscription 1.5-meters wide and 8 meters high, the 9 rows of script leaning at a 150-degree angle. The face of the rock is light tannish pink and shows water scouring. The letters are 6 to 8 mm wide, 4 to 5 mm deep and 40 mm long. There are 12 large, blue gray spall scars, some of the characters chiseled into these scars. Smaller spall scars are scored around some of the individual letters, which seem to have been sharpened by a steel mason's chisel.

The enormous interest concerning the origin and meaning of the "Mystery Stone" is a reward in and of itself, and, to some, equal to any alternative or definitive answers that may be found to its riddles. The eleven known hypotheses about the Stone would, each in their own right, provide tantalizing plots for tales of New Mexico's past. Seven investigations can be considered minor in that the researchers did not carry out extensive translation of the Stone's message, drawing only inferences patched together from bits of historical information, some knowledge of ancient writing and a lot of lore and legend. Some investigators merely projected their favorite theme based upon little or no physical evidence. However, each commentary about the Stone stands as a distinct and intriguing premise.

Lewis R. Church claimed that the carvings describe the location of a gold cache that was hidden by the Acoma Pueblo people preceding the eruption of Mount Taylor (Church). Bill Mack asserted that the message on the Stone was left by a settlement of Romans who prospered in the Southwest as early as the 9th Century A.D. (Mack). H.W. Stowell claimed that the Stone's glyph was made by one of the ten lost Tribes of Israel (Stonwell). Jack Kutz proposed that the site was visited in Biblical times by an extra-terrestrial who left "a coded message within a message within a message — the Ten Commandments." (49)

A comprehensive discussion by Barry Fell considers the entirety of the inscriptions, pictographs, petroglyphs, coins and cairns that were supposedly left by visitors to North America who might have come from Europe, Africa or Asia. Fell's examination of the evidence persuaded him to propose a number of hypotheses about the early presence of these foreigners.

His proposed scenarios include: the arrival of Carthaginian traders and Phoenician manufacturers that crossed the North American continent in 325 BC; early visitations by Libyan, Greek, Iberian, or Roman traders; the appearance of Jewish emigrants after the destruction of Jerusalem in 69AD; the entrance of Jews emigrating after the second Jewish revolution in 13AD; a landing by North African Christian emigrants running from the Vandals; Libyan emigrants arriving in 559 AD; Moslem and Christian Celts coming after 700AD, and, later, the advent of a Viking and Norman presence (28).

Professor Pfeiffer, a Harvard Professor from the Semitic Museum and the only Stone interpreter with expertise in Semitic languages, completed a translation in 1949 that reads—"Line I: I am Yahweh thy God who brought thee out of the land. Line 2: (added) There shall not be unto them other gods before Me. Line 3: …of Egypt, out of the house of bondage. Thou shalt not make unto thee a graven image. Thou shalt not take. Line 4: The name of Yahweh in vain. Remember the day Line 5: of the Sabbath to sanctify it. Honor thy father and mother that…Line 6: Thy days shall be long on the soil which Yahweh thy God Line 7: … giveth thee. Thou shalt not kill. Thou shalt not commit adultery. Thou shalt not steal. Thou shalt not Line 8: testify falsely against thy neighbor. Thou shalt not covet thy neighbor's wife." (65)

Frank Hibben of the Anthropology Department at the University of New Mexico and Ferenc Szasz and Frank Wozniak of the UNM History Department all recognize Pfeiffer's translation, but do not accept its derivation as being from the Near East (80). Hibben suggests that the Mormons created the inscription when they first came into the West. Szasz and

Ancient Greek and Phoenician language

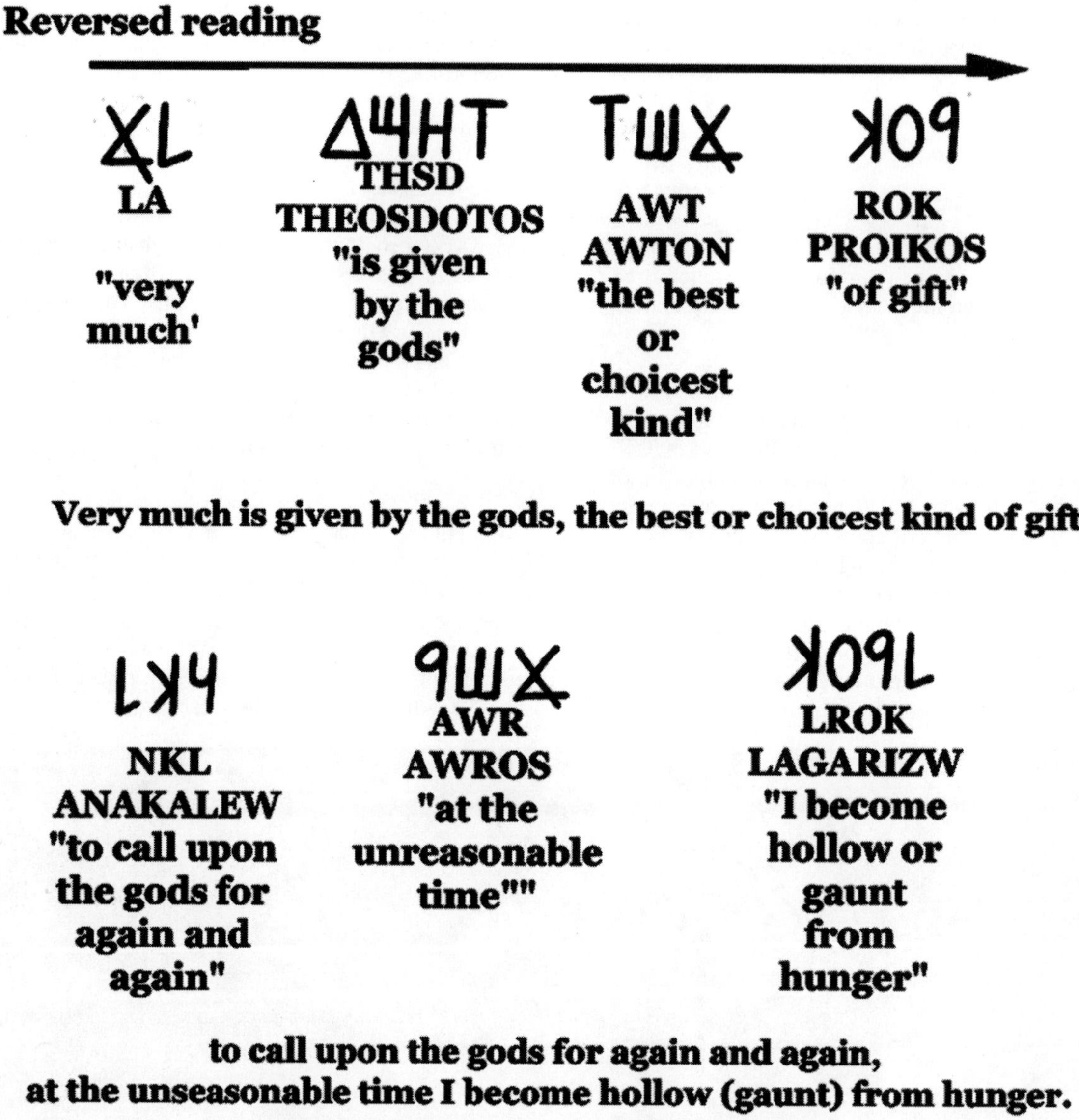

Reversed reading

XL
LA

"very much'

Δ4HT
THSD
THEOSDOTOS
"is given by the gods"

TШX
AWT
AWTON
"the best or choicest kind"

ꓘO9
ROK
PROIKOS
"of gift"

Very much is given by the gods, the best or choicest kind of gift,

LꓘႷ
NKL
ANAKALEW
"to call upon the gods for again and again"

9ШX
AWR
AWROS
"at the unreasonable time""

ꓘO9L
LROK
LAGARIZW
"I become hollow or gaunt from hunger"

to call upon the gods for again and again,
at the unseasonable time I become hollow (gaunt) from hunger.

Transalation of the Mystery Stone by Dixie Perkins

Wosniak, who held professional historical credentials, declared the inscription to be of recent, but legitimate, origin They claimed that it was carved by Andres Muniz, an interpreter for the Dominquez-Escalante Expedition, in 1776 AD.

They based their conclusions on the existence of the flowery initials, "A.M." near the inscription. They analyzed the "A.M." and compared it to the one left at El Morro Monument. El Morro was a watering hole and stopping off point in prehistoric times, and was also used by the Conquistadors who made their marks on the soft sandstone walls. Szasz and Wosniak note that Muniz is a Jewish name. Therefore, they concluded that Muniz, who was

secretly a Jew, had camped nearby. Muniz had become dissatisfied with Escalante and as a Jew, used the Old Testament to rebuke him. (80)

In addition to Pfieffer's earliest translation there were two other investigators, each of whom did extensive translations of the inscription. Like Pfieffer, these individuals possessed distinctive, but different, backgrounds and skill mixes. In 1964, Robert H. La Follette provided one of the more complex and bizarre renderings of the Stone's glyphs (50, Pg. 10-11). Employing his knowledge of the Phoenician, Hebrew, Cyrillic, Etruscan, and Egyptian languages, he applied Navajo meaning to the oral pronunciations of the words he formulated, claiming that the words were composed around 2000 BC by ancestors of Navajo emigrating to North America from the Palestine-Phoenician regions.

According to La Follette the inscription read: "We retreated while under attack, continually moving ahead; then we traveled over the surface of the water; then we climbed, without eating. They surrounded us from above, some hiding among rocks, scattered and alone, while part of them remained together and took us by surprise. We found that they were afraid, so we did a fearful thing to them, for their coming against us! Just when we were greatly in need of water, we had rain. They were surprised to see us wearing shoes for crossing the land along the trail behind us. It is good hanging down the meat (we learned from them) and it was soon ready. We were grateful for what they gave us to carry away.

We were about to run away, but found they went about the land and we found there was a change of weather on the land." (50)

The most intriguing interpretation of the origin and meaning of the Mystery Stone, one determined by a multidisciplinary approach, was published in 1979 by Dixie L. Perkins, (65). Whether true or not, the story she pried from the Stone's face is an epoch of awesome proportions. Perkins heard about the Stone on a program entitled "Mysteries of the Desert," broadcast in the early 1970's by KOB-TV in Albuquerque, New Mexico. Ms. Perkins had an interesting repertoire of skills — a proficiency in epigraphy, a deep grasp of ancient history and a facility with ancient languages. She also had considerable experience in decipherment and translation of ancient 3500-year-old cuneiform.

Although we were afraid, we proceeded to the river, throwing our bodies and feet in the water, and bringing water back to the others who carried the burdens in the hot sun as they climbed the side of the hill. Then an omen or sign in front of us on the slope or ledge pointed at (to stop and camp). In the water we sat down. Then we found something still farther on. It was on the shore of the river. It was discovered that they were all meeting us to help us build and get our dwellings ready. In the water we sat down and camped on the surface above where we took land.

Ms. Perkins undergirds her thesis by stating that at the time of her research, archaeologists and epigraphers acknowledged the authenticity of many ancient rock inscriptions. Quoting Barry Fell, she claimed that such inscriptions had been carved by Old World peoples centuries before Christ. Ms. Perkins cited the New Mexico Mystery Stone inscription as one of the finest pre-Colombian examples ever found in terms of its completeness, length and lucidity. She first addresses the issue of whether or not there is sufficient evidence to support the claim that ancient Old World travelers came to the Western Hemisphere before the Vikings and Columbus.

In her affirmative response to this concern, Perkins submits that the intense activity around the Mediterranean generated the essential knowledge for sea travel. Her line of reasoning suggests that such

View eastward from the canyon

skills were owned by the Phoenicians, who were fearless navigators. Furthermore, Perkins claims that trade and freedom were the motives for exploration. Evidence of a Libyan presence in Polynesia was surfacing at the time of her research.

The Phoenicians established colonies, and gained sophisticated information about sea currents and winds, information then acquired by Greek sailors. Mariners traveled to other lands to explore, trade and settle the land. But, it was profit that drove these sailors to find the New World centuries before Christ. According to Perkins, records of old-world excursions across the globe and into the Western Hemisphere were destroyed when the Romans burned Carthage, an act that halted sea travel beyond the Mediterranean for many centuries.

A second issue addressed by Perkins involves evidence in support of the position that the writing chiseled on the rock on Hidden Mountain was concurrent with what was in use 2,500 years ago on the Greek island of Samos. Perkins' analysis attempts to establish the writing as that of the Phoenician-Greek alphabet used in 500 BC, postulating that the particular use of the symbol "W" for an "O" was used on Samos in 500 BC. Writing from right to left, the absence of vowels and the exclusive use of capital letters were said to be characteristic of writing at that time. The absence of vowels (which were in a sense understood in the discourse) made it possible to say a lot in a little space, as was the case in the Mystery

Stone inscription. Ms. Perkins' facility in decipherment, her knowledge of ancient Phoenician-Greek, and the assistance of a several other scholars in ancient languages established the plausibility Perkins' interpretation of the Stone's origin and meaning.

The third issue addressed by Ms. Perkins builds an argument in support of an early Greek arrival, those travelers having had the capability, and no doubt the desire, to chisel a story on the face of a lava rock. Perkins claims that Zakyneros came from Greece's Island of Samos, which is located at the eastern end of the Mediterranean. She maintains that his visit was the first of its kind into New Mexico, and that it was recorded due to his knowledge of ancient sea travel and his writing ability, skills representing the enormous achievements of the Mediterranean peoples.

Perkins' hypotheses challenged the prevalent attitude in the 1907's that inscription by ancient cultures from Europe, Africa and Asia could not be present in the "New World." Perkins pointed out that hundreds of inscribed rocks carved by Europeans and North Africans who lived in 800-200 BC had recently been uncovered in the Americas by "scholars." She points to evidence of pioneering Celts, Phoenician traders from the Iberian Peninsula and Egyptian-Libyan sailors having left rock records from the Gulf of Mexico to the middle western states. Perkins offers evidence of the hundreds of detailed decipherments done by researcher Barry Fell (28) to support the visitations of the Old World travelers. Gravestones of an early 800-600 BC settlement in the Susquehanna River Valley of Pennsylvania contain-

The Rio Puerco once flowed

ing early Celtic, Iberian, Basque and Phoenician writing are offered as specific data supporting her position.

Perkins notes as well the existence of light skinned, blue-eyed people among Native Americans, physical characteristics observed by early explorers, particularly among the Mandan Nation, as evidence of early contact and colonizations by the Old World. Many tribes, including the Mayas and the Incas, have oral traditions mentioning contact with "white" and "bearded" men. Exploration in the Old World was in fact discouraged. In order to protect their trade resources, Phoenician-Carthaginian sailors allegedly manufactured the presence of giant sea monsters and spoke of the terror of entrapment in endless seas of seaweed, hoping to frighten those who might enter their territory.

The fourth and key question that Perkins addressed was her translation and interpretation of what Zakyneros recorded on the Mystery Stone. First, she had to identify each letter of the Phoenician-Greek alphabet. From the micro-translation of individual letters, the more complex task of determining and defining each word in the narrative was carried out and verified by a number of other scholars. The ancient Greek words were then transcribed into English words, phases and sentences. The specifics of Perkins' step by step translation can be found in her monograph, THE MEANING OF THE NEW MEXICO MYSTERY STONE, by Dixie L. Perkins, published by Sun Books, Sun Publishing Co., Albuquerque, New Mexico. (65)

According to Perkins, climatological and natural history research indicates that Zakyneros entered a relatively empty central New Mexico in 500 BC. He probably traveled from the Gulf of Mexico up the Rio Grande to the place where the Rio Puerco River joins the Rio Grande. One can only surmise why he chose to go up the Rio Puerco. As his message suggests, he may have been running from his pursuers. At that time, the mesas of central New Mexico were covered with spruce and stretched far to the north along the Lucero Basin, where a crack in tectonic plates make up what is called the Rio Grande Trough.

The Anasazi had not yet arrived, and only scattered Paleo Indian bands wandered the land gathering berries and fruit and hunting the bison and wooly mammoth. Perkins discusses detailed evidence of a very wet climate being present in the time of Zakyneros's stay. Such a rainy climate would provide ample flora and fauna along the Rio Puerco to sustain the exiled sailor. Zakyneros, totally alone in his refuge above the Rio Puerco River, recorded a weather report, laying claim as the first New Mexico weatherman.

Perkins discussed the fact that it was fairly common for Greeks of that time to register their feelings, ideas and experiences. Zakyneros, apparently unfazed by the rigors of daily existence, had time to carve his story with an iron or bronze tool. Iron or bronze tools of European origin have been found in the United States. If an individual named Zakyneros actually wrote the message, it is the most detailed inscription recorded in the Southwest, one whose impression reaches far across time. Perkins' translation of the inscription reads as follows:

"The other one (another) met with an untimely death one year ago; dishonored, insulted, and stripped of flesh; the men thought him to be an object of care, whom I looked after, considered crazed, wandering, in mind, to be tossed about as if in a wind; to perish, streaked with blood. On Samos I was respected and honored of blessed lot or fortune, with a body of slaves and so many olive trees; also, I set (planted) them, a peg to hang anything upon! Men punished me with exile to exact retribution for a debt; meanwhile I remain or stay a hare (rabbit). I, Zakyneros, just as, (just like) a soothsayer or prophet, out of reach of mortal man, I am fleeing and am very afraid.

I am dross, scum, refuse, just as (just like) on board ship, a soft, effeminate sailor (seaman) is flogged with an animal's hide or all who speak incorrectly or, offensively are lashed or beaten with a cane; but after a little, or a very short time the hurtful and destructive ones may be sated (satisfied); at an unseasonable time I remain (stay) to protect (guard) from the west, many south or southwest winds, the hollow (ravine). Very much is harvest, (ripe fruits or crop) is gathered in; very much is in the woody dell and glen, very much (many) bags of young deer. Very much (many) bands or hides with delicate, luxuriant hair; by the channel of a river, swift-flowing. Very much is given by the gods, the best or choicest kind of gift, to call upon the gods for again and again, at the unseasonable time I become hollow (gaunt) from hunger." (65, pgs. 41-53)

Perkins not only applied her knowledge of language and ability at deciphering, but also her knowledge of ancient societies, particularly Greece, to flesh out an interpretation of Zakyneros' story. "Come up" suggests that Zakyneros was situated in a safe harbor near Hidden Mountain, and that he journeyed up the Rio Grande and the Rio Puerco to escape and forge for food. Zakyneros apparently had a companion who, being either mentally retarded or imbalanced, irritated the group, causing him to be whipped to death.

Individuals were enslaved and exiled either for debt and/or political reasons, and Zakyneros does say that his exile was due to debt. It was common in Ancient Greece to exile political rivals or debtors for periods of up to ten years without dispossessing them of either their citizenship or their material wealth. Zakyneros mentioned his wealth in Olive trees and his ownership of slaves. The reference to Olive trees and the use of the "W" symbol for "O" was identified by Perkins as evidence of Zakyneros' Samos origins.

Perkins' interpretation of the Mystery Stone weaves a fascinating tale about a man who escaped and lived at the Hidden Mountain site for a year, a man who considered himself alone and removed from the main stream of civilization like the prophets of his day. Perkins' familiarity with ancient history led her to believe that Zakyneros' statement of "being like a flayed seaman" supports historical data stating that, in Zakyneros' day, individuals were flogged for bad grammar by the highly literate Greeks.

Zakyneros describes rainy weather and the threat of southwest winds to his harvest, one probably made up of berries, nuts and some local grains, possibly even primitive corn. The Rio Puerco would have supplied him with plenty of water and fish. Perkins maintains that his reference to deer and hides confirm the high value Greeks placed on leather and fur. Finally, Zakyneros' expression of gratitude to the Gods that he felt had saved him from starvation, and who continued to sustain his life, was characteristic of the spiritual orientation of the times.

Perkins uses an example in her translation of the key word in the opening of the inscription—ANKM. By filling in the necessary roots and vowels, the Greek word ANIKNEOMAI emerges, which translates into English as "I have come up to this point or place." Details and illustrations of the original letters and words, their decipherment into Greek words and their final translation to English are included in the Sun Publishing monograph.

Fascination abounds concerning the premise of a Greek sailor's visit to New Mexico 2,500 years ago. The proposition stimulates the imagination, and would make a superb tale for a creative non-fiction movie. But, the adage that "truth is stranger than fiction" prevails in the case of the Mystery Stone, and the real value of any phenomenon can only be increased with each bit of scientific evidence supporting or negating its hypothetical origins and meanings.

Finally, a number of individuals propose the Mystery Stone inscription to be only a turn of the century hoax by college pranksters.

Two major questions remain to be answered about the Stone. What does the Stone mean? Who made it and where did they come from? Winters suggests that the answers to these questions can be divided into three major hypothetical dramas: a) An ancient group of Near Eastern visitor(s) created the inscription, or, b) It was produced by Native Americans or other Americans with a knowledge of Phoenician-like writing, or, c) It is a hoax.

Joseph C. Winter (92) in an unpublished white paper provided by the New Mexico State Land Office attacks the two major hypotheses from several vantage points. First, he rejects the hypothesis of "evidence of contact" by pre-Columbian visitors from the Near East or other parts of world on the basis that there is no supporting evidence — no artifacts, manuscripts, walls, rooms or cities. All inferences are based on nothing but the glyphs. Second, Winter points out errors or variances in translations, which produce three totally diverse interpretations. Rather than scientific evidence, Winter claims that the three translations and interpretations are projections and bizarre extrapolations on the part of the translators. Third, Winter maintains that Perkins was not a professional, but was considered a "layman" with little expertise in languages, and that she used roundabout interpretations. Fourth, Winters accepts Pfeiffer as a respected expert on ancient Semitic languages. He points out that the translation is logical and coherent, and that there is a confirmed origin of characters, those being Phoenician, Moabitic and Greek. However, the Semitic nature of the characters used to inscribe the Ten Commandments could have been carved by Mormons or Hispanics or some other group of people.

Winter chooses to support the hypothesis of a turn of the century hoax, one perpetuated by university students from the University of New Mexico or New Mexico A & M. He provides six lines of reasoning, citing evidence or lack thereof, to support the Hoax hypothesis.

1. Alternative explanations lack logic and offer no physical evidence to support such scenarios. Winter declares that there is no evidence of any Eastern-Mormon-Hispanic connections to the Mystery Stone — no artifacts, documents or structures. He states that the initials "AM" could mean anything, and that there are no reports of AM being a secret Jew much less of his camping there with the Escalante Expedition.

2. Winters cites physical evidence suggesting that the chisel cuts are of relatively recent origin. In support of this, he points out that the spell scars are gray-blue, rendering them recent and fresh. Although he observed that the chisel marks are crisp and clear, he feels they were executed by an inexperienced person, the effort resulting in large spalls with letters inside them. Also, no lichen, desert varnish, or weathering is evident on the carvings. Winters estimates the carvings to be 50 to 60 years old, and bases this estimate on his experience in dating petroglyphs and pictoglyphs.

3. Early researchers and students who studied the Stone had often found questionable alleged evidence that the inscription was known before 1911 (report by the Ranch family). However, the site was visited in the 1930's, and the only documentation of the Stone's existence that can be found to date was that recorded in 1936 by Frank Hibben of the Anthropology Department at UNM.

Hibben claimed that Mormons executed the inscription when they first came to the West. The most damming evidence against an ancient origin was found, or shall we say, not found, in Adolph Bandelier's description of the Anasazi Village atop Hidden Mountain. In 1883, using a local guide, Bandelier climbed to top of the Mountain, constructing a detailed map of the village and the mountain-top. Bandelier made no mention of an inscription, a fact even more revealing in that the only physical trail to top went right past the rock.

4. In the 1930's, it was widely believed that the inscription was of student production. Consensual oral history of former University of New Mexico professors and scholars asserts that the inscription was created in the 1930's. Professors Reiter and Hill of the University of New Mexico Anthropology Department always maintained that the carvings were inscribed around 1936. Reiter's widow confirmed this opinion. It was also suggested that someone from the Soccoro School of Mines produced it. Lez Hass of the UNM Art Department. was told by Professor Hill that anthropology students did the deed and were almost expelled for it. Florence Ellis of the University of New Mexico Anthropology Department went so far as to maintain that there was nothing to the inscription from a scientific standpoint.

5. Resources were accessible for the Mystery Stone's creation. Phoenician, Hebrew and Greek dictionaries, alphabets and grammar books were available in the University of New Mexico library. There were also polylingual Greek-Hebrew bibles containing the Ten Commandments, written in Phoenician. The availability of these resources would have made it very easy to construct a legitimate looking version of Ten Commandments in Phoenician, Moabite (Paleo-Hebrew) and Greek.

6. The high correlation of the elements characteristic of the Mystery Stone carvings with the inscription, "HOVE/EVA/3-9-30" suggests common authors. "HOBE/EVA/3-9-30" at the Mystery Stone Inscription site and the "Sore Foot Canyon" glyph are close enough in size, chisel marks and other features to suggest that they were done by the same person(s) at the same time.

The scientific tradition precludes "proving" any fact, concept or theory. Only observations in support of or contrary to a position (hypothesis) are gathered and analyzed by the relevant disciplines. Then, an accepted regimen must be applied to provide answers to any of the riddles that the Mystery Stone presents. The presence of and inscription by a Greek sailor in his exile at the Las Lunas site in 500 BC enthralls the imagination and appeals to the romantic bent in all of us, even hard core social scientists. Like any other phenomenon, more sophisticated observations, new techniques and the growth of related fields of knowledge can be used to shed more light on the origin and meaning of the Mystery Stone.

While it appears that current sets of observations and logic suggest that the origin of the inscriptions occurred in the last hundred years and were carved by persons unknown for unknown reasons, it would be premature to suggest that it was a hoax. Further observations may well add new information concerning the enigma of the Stone. Excavation for archaeological material at the site has never been done. A microscopic and metallurgic analysis of the inscripted chisel marks for metallic residues could be carried out to ascertain the nature of the carving tool. Carbon dating could be applied to any desert varnish that might have accumulated on the letters and be compared to nearby samples. The analysis and interpretation of the inscription could be independently confirmed by a scholar from the Mediterranean, one with no knowledge of the location and background of the Stone.

As in the case of the famous cold fusion discovery at the University of Utah, the validity of the process would not be replicated and confirmed by other sci-

The 500 Foot Totem Pole

The Land of Time Enough and Room Enough

entists. In the case of the Shroud of Turin, for example, new evidence continually emerges, revising the evaluations made of its nature and origins.
Hopefully, someone will initiate further study of the Stone before time and people obliterate it, relegating it to the realm of unsolved mysteries. In the meantime, an enjoyable evening can certainly be spent contemplating the eleven explanations of the Mystery Stone's meaning.

In any event, the case for Zakyneros' presence in 500 BC in a canyon refuge on Hidden Mountain will continue to be the subject of campfire discussion across northern Arizona and New Mexico for years to come. Those who "obsess to possess" the quintessentials of Route 66 can, thanks to Dixie Perkins, now aspire to know the secret of the first tourist and the first motel on New Mexico's Route 66.

Selected Bibliography

1. Aaseng, Nathan. NAVAJO CODE TALKERS. New York: Walker, 1992.

2. ARIZONA HIGHWAYS MAGAZINE. April, 1992.

3. Baars, Donald L. BEYOND THE SPECTACULAR IN MONUMENT VALLEY, NAVAJO TRIBAL PARK: A VISITOR'S INTRODUCTION. Grand Junction, Colorado: Cañon-Publishers, 1998.

4. Babbitt, James. "Historic Trading Posts-Trading Posts along the Little Colorado River." PLATEAU MAGAZINE, Flagstaff, Arizona: Museum of Northern Arizona, Volume. 576, No.3, 1986.

5. BAKER, Arthur A. GEOLOGY OF THE MONUMENT VALLEY- NAVAJO MOUNTAIN REGION, SAN JUAN COUNTY, UTAH. WASHINGTON. D.C, U.S. GOVERNMENT PRINTING OFFICE, 1936.

6. Banks, Leo W. "Holbrook Violence and Blood Triggered its Legend." ARIZONA HIGHWAYS, July 1992.

7. Barnes, Will C. (Will Croft). TALES FROM THE X-BAR HORSE CAMP: THE BLUE-ROAN 'OUTLAW' AND OTHER STORIES. Chicago, IL: The Breeders' Gazette, 1920.

8. Barnes, Will C. (Will Croft). GUNFIGHT IN APACHE COUNTY, 1887: THE SHOOTOUT BETWEEN SHERIFF C. P. OWENS AND THE BLEVINS BROTHERS IN HOLBROOK, ARIZONA. Tucson, AZ: Trail To Yesterday Books, 1997.

9. Barnes, Will C. ARIZONA PLACE NAMES. Tucson, Arizona: University of Arizona Press, 1935.

10. Barringer, D. Moreau. "Meteorite Search." NATURAL HISTORY MAGAZINE, May 1964.

11. Billison, Dr. Samuel. President, Navajo Code Talkers. Personal Interview by Author, 2001.

12. Bixler, Margaret. THE WINDS OF FREEDOM: THE STORY OF THE NAVAJO CODE TALKERS OF WORLD WAR II. Darien: Two Bytes, 1992.

13. CENTENNIAL MEMORIES-1981, City of Holbrook, 1981.

14. Intertribal Indian Ceremonial Committee. CEREMONIAL MAGAZINE - 1958, Gallup, New Mexico: Ceremonial Committee, August 1958.

15. Chronic, Halka. ROADSIDE GEOLOGY OF ARIZONA. Missoula: Mountain Press Publishing Company, 1983.

16. Church, Lewis R. "New Mexico's Lost City of Gold." WESTERN TREASURES, August 1968.

17. Colton, H. S. "A Brief Summary of the Early Expeditions into Northern Arizona." NORTHERN ARIZONA MUSEUM NOTES 2 (1930) 9.

18. Coues, Elliot. ON THE TRAIL OF A SPANISH PIONEER: THE DIARY AND ITINERARY OF FRANCISCO GARCES (MISSIONARY PRIEST) IN HIS TRAVELS THROUGH SONORA, ARIZONA, AND CALIFORNIA, 1775-1776.New York: F.P. Harper, 1900.

19. Creamer, Winifred and Hass, Jonathan. "Search for the Ancient Ones' Pueblo." NATIONAL GEOGRAPHIC, 180 (1991) 4: 84-99.

20. Crozier, Bruce. Personal Interview by Author. November, 2000.

21. Davis, Ronald L. JOHN FORD: HOLLYWOOD'S OLD MASTER. Norman: University of Oklahoma, 1995.

22. De Roos, Robert William. MONUMENT VALLEY: AN EXPLORATION OF A RED-ROCK LAND WHERE THE DESERT BECOMES MAGIC AND WONDER. Flagstaff, Arizona: Northland Press, 1965.

23. Dedera, Don. A LITTLE WAR OF OUR OWN: THE PLEASANT VALLEY FEUD REVISITED. Flagstaff, Arizona: Northland Press, 1988.

24. DenDooven, K. Camille. MONUMENT VALLEY: THE STORY BEHIND THE SCENERY. Las Vegas, Nevada: KC Publications, 1992.

25. Dodge, Col. Richard Irving. THIRTY-THREE YEARS AMONG OUR WILD INDIANS. Hartford, Connecticut: A.D. Worthington and Company, 1882.

26. Draper, Teddy, Jr., Marine Corporal, Navajo Code Talker. Personal Interview by Author. May, 1995.

27. Favour, A. H. (Alpheus H.). OLD BILL WILLIAMS MOUNTAIN MAN. Chapel Hill: University of North Carolina Press, 1936.

28. Fell, Barry. SAGA AMERICA. New York. Times Books, 1980.

29. Fergusson, Erna. OUR SOUTHWEST. New York: Alfred A Knopf, 1940, 265.

30. Fireman, Bert M. "The Honeymoon Trail." ARIZONA HIGHWAYS, May 1978.

31. Fisher, Leonard Everett. TRACKS ACROSS AMERICA: THE STORY OF THE AMERICAN RAILROAD, 1825 - 1900. Holiday House, 1992.

32. Flynn, Errol. Letter written and mailed from Flagstaff, Arizona: unpublished document, November 1939.

33. Forrest, Earle R. ARIZONA'S DARK AND BLOODY GROUND. Caldwell, Idaho: Caxton

Printers, 1936.

34. Franklin, Garnette. Personal Interview based on article she wrote in the Arizona Republic, 2001.

35. Gillette, Lil and Fenton, Katherine, "The Los Lunas Mystery Rock." NEW MEXICO MAGAZINE, September, 1975.

36. Grattan, Virginia. MARY COLTER, BUILDER UPON THE RED EARTH. Grand Canyon, Arizona: Grand Canyon Natural History Association, 1992.

37. Gregory, Leslie. "Arizona's Haunted Walls of Silence." ARIZONA HIGHWAYS, October, 1947.

38. Griffith, Jance. Director, Interview, Old Trails Museum, Winslow, Arizona

39. Griffth, Kenny A. "Old Solitaire-Bill Williams." TRUE WEST, Volume. 17, No. 1, Sept.-Oct., 1969.

40. Hanchett, Leland J. ARIZONA'S GRAHAM-TEWKSBURY FEUD. Phoenix, Arizona: Pine Rim Publishing, 1994

41. Harvik, Dan. "Canyon Diablo Train Robbery." FRONTIER TIMES, Volume. 45, No.1, December-January, 1971

42. Hayden, Scott. "Old Bill Williams' Favorite Mountain." ARIZONA HIGHWAYS, Volume. 33, No. 3, March, 1957

43. Houk, Rose. "Five dead outlaws leave no clues to $125,000 in buried loot. (1881 stage-coach robbery near Canyon Diablo in Arizona)." ARIZONA HIGHWAYS, v. 70, April, 1994, p. 48-9.

44. Jones, Catherine. NAVAJO CODE TALKERS: NATIVE AMERICAN HEROES. Greensboro: Tudor Publishers, 1997.

45. Kant, Candace C. ZANE GREY'S ARIZONA. Flagstaff, Arizona: Northland Press, 1984.

46. Kildare, Maurice. (A Pen Name for Gladwell Richardson), "Apache Death Cave." BIG WEST, December, 1967.

47. Kildare, Maurice. (A Pen Name for Gladwell Richardson). "Cave of Death." DESERT MAGAZINE, September, 1967.

48. Klinck, Richard E. LAND OF ROOM ENOUGH AND TIME ENOUGH. Salt Lake City: G.M. Smith, Publisher, 1984.

49. Kutz, Jack. "New Mexico's Mystery Stone." DESERT MAGAZINE, 1973.

50. La Follette, Robert Hoath. THE ROCK THAT GIVES EVERY WORD WISHED. Dallas: Triangle Publishing Co., 1964.

51. Lagerquist, Syble. PHILIP JOHNSTON AND THE NAVAJO CODE TALKERS. Billings: Reading Publications, Montana Indian Publication Fund, 1975

52. Mack, Bill. "An Ancient Roman Settlement in America." ARGOSY, March, 1972

53. Martin, Judy. ARIZONA WALLS: IF ONLY THEY COULD SPEAK. Phoenix, Arizona: Double B Publications, 1997.

54. Mays, Carelton. "Broken-Hand Fitzpatrick, Mountain Man Extraordinary." REAL WEST, Volume. IX, No. 47, May 1966.

55. Mike, Richard. Son of Marine Navajo Code Talker, King Mike. Personal Interview by Author.

56. Miller, Joseph. MONUMENT VALLEY AND THE NAVAJO COUNTRY, ARIZONA & UTAH. New York: Hastings House, 1951.

57. Moody, Ralph. THE OLD TRAILS WEST. New York, T. Y. Crowell Co., 1963.

58. Moon, Samuel. TALL SHEEP - HARRY GOULDING, MONUMENT VALLEY TRADER. Norman, OK: University of Oklahoma Press, 1992.

59. Nelson, Gary. Personal Interview by Author, 2001.

60. Newman, Dr. Terrance. Personal Interview by Author, 2000.

61. Nininger, H. H. "Visitor from A Distant Planet." DESERT MAGAZINE, July, 1942.

62. Noe, Sally W. GREETINGS FROM GALLUP: SIX DECADES OF ROUTE 66. Gallup, N.M.: Gallup Downtown Development Group, 1991.

63. Patterson, Alex A. FIELD GUIDE TO ROCK ART SYMBOLS OF THE GREATER SOUTHWEST. Boulder, Colorado: Johnson Printing Company, 1992.

64. Paul, Doris Atkinson. THE NAVAJO CODE TALKERS. Philadelphia: Dorrance, 1973.

65. Perkins, Dixie L. THE MEANING OF THE NEW MEXICO MYSTERY STONE. Sun Books. Albuquerque: Sun Publishing Co. 1979.

66. Poling-Kempes, Lesley. THE HARVEY GIRLS: WOMEN WHO OPENED THE WEST. New York: Paragon House, 1989.

67. Poling-Kempes, Lesley. ALBUQUERQUE MORNING JOURNAL, July 29, 1911.

68. Potter, Albert F. Unpublished document, 1974.

69. Richardson, Gladwell. "Old Wolf Trading Post," Serially in the WINSLOW MAIL and THE (Flagstaff) COCONINO SUN, 1939.

70. Richardson, Gladwell. "A Drink for the Dead." ARIZONA HIGHWAYS, Volume. 39, No. 6. June, 1963.

71. Richardson, Gladwell. TWO GUNS, ARIZONA, Series of Americana: No. 15, Santa Fe, New Mexico: Press of the Territorian, 1967.

72. Richardson, Gladwell. ."Arizona's Mystery Cave." ARIZONA MAGAZINE, December 3, 1967.

73. Wilson, Roscoe. ARIZONA REPUBLIC, 1975

74. Sheffer, H. Henry. THE PLEASANT VALLEY

WAR: CATTLE AND SHEEP DON'T MIX. Apache Junction, Arizona: Norseman Publications, Elite Promotions, 1995.

75. Sparks, William. THE APACHE KID - A BEAR FIGHT, AND OTHER TRUE STORIES OF THE OLD WEST. Los Angeles: Skelton, 1926.

76. Stanton, Bette L. (Bette Larsen). WHERE GOD PUT THE WEST: MOVIE MAKING IN THE DESERT - A MOAB-MONUMENT VALLEY MOVIE HISTORY. Moab, Utah: Four Corners Publications, 1994

77. Stocker, Joseph. "Arizona's Wonderful Hole in the Ground." ARIZONA DAYS AND WAYS MAGAZINE, November 16, 1958.

78. Stores, James. Personal Interview by Author. 2001.

79. Stowell, H.W. "Mystery Inscription." NEW MEXICO, August, 1961.

80. Szasz, Ferenc M. and Wozniak, Frank E. "Pre-Columbian Contacts in the American Southwest: Theories and Evidence." NEW MEXICO HUMANITIES REVIEW, 1 982.

81. THE RAILROAD GAZZETTE, May, 1882.

82. Thomas, Bob. "Shoot-out in Canyon Diablo." ARIZONA HIGHWAYS, Volume. 75, No 9 (September, 1999).

83. Thomas, Gail Ingledew. Personal Inteview, 2000.

84. Trimble, Marshall. ROADSIDE HISTORY OF ARIZONA, ROADSIDE HISTORY SERIES, Missoula: Mountain Press Publishing Co., 1986.

85. Tuska, Jon. THE AMERICAN WEST IN FILM-CRITICAL APPROACHES TO THE WEST-ERN. Westport, Connecticut: Greenwood Press, 1985.

86. Udall, Stewart L. CORONADO AND OUR SPANISH LEGACY TO THE INLAND EMPIRE. 1987

87. Berlin: New York: Wasson, John T. METE-ORITES: CLASSIFICATION AND PROPER-TIES. Berlin; New York: Springer-Verlag, 1974.

88. Wayte, Harold C., Jr. "Old Blevins House Was Scene of Famous Gunfight." A HISTORY OF HOLBROOK AND THE LITTLE COLORADO COUNTRY (1540-1962). Thesis (M.A.) - University of Arizona. Tucson: University of Arizona, 1962.

89. Willis, Larry. "Commodore Perry Owens." TRUE WEST LEGENDS, Volume. 46, No. 8, August 1, 1999.

90. Wilson, Roscoe. ARIZONA REPUBLIC, 1975

91. Winslowe, John R. "The Devils Canyon," THRILLING WESTERN, July, 1950.

92. Winter, Joseph C. "Mystery of the Mystery Stone," Unpublished paper. Albuquerque: New Mexico Land Commission, 1984.

93. ARIZONA (PHEONIX) REPUBLIC, 1926-2001.

94. COCONINO (FLAGSTAFF) SUN, 1936-1939.

95. ARIZONA HISTORICAL REVIEW, 1926-1936.

96. THE GALLUP INDEPENDENT, 1930-1946.

97. NAVAJO COUNTY HISTORICAL SOCIETY, Unpublished document, 1987.

98. WINSLOW MAIL, 1993.

99. ALBUQUERQUE MORNING JOURNAL, 1911.

100. THE SANTA FE MAGAZINE, 1943.

Harvey Indian Detour Headquarters in Santa Fe, New Mexico

Map Legends

Symbols

CITIES AND TOWNS   Ⓦ

HISTORICAL SITES   23

PHYSICAL FEATURES   34

HIGHWAYS AND ROADS

Interstate

U.S. Highways

State Highways   93

Navajo Nation   60

Unimproved Local   ◆

Guidance for Visiting Various Sites

Many of the sites discussed in Volume One of Chronicles are hard to access, but certainly worth investigating for the thrill of adventure and going back-of-the-beyond in Route 66 country. For many, as it was with the author, the journey will be as exciting as exploring the destination. There is nothing like being at the spot where it happened. Each site and area has its own particular requirements for access — in terms of transportation, safety, and the right of passage. Many sites listed as "unimproved roads" require high center four wheel drives. Past and immediate weather conditions should be studied and locals asked about road conditions.

Appropriate clothing, shelter, food and water should be taken in case of inability to complete trips within one day. Caution should be taken climbing around rough canyon country. Being on the look out for snakes by avoiding heavy brush along streams and not reaching up into unseen canyon niches will serve you well The author has found that Mother Nature is unforgiving. Is important to be prepared for heat or cold.

While many lands are public, many of the sites noted are within land controlled either by the State, private entities or the Navajo and Hopi Nations. Private areas require permission and in some cases, special arrangements must be made to visit a site. The Navajo Nation yet remains as one of the few free

and open areas of the Southwest. Special care must be taken to close gates and not to go directly into sheep camp areas. When in doubt it is best to ask for permission from the local people, either at the sheep camp or at the local governmental unit, a Chapter House, which is found in most small centers.

Keeping our Southwest open for continued access for exploration and trekking into the unknown depends on how much respect is given to the land and its people.

Guide to Arizona West Map

TOWNS AND CITIES

Ashfork	R
Bullhead City	S
Kingman	T
Lake Havasu City	U
Needles, California	V
Peach Springs	W
Prescott	X
Seligman	Y
Williams, Arizona	Z

SITES-HISTORICAL AND NATURAL

Arizona Strip	70
Bill Williams Creek	71
Bill Williams Mt.	72
Boulder Dam	73
Colorado River	74
Grand Canyon 1	75
Havasupai Nation	76
Lake Mead	77
Wualpai Nation	78
Oatman	79

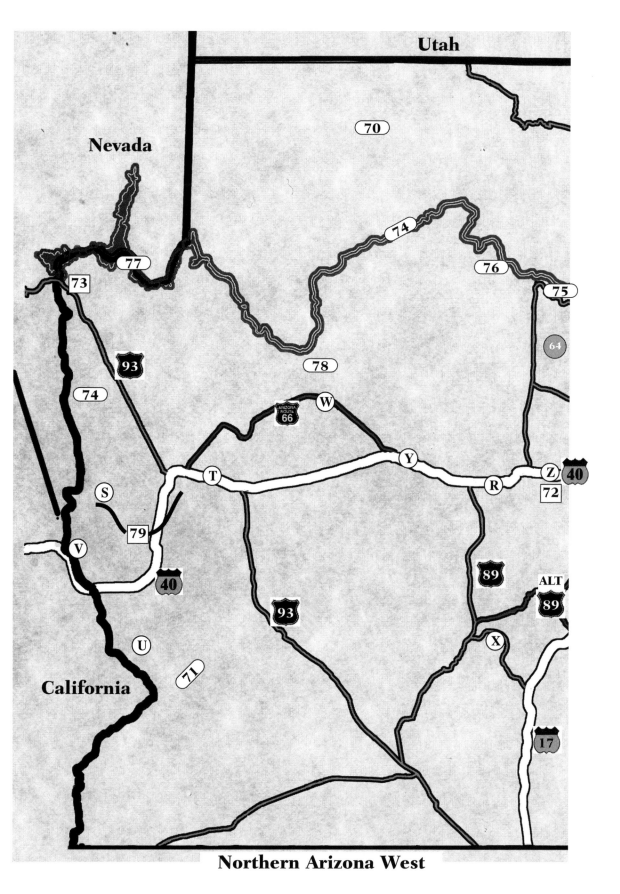

Northern Arizona West

Guide to Arizona East Map

TOWNS AND CITIES

Cameron,	A
Chinle	B
Flagstaff	C
Fort Defiance	D
Holbrook, Arizona	E
Hopi Villages	F
Joseph City	G
Kayenta.	H
Luepp	I
Payson	K
Page	J
Sedona	L
WIndow Rockm	M
Winslow	N

SITES

Brigham City.	1
Canyon Diablo	2
Cave of Death	3
Chevron Hills	4
Foxborro Ranch	5
Lee's Ferry	6
Painted Desert Inn	8
Sunset Crossing/Sunset	7
Tolchalco	9
Two Guns	10
Wolf's Trading Post	11

PHYSICAL FEATURES

Canyon de Chelly	12
Canyon Diablo	13
Chavez Pass	14
Cinder country	15
Clear Creek	16
Colorado River	17
Cottonwood Wash	18
Grand Falls	19
Hopi Buttes	20
Hoskannini Hideout	21
Lake Bitahochi	22
Lake Powell	23
Little Colorado River	24
Melgosa Desert	25
Meteor Crater	26
Moencopi Cliffs	27
Mogollon Rim	28
Monument Valley	29
Mormon Crossing	30
Mormon Lake	31
Oak Creek Canyon	32
Padre / Diablo Junction	33
Painted Desert	34
Petrified Forest	35
Pinta Road	36

Pleasant Valley	36
San Francisco Peaks	37
Schnebly Hill	38
Sunset Crater	39
Sunset Pass	40
Tucker Flat	41
Verde Valley	42
White Mountains	43

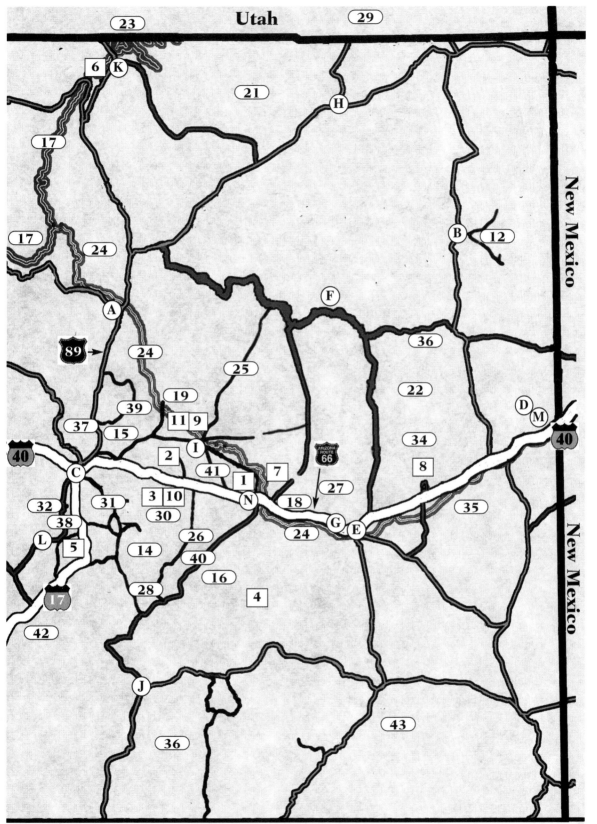

Northern Arizona East

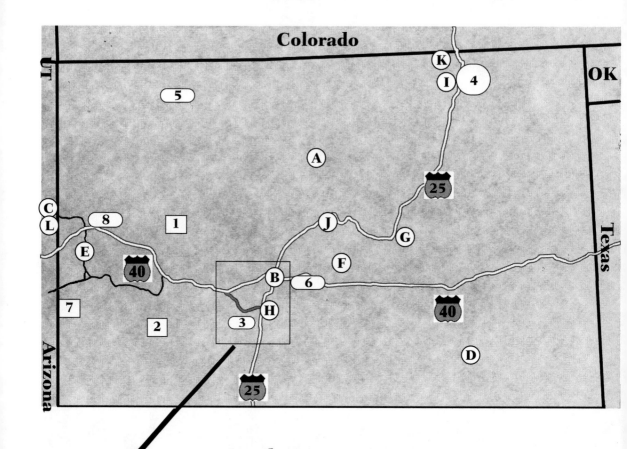

Northern New Mexico

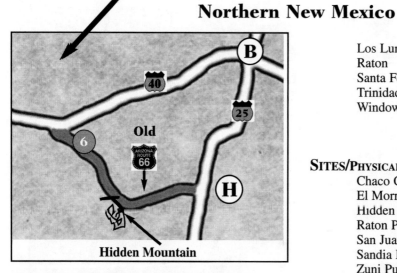

Hidden Mountain

Guide to Northern New Mexico

TOWNS AND CITIES

Taos	A
Albuquerque	B
Fort Defiance, Arizona	C
Fort Sumner	D
Gallup	E
Lamy	F
Las Vegas	G
Los Lunas	H
Raton	I
Santa Fe	J
Trinidad, Colorado	K
Window Rock, Arizona	L

SITES/PHYSICAL FEATURES

Chaco Canyon	1
El Morro National Monument	2
Hidden Mountain	3
Raton Pass	4
San Juan River	5
Sandia Mountains	6
Zuni Pueblo	7
Red Rock State Park	8

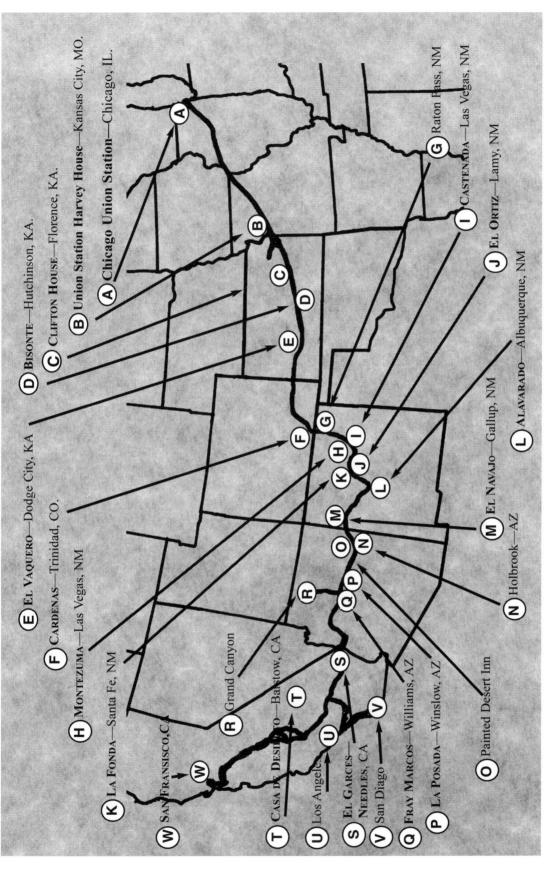

The Harvey Houses

A Chicago Union Station—Chicago, IL.
B Union Station Harvey House—Kansas City, MO.
C Clifton House—Florence, KA.
D Bisonte—Hutchinson, KA.
E El Vaquero—Dodge City, KA
F Cardenas—Trinidad, CO.
G Raton Pass, NM
H Montezuma—Las Vegas, NM
I Castenada—Las Vegas, NM
J El Ortiz—Lamy, NM
K La Fonda—Santa Fe, NM
L Alavarado—Albuquerque, NM
M El Navajo—Gallup, NM
N Holbrook—AZ
O Painted Desert Inn
P La Posada—Winslow, AZ
Q Fray Marcos—Williams, AZ
R Grand Canyon
S El Garces—Needles, CA
T Casa De Desierto—Barstow, CA
U Los Angeles, CA
V San Diago
W San Fransisco, CA

Montezuma Castle in Northern Arizona

Photo Credits

*Schauermann small and full size colored prints
may be accessed at *www.jwsoriginals.com*

Austin, Matthew -Kayenta, Arizona— (87)tl.

Brothers, Anne Mason

**Center for Southwest Research- Universilty of
New Mexico**— (19)tl; (33)tcp; (70)tr.

Coconino Sun ~ Flagstaff, Arizona— (28)tcp;
(108)tcp; (114)ml; br.

Cogdill, Mrs. Janie Severson— (133)ml; br;
(142)tl; tr; (143)tr; (144)tl; mr.

Colorado Historical Society— (22)bl; (40)tcp;
(42)tcp.

Crawley, Bill -Monument Valley Tours—
Monument Valley and John Wayne photos.

Crozier, Bruce— (115)tcp.

**Curt Teich-Lake Forest Discovery Museum, Lake
Forest, Illinois**— (48)tcp; (130)tcp; (140)mr;

Draper, Teddy-Chinle, Arizona— (122)mr.

Gallup Independent ~ Gallup, New Mexico

**Gallup Inter~Tribal Indian Ceremonial
Association**— (50)mr; (85)tcp; (93)mr; (96)tr.

Knowles Archives

La Font Monument Valley Lodge— (31)bcp;
(86)tcp; br; (88)tl; bl; br; (89)tl; tr; (90)bl; tr;
(91)tcp; (103)mr;

McCubbin, Robert G. -El Paso, Texas— (66)mr.

Mike, Richard~Kayenta, Arizona— (124)bl; br;
(125)tl; bl; mr; (126)tl; bl; tr; br; (127)bl.

**Museum of Albuquerque ~ City of
Albuquerque**— (103)tl; (121)tr; (138)tcp.

Navajo County Museum— (18)tl; (63)bcp.

New Mexico Department of Tourism— (14)mcp.

Northern Arizona Pioneer Historical Society—
(24)br; (41)bl; tr; (52)bl;

Northern Arizona University— (28)tcp; (32)tcp;
(37)tl; (39)tcp; (47)tl; (52)tr; (83)tl; (84)tcp;
(103)tcp; (113)tl; (124)tcp.

Old Trails Museum ~ Winslow, Arizona— (70)ml;
(71)bl; (72)ml; (73)tr; (77)tl; (131)ml.

Perkins, Dixie— (154)tcp.

**Ration Museum, Mr. Joe Sanchez ~ Raton, New
Mexico**— (128)tcp; (135)tl; ml; (141)mr;
(148)bcp; (149)tcp,ml,br; (165)tcp; (176)tcp.

Rodgers Townsend~St. Louis, Missouri—
(122)tcp.

***Schauerman, Judy**— (138)bcp.

**Stagmeir, George - Arizona Route 66
Association**— (51)tr.

The Navajo Nation— (115)tr.

Trimble, Marshall ~Southwest Studies— (62)tcp.

**U.S. Department of the Interior - National
Parks**— (113)bcp.

U.S. Geological Survey Map— (41)br.

Unknown origin and author— (15)ml; (16) tl;
(16)bl; (34)tr; (61)tcp; (64)tr; (71)tl; (93)bcp;
(108)br; (133)tr; (134)tl; tr; (137)bcp.

Index

Franciscan mission atop Enchanted Mesa at Acoma Pueblo